BY AARON MAHNKE

Destiny: A Fairy Tale
Indian Summer
Consumed
Grave Suspicion

THE WORLD OF LORE
Monstrous Creatures
Wicked Mortals
Dreadful Places

THE WORLD OF
LORE

DREADFUL PLACES

New York

AARON MAHNKE

THE WORLD OF

LORE

DREADFUL PLACES

2024 Del Rey Trade Paperback Edition

Copyright © 2018 by Aaron Mahnke

Published in the United States by Del Rey, an imprint of Random
House, a division of Penguin Random House LLC, New York.

DEL REY and the CIRCLE colophon are registered trademarks of
Penguin Random House LLC.

Most of the text in this work is based on the author's podcast, *Lore*.

Originally published in hardcover in the United States by Del Rey,
an imprint of Random House, a division of Penguin Random House
LLC, in 2018.

LIBRARY OF CONGRESS CATALOGING-IN-PUBLICATION DATA
Names: Mahnke, Aaron, author.
Title: The world of lore. Dreadful places / Aaron Mahnke.
Description: New York: Del Rey, 2018. | Includes bibliographical
references.
Identifiers: LCCN 2018019465 | ISBN 9781524798048 (paperback) |
ISBN 9781524798031 (ebook)
Subjects: LCSH: Haunted places.
Classification: LCC BF1461 .M3395 2018 | DDC 133.1/2—dc23
LC record available at https://lccn.loc.gov/2018019465

Printed in the United States of America on acid-free paper

Artwork designed by M. S. Corley

randomhousebooks.com

1st Printing

Book design by Simon M. Sullivan

For Mom and Dad.
You spent my whole childhood encouraging me to do what I love instead of whatever you might have dreamed up for me. Thank you for having the selfless love it takes to set your son free, and for giving me the courage I needed to fly.

Searchers after horror haunt strange, far places.

—H. P. Lovecraft,
"The Picture in the House"

CONTENTS

 **CITIES OF SHADOW**

Dark Imports 3
A Dead End 16
Everything Floats 27
Downriver 37
A Way Inside 47
Behind Closed Doors 58

 INSIDE THESE WALLS

Echoes 71
Southern Drama 78
Behind the Door 81
A Bad Spirit 85
Steam and Gas 90
In the Bag 100
If Walls Could Talk 110
Withering Heights 120
Locked Away 131

 DISTANT SHORES

Bite Marks 145
The Cave 154
The King 163

The Mountain 172
Within the Walls 181
The Tainted Well 193

 DEEP AND DARK

Rope and Railing 207
I Die 216
All Gone 219
Rearranged 222
The Big Chill 225
When the Bow Breaks 236

 OFF THE BEATEN PATH

In the Dark 247
An Angel Among Us 250
A Bridge Too Far 254
A Leg Up 258
A Head of Steam 261
A Deadly Past 265
For Want of Cider 268
In the Woods 272
Broken Fingernails 278
Going Viral 289
The Red Coats 299

Acknowledgments 313
Bibliography 315

CITIES OF SHADOW

Dark Imports

THE PLACES WE live have a way of coming to look like us over time. It's almost as if people inject their true nature—those passions and priorities and all the intimate details of the heart—into the very fabric of the place they call home.

Just look at the big cities of the world, and you'll see human nature written in their architecture. The beautiful façades of London, one of the world's leading financial centers, practically drip with wealth and power. The glassy skyscrapers of Dubai stand as an outward expression of an inward love of achievement. When we spend enough time somewhere, we have a tendency to build it in our own likeness.

And that's true of the darker aspects of life as well. Think of the number of cities in America with neighborhoods built around social status or ethnic identity. Or the bright, attractive lights of Las Vegas surrounded by barren desert, as if that tug-of-war between our desperation and dreams had come to life. Our cities are a part of us. In some ways, they *are* us.

Cities are often described as being alive, as having a pulse and a heart, and we, the people, are their blood. We personify them to the point where they are indistinguishable from the humans who built them. In 1946, the well-known American-turned-British-aristocrat Lady Astor visited the city of Savannah, Georgia, and described it as "very much like a beautiful woman with a dirty face." It had an aura about it, something dark and unclean, that seemed to blur the obvious beauty of the place. And maybe she was on to something. In the decades since, Savannah has become known as the most haunted city in America.

Now, I'm not sure how you measure that sort of characteristic, or if you can even declare something like that to be an indisputable fact. Still, according to those who live there, Savannah is home to a lot more darkness than we might realize.

And considering its grim past, it's easy to understand why.

Ebb and Flow

When Americans talk about the original thirteen colonies, they're talking about the seeds that grew into the country we have today. Thirteen separate settlements that grew into territories, and then—eventually—the first thirteen American states. The oldest colony, Virginia, dates back to 1607, while Georgia didn't receive a charter until over a century later, in 1732. They were the last to show up at the party, so to speak.

The leader of the Georgia colony was a man named James Oglethorpe, and he had two very specific goals for the settlement there. First, it would be a buffer territory between the other British colonies to the north and the Spanish to the south. And so slavery was actually illegal, because Oglethorpe didn't want a colony full of soft, lazy white men; he wanted soldiers.

Second, he envisioned Georgia as a new home for the hopeless of England. People who had served time in jail for debt but were trying to rebuild their lives. Or—as Oglethorpe described them— the "worthy" poor. It was meant to be a humble community, with smaller estates and more purpose behind the land division.

Oglethorpe and his team of 120 colonists arrived on February 12, 1733, and immediately did what English settlers were experts at doing: they approached the indigenous people who already lived there and negotiated for the best land. As a result, those original native inhabitants had to move inland. Shocking, I know.

Oglethorpe's prize was a bluff overlooking the mouth of the

river, and it was there that he laid the foundation for a new city. He called it Savannah, named after the river itself, and set about planning every square foot of the place. In fact, it was America's first planned city, with an almost obsessive arrangement of public squares surrounded by streets aligned to a tidy grid. And I'm going to be honest with you—as a former designer, I love it.

Four decades later, after the colonies broke off from England, Georgia legalized the ownership and forced labor of other human beings, allowing rich white Georgians to build a powerful economy on the backs of slaves. In fact, years later, in 1859, Savannah would be the location of one of the largest sales of human lives in American history. Nearly 450 men, women, and children were sold over the course of two days, breaking up nearly a hundred families. It's said that torrential rains fell during the entire event, leading those who were trapped in that system to refer to it as "the Weeping Time," as if the heavens themselves were broken by the tragedy of it all.

Slavery allowed the rich to get richer in Georgia, and as *the* port city, Savannah became the place through which all that wealth flowed. But it wasn't all sunshine and roses for the white people of Savannah. As the years ticked by, the community there had to endure a number of darker events, moments of tragedy that left bruises on the city's history. And the first of those happened in 1796.

That was the year that a fire broke out in the bakery owned by one Mr. Grommet. On the evening of November 26, a fire started in his unoccupied shop and then moved to neighboring structures. Thanks to a two-month-long drought and an inadequate fire service, the blaze spread quickly and eventually destroyed more than two hundred homes and 150 other buildings—roughly one-third of the entire city.

Another fire occurred in January 1820, destroying nearly five hundred buildings and leaving two-thirds of the city's inhabitants completely homeless. Later that year, while so many people were outdoors rebuilding their homes, heavy rain and hot weather led to a perfect breeding ground for mosquitos, which began the spread of yellow fever. By the time it finally ran its course, the epidemic had claimed nearly seven hundred lives, more than 20 percent of the city's population. It was described by one witness as a "scene of sickness, misery and ruin."

Forty years later, after capturing Atlanta in September 1864, Union General William Tecumseh Sherman led sixty-two thousand soldiers south toward Savannah. Less than a month after their arrival, the city fell. And while the city was spared the destruction that Sherman had built a reputation for, smaller battles around the city took hundreds of lives. Five months later, the war was over.

A decade after that, yellow fever returned, moving across the city like a tidal wave and taking another thousand lives with it. There are rumors that city officials hid many of the bodies in underground tunnels beneath the former Candler Hospital in an effort to hide the severity of the outbreak. While those stories can't be entirely validated, we do know those same tunnels were once used by the hospital for autopsies.

Everywhere you go in Savannah, it seems there's a bit of history lurking in the background. It's an ancient city, at least by American standards, and you can feel it in the genteel pre–Civil War architecture. Just take a walk along historic River Street, past the centuries-old warehouses that now play host to taverns, hotels, and boutiques, and you'll see what I mean. It's beautiful, in a haunting sort of way.

There's something else, though. Something lurking at the edges like a shadowy figure, waiting to reveal itself. Maybe it's the gloom of those shady squares, or the tangle of Spanish moss that hangs off so many of the trees like the web of some unnatural spider. Savannah has just as much darkness as it does beauty.

And then, of course, there are the ghosts.

DUELING FATES

I'm going to be honest with you: James Stark was a bit of a jerk. On the surface, he was everything you would expect from a southern gentleman in 1830. He was young, rich, and quite fond of climbing the social ladder. But like I said, he wasn't the nicest of people.

He seemed to have a problem with another of the men in his circle, Philip Minis. That's because, while Stark was descended from English plantation owners, Minis was the son of the first Jewish settlers in the area. So Stark, believing that someone's ancestry somehow made them inferior, used every opportunity he could find to mock and insult poor Minis.

In the spring of 1832, this apparently led to a confrontation between the two of them. One version of the legend says that the pair had been playing a game of horseshoes and that Stark became angry when Minis beat him. Stark called the other man some derogatory and racially based names, and Minis demanded an apology. Stark refused, and instead offered a different solution: they should settle it with a duel.

Minis agreed, and both parties began to prepare for the appointed day. Except something came up and Minis couldn't make it. He told Stark, but his request for a delay was ignored. So on the day of the duel, Stark arrived in his finest coat and pulled out an ornate and expensive dueling pistol. After waiting for a while for his opponent to arrive, he simply fired it into the air, and then declared Philip Minis a coward.

But you can't do something like that without word spreading, and eventually Minis caught wind of what had happened. Naturally, he was outraged, and went looking for Stark. According to the story, he tracked him down to the City Hotel, and on August 10, 1832, he made his way there, took a seat at the bar, and had one of the staff take a message up to Stark's room. And then . . . he waited.

A few minutes later, Stark descended the stairs and locked eyes with Minis. There was a moment of intense, palpable tension, and then Philip Minis shouted across the room, "I pronounce you, James Stark, a coward!"

Both men reached for their pistols, but Minis was faster. He fired just once, and Stark toppled over, landing at the foot of the stairs in a puddle of his own blood. He never stood back up.

After a short trial that ended in his acquittal, Minis moved north to Maryland, where he served as a physician to the Native Americans in the Baltimore area, and died there decades later of natural causes. James Stark, though, seems to have never left the City Hotel. The building later became a hospital and is now home to a brewery, and sightings of his ghost there are as common as the sweet smell of beer.

Eight years after that fateful duel, architect Charles Cluskey was supervising the final touches on an enormous 16,000-square-foot mansion at the intersection of Bull and Harris Streets. The owner was a wealthy shipping merchant who had moved there from Haiti, where his family had long owned a large and profitable plantation. Judging by how many secrets he had to hide, he was going to need every single spare room in that house.

For starters, he had moved to Savannah at a time when there were more slaves in the city than white European Americans. That social divide was ever-present, like a cultural Grand Canyon, and people were very good at maintaining the status quo. Which presented a challenge to François Sorrel des Rivières, because in addition to speaking French, he had the blood of African slaves in his veins.

After moving to Savannah in 1812, François transformed himself. He learned to speak perfect English, changed his name to Francis Sorrel, and pushed his ancestry deep into the dark. And it seems to have worked, however tragic it is that he had to do that at all.

His first wife, Lucinda, passed away from yellow fever in 1817, leaving him alone with three children. He married again two years later to a woman named Matilda, and they went on to have eight children of their own. Together, the family filled that mansion with laughter and noise and . . . well . . . more secrets, apparently.

Matilda was said to struggle with severe depression, and would often stay in bed for days or weeks at a time. Her needs, along with those of Francis and the children, were all taken care of, though, because the family, in a textbook example of irony, actually owned a large number of slaves.

One of those slaves, according to the legend, was a young woman named Molly, whose beauty caught the eye of Francis. So much so that he carried on an affair with her, right under the same roof as his wife. It was bold, and—if history has taught us anything about slave owners and the way they treated the women they owned—it was also probably against Molly's consent.

This went on for some time, until one day Matilda opened a door to one of the bedrooms, only to find Francis in bed with Molly. It's said that the discovery was so shocking that Matilda ran back to her own bedroom, threw open the balcony doors, and jumped out. She died where she landed on the street below. A few days later, Molly ended her own life in the carriage house.

With a past that bloody, it's no wonder that for many decades visitors to the house have claimed to experience unusual phenomena. Tourists have reported being touched by unseen hands, or feeling the pain of being struck by an invisible force. Others have described shadowy figures that move across hallways and the sounds of voices crying out from different parts of the house. If these stories are true, the house might be unoccupied, but it's certainly not empty.

Whether or not the reports are true, this series of events is far from the darkest tale to have come out of Savannah. The city's past is checkered with moments of violence and evil, and it's easy to get lost in the shadows. But the most tragic story of all happened just two years after the city was founded.

It seems that the first settlers of Savannah brought more than hope to the New World; they also brought *death*.

BOUND AND GAGGED

Oglethorpe had a lofty goal for the colony of Georgia. On the surface, it seemed like a great opportunity: either you could stay in jail for the debts you might never be able to pay back, or you could board a ship and travel to the New World and make a fresh start. You just had to work hard and be willing to take up arms if there was a need. To get the word out, Oglethorpe used agents in England and Ireland to recruit new settlers. As you would expect, the terms were spelled out clearly to these candidates.

Except you know how tricky contracts can be, right? Phrases that sound good on the surface but hide a catch or a trap that you don't notice. This was indentured servitude, sometimes called debt bondage, because once you agreed to the deal, you were barely better off than a slave for the next seven years.

That's the path Alice Riley took to reach Savannah. She'd been recruited from Ireland, and boarded a ship with nearly a hundred others just like her—poor, Irish, young, and single. The Atlantic crossing was treacherous, though, and by the time the ship arrived in Georgia, winter storms and a lack of food had left only six women and thirty-four men alive. Alice was thankful to be among the living.

She served for a brief time in the home of a widower named Richard Cannon, but she was eventually reassigned to a farm on a small island in the river, called Hutchinson's Island. Her new master there was an old, unhealthy man named William Wise, and he was quite the piece of work.

William Wise was a gentleman of status who had lost his family fortune back in England. He had requested permission to travel to Georgia, boarded the ship with a woman he claimed was his daughter, and then set sail. A day or two later, his request was denied, but it was too late. And that "daughter" turned out to actually be a prostitute. Needless to say, most people didn't like William Wise.

Still, Savannah represented the same hope for him as it did for people like poor Alice—a chance to start over and build something better. However, he did so on the backs of others, with a number of indentured servants working on his farm and in the home. We've already met Alice, but another of those servants was a young man named Richard White.

Richard and Alice became fast friends, and because both of them were assigned to work inside the house, they saw a lot of each other. They also, if the legend is true, saw far more of William Wise than either of them wanted, because they were in charge of his bathing.

While Wise sat in the large basin, it was Alice's job to clean his body and wash his hair. Richard would then dry and comb it. The journey from England had made Wise rather ill, and he spent most of his days alone in bed, but those moments in the water were different. He came alive, tormenting both Alice and Richard. And they hated it.

As you can imagine, this was a lot to deal with. It pushed the limits of their patience, and dehumanized them in a way that neither of them had ever experienced before, whether back home or here in this new land of hope. But thanks to the legal constraints of their agreement, they could do nothing other than grin and bear it. They were little more than prisoners in that house, so they pushed their disgust and hatred deep down inside themselves.

We don't know exactly what happened on March 1, 1734, to set Alice and Richard off. We don't have a recording of what they experienced, or even a full understanding of what the months leading up to it had been like. But we can all agree that everyone has a breaking point. For some, it's right below the surface, while others have more endurance. What we do know is that Alice and Richard both hit theirs on the same day.

It happened during one of those baths. Wise provided more of his typical rude and creepy behavior, and continued to humiliate Alice and Richard. Then, with her anger finally reaching a boiling point, Alice took the rag that she was cleaning the old man with and wrapped it around his throat.

Rather than stop her, Richard moved closer to help, forcing the old man's head beneath the surface of the water. Together, both servants held their breath as they waited for his to run out. Soon enough, it did; William Wise was dead.

They ran, of course—attempting to make their way to the Isle of Hope, ironically—but they were easily captured. Then they were held until James Oglethorpe was available to preside over their trial. They were guilty of the first murder in Georgia, after all. This had to be done right. But when it came time for a verdict, Alice threw a wrench in their plans, telling them all that she was pregnant.

Sure enough, she was. Judging by the events that led up to her trial, we can probably guess that Richard White was the father, although I think it's impossible to rule out William Wise. Either way, that pregnancy delayed her fate . . . for a while, at least.

In late December 1734, Alice gave birth to a baby boy. Perhaps in an effort to sway Oglethorpe's decision, she named the child James, after him. It didn't work, though; the child was taken away and she was placed in jail to await her execution. She never held her baby again.

There's no record of what happened to Richard White, although without a pregnancy of his own, the odds are pretty high that he'd been executed months before the birth. On January 19, 1735, Alice was taken from her jail cell and transported to the place where she would meet the same fate. She rode in the back of a horse-drawn wagon that brought her to Wright Square, where it parked beneath a tall tree.

Then she was asked to stand, and a rope was thrown over a high branch, one end looped around her neck. She screamed for her baby, calling out his name and scanning the gathered onlookers for someone who might have been cruel enough to bring James to his mother's execution, but he wasn't there.

They say she cursed everyone there, but that's not unique. We've all heard stories of curses muttered from the gallows, and it's one of those elements that always adds an extra bit of drama to the tale. Still, she cursed them. She cursed Oglethorpe, the man who drove the wagon, even the trees there in the park.

When she was done, someone gave a nod, and the horse slowly walked away, pulling the wagon out from under her.

Moments later, Alice Riley was dead.

IMPORTS AND EXPORTS

Every city has a nuanced history. Sure, not all are as old as Savannah, but there's no shortage of places where humans have settled in and built new lives. But we're far from perfect, and if Savannah is any indication, people brought a lot more than their hopes and dreams to its port; they brought their flaws.

Today you can still walk past the old cotton warehouses on River Street where slaves worked under horrible conditions, ground down by the economic machine. Some of these warehouses still have stalls with chains in them, where newly arrived slaves were locked up until they were sold.

And if you have a chance, visit the First African Baptist Church, one of the first black churches in America, and look for holes in the wood floor. They're small holes, maybe the diameter of a pencil, arranged in an old African pattern. But they're also breathing holes. The church, you see, was once part of the Underground Railroad, and slaves who passed through would hide beneath the floorboards until it was safe to move on.

It's a past we'd like to forget, and at the same time we would do well to remember it. Humans aren't just debris floating through life on a river of tragedy; most of the time, we craft that pain ourselves.

For Alice Riley and Richard White, that pain and suffering ended up destroying their lives. It's said that Alice's body was left hanging from that tree for three days before it was taken down. Less than two months later, her infant son, James, passed away as well. It's a tragic story that's left a dark mark on the pages of Savannah's history—a mark that some say can still be found, if you know where to look.

Local legend says that the tree from which Alice was hanged in Wright Square is the only one there with no Spanish moss growing on it. It's a sign, they say, of the blood that was spilled so cruelly. Or maybe it's a product of the curse Alice shouted out from beneath it. Whatever the reason, it's a reminder of what she did, and the price she paid.

Back on Hutchinson's Island, where Alice and Richard worked for William Wise, other remnants of their grim tale can be found. Some visitors to the island have reported seeing a man and woman in eighteenth-century clothing. They're always described as hiding in the shadows, huddled together as if avoiding someone, but disappear the moment you glance away.

The most common report, though, is that of a pale woman seen walking through Wright Square. They say she wears an old, weathered dress, and approaches people at night with thin, out-stretched arms.

"Do you know where he is?" she asks the people who see her, a mournful expression on her face. "Where's my baby?"

EPILOGUE

ACROSS the street from the southeastern corner of Lafayette Square, on Abercorn Street, is a large, historic mansion with a complex past. It's old, too, having been built in 1873 for a wealthy man named Samuel Hamilton. He earned his fortune a variety of ways, including war profiteering during the Civil War, and set up his home to be a reflection of his social status and achievements. He would even go on to be mayor of the city for a time.

He was also an avid collector of art, in much the same way as his contemporary in Boston, Isabella Stewart Gardner. His mansion there on Abercorn Street was full of valuable paintings that he loved to show off. So much so that he set up the house as a private museum of sorts, which included protecting what was inside. Guards worked in the house around the clock, including a man on the roof armed with a rifle.

Local legend says that one morning, after it was noticed that the guard had failed to come down from the top of the mansion, someone was sent up to retrieve him. What they discovered, though, was the man's corpse lying in a pool of his own blood, but no discernible cause of death or sign of theft inside the house. When other guards refused to take his place, Hamilton himself sat up through the night, rifle in hand, for a number of months—that is, until he became ill and passed away in 1899.

The second owner of the house, Dr. Francis Turner, took over in 1915, and set up his medical practice in the basement of the building. Turner was also well respected and socially prominent, hosting frequent parties at the mansion. Whenever he did, though, it was said that his children were forced to stay upstairs, where they would be out of the way.

They usually passed the time playing billiards, but on one fateful night the girls became bored and rolled a few of the balls down the staircase. One of the girls slipped, though, and tumbled down the steps. Her injuries, they say, were fatal.

Today the mansion serves as a local inn, but it's also home to a number of unexplainable sights and sounds. The figure of an older man smoking a cigar has been reported on the roof of the building, while guests indoors have heard sounds they can only describe as billiard balls dropping to the floor somewhere above them.

Savannah is indeed a beautiful city, but like so many old communities in our world, that façade hides a darker underbelly. The people who live there today may no longer have to deal with yellow fever or slave markets, but there are still shadows everywhere.

And if the Hamilton-Turner Inn is any indication, that darkness has never really checked out.

A Dead End

WHEN THE TRUCKER pulled up to the tollbooth on Route 895 in Virginia, it was the middle of the night and the look on his face was one of confusion and fear. The tollbooth attendant listened to the man's story, and then sent him on his way.

The state highway is referred to as the Pocahontas Parkway, so maybe the man's story was just a play on the name's motif. But when the highway department received more than a few phone calls that night from distressed motorists, each telling essentially the same story, the authorities began to take notice.

What the trucker saw—what all of them claimed to have seen—was a small group of Native Americans standing on the median between the eastbound and westbound lanes of traffic near Mill Road. The trucker described them as standing motionless in the grass, each holding a burning torch. He'd assumed they were picketing, of course. After all, the parkway is rumored to cut through land that's sacred to local Native American tribes. But the middle of the night didn't seem like the right time for a peaceful protest. So it didn't sit well with him. Or the others who claimed to see the very same thing.

The *Times-Dispatch* caught wind of the story, and soon people were flocking to the Mill Street overpass to see if they, too, could catch a glimpse of the ghosts. And that's what it all comes down to, isn't it? We all want to see the ghosts. To witness history press its face against the glass of the present. To cheat reality, in a sense.

Each year, thousands of people around the world claim that they have seen a ghost. They tell their stories, and pass along their goosebumps like some communicable disease. But the reality is that most of us never see a thing. History is often nothing more than a distant memory.

In some places, though, that history floats a bit closer to the surface.

A SEAT OF CONFLICT

When the English arrived in what is now Virginia way back in 1607, they found the land heavily populated by the original inhabitants of the region. The English called them the Powhatan, although that was just the name of their leader. If you don't recognize his name, that's understandable, but everyone certainly remembers his daughter, Pocahontas.

Before Richmond was Richmond, the land where it now stands was an important Powhatan settlement. In 1607, a party from Jamestown traveled inland and claimed the location as their own. Possession of the land bounced back and forth between the Native Americans and the English for years, but in 1737 the tribe finally lost and Richmond was born.

Early on, Richmond played host to important figures in the American Revolution. Patrick Henry, the man who shouted "Give me liberty, or give me death!," did so from St. John's Church right there in town. And in the middle of the Revolutionary War, Thomas Jefferson served as the governor of Virginia out of Richmond.

Less than a century later, Richmond became a key city in the Confederacy as the Civil War tore the country apart. From its munitions factory and railroad system to the seat of the new government under Jefferson Davis, the city was powerful. And right at the center of it all is Belle Isle.

It sits right there in the James River, between Hollywood Cemetery to the north and Forest Hill to the south. It's easy to over-look on the map, but far from being an afterthought, Belle Isle is actually home to some of the most painful memories in the history of the city.

Before the English arrived and Captain John Smith stood atop the rocks there, it belonged to the Powhatan. Shortly after the English took control of it in the early 1700s, it was a fishery, and then in 1814 the Old Dominion Iron and Nail Company built a factory there. Positioned on the river, where the strong current never tired, it was in the perfect location to harness the power of the water.

As the ironworks grew, so did its footprint. The factory expanded. A village was built around it, and a general store even popped up to serve the hundreds of people who called the island home. But they wouldn't be the only ones to live there.

In 1862, Confederate forces moved onto the island and began to fortify it. Their plan was to use the isolated island as a prison camp, and they began to transport Union captives there by the thousands. Over the three years it was in operation, the prison played host to more than thirty thousand Union soldiers, sometimes more than ten thousand at a time. And the crowded space and resentful feelings between the Confederate and Union sides led to deplorable conditions.

In 1882, after living with memories of the prison camp for nearly two decades, New York cavalry officer William H. Wood wrote to the editor of the *National Tribune* with his observations.

> *Many froze to death during the winter, others were tortured in the most barbarous manner. I have seen men put astride a wooden horse such as masons use, say five feet high, with their feet tied to stakes in the ground, and there left for an hour or more on a cold winter morning. Often their feet would freeze and burst open.*

He also wrote of their lack of food:

> *A lieutenant's dog was once enticed over the bank and taken into an old tent where it was killed and eaten raw. Your humble*

servant had a piece of it. For this act of hungry men, the entire camp was kept out of rations all day.

There were only a few wooden shacks to house the prisoners, so they lived out their days completely exposed to the elements. Blistering heat, freezing cold, rain, and frost. All of it contributed to the suffering of the men who were held there. Estimates vary depending on the source, but it's thought that nearly half of those who were brought there—that's close to fifteen thousand—never left alive.

Today, Belle Isle is a public park haunted by a dark past, and by those who lived and died there long ago. You can't see their ghosts, but you can certainly feel them. It's a heavy place. Visitors to the island claim to have felt its dark past in the air, like the stifling heat of an iron forge.

But there are other places in Richmond that are said to be haunted as well. Unlike Belle Isle, though, these locations aren't in ruins, or nearly forgotten by the living. They're right in the middle of everyday life, and each one has a unique story to tell.

They have their own past. And according to those who have been there, it can still be seen.

MEMORIES LOST

Technically, Wrexham Hall is in Chesterfield County, just south of Richmond. But when you speak to people about the city's deeply haunting past, it's always brought up as a perfect example of local lore. And while it doesn't have a large number of stories to tell, what it does offer is chilling enough.

The house was built at the end of the eighteenth century by Archibald Walthall, who left the home to his two daughters, Polly and Susannah. It was Susannah who later sold her childhood home, but she stipulated that the new owners must always preserve the family graveyard.

Time and the elements, though, have allowed the site of the burial ground to slip from memory. And according to some, that's why Susannah has returned to Wrexham Hall, perhaps in an effort to make sure some piece of the past is remembered.

It was years after her death, when the home was owned by a man named Stanley Hague. He and a handful of other men had been working in the field near the house when they looked up to see a woman in a red dress sitting on the front porch. They all saw her, and even commented to each other about it. It was hard to miss that bright red against the white home.

Later, when Stanley headed home, he asked his wife if her mother had been on the porch that day. No, she told him. She'd been away all day in Richmond.

In Hollywood Cemetery, just north of Belle Isle, there are other stories afoot. The graveyard was established in 1849, and it is the final resting place of a number of important figures. Former U.S. presidents James Monroe and John Tyler are buried there, along with Confederate president Jefferson Davis. There are also two Supreme Court justices buried there, along with twenty-two Confederate generals and more than eighteen thousand soldiers.

The soldiers are honored with an enormous stone pyramid that reaches up beyond the trees, and even though no one is buried beneath it, there have been several reports of moans heard coming from the stones. Others have claimed to have felt cold spots near the base. But it's really a nearby grave that's the site of the most activity there.

The grave belongs to a little girl who died at the age of three from a childhood illness. And standing beside her tombstone is a large cast-iron dog. According to the local legend, the dog once stood outside her father's grocery store, but when she passed away in 1862, it was moved to her grave to look after her.

That might not be completely accurate, though. In the early 1860s, many iron objects were melted down to be used for military purposes, and so the dog was most likely moved to the cemetery as a way of protecting it. That hasn't stopped the stories, though—stories that include visions of a little girl playing near the grave, or the sounds of barking in the middle of the night.

Nearby on Cary Street is the historic Byrd Theatre. It was built in 1928 and named after the founder of Richmond himself, Wil-

liam Byrd. The space inside is enormous; it can seat over nine hundred on the lower level, and another four hundred or so in the balcony. And it's up there that some of the oddest experiences have taken place.

When the theater opened its doors in December 1928, Robert Coulter was the manager, and he continued to serve in that role all the way up to 1971, when he passed away. For over four decades, he was a permanent fixture in the theater, often found sitting in his favorite seat up on one side of the balcony. And if we can believe the stories, Robert never left.

The current manager has been told by a number of people that they've seen a tall man in a suit sitting in the balcony at times when no one else was up there. Others have physically felt someone pass by them while they were operating the projector. The former manager has even been seen on more than one occasion by employees locking the front doors at night, as if he were coming out to help them.

The stories that are whispered about places like the Byrd Theatre aren't alone. There are dozens of locations across the city that claim unusual activity and equally eerie stories. But none can claim to have played host to a flesh-and-blood monster.

None, that is, except for one.

Dead Ends

In 1875, the Chesapeake and Ohio Railway was looking to connect some track in Richmond to another spur seventy-five miles to the south. Newport News was down that way, and that meant the ocean and shipping. It was a gamble to make their railroad more profitable in the wake of the Industrial Revolution and its increasing demand for things like coal, something mined in western Virginia.

Part of the new railway line would cut through Richmond near Jefferson Park, and it was decided that a tunnel would be constructed for the track to pass through. Trains would enter on 18th Street, and then exit four thousand feet away on the eastern end, near 31st Street. It was one of those ideas that sounded perfect on paper. Reality, though, had a few complications to throw at them.

Richmond sits on a geological foundation of clay, as opposed to the bedrock found in other parts of the state. It's the kind of soil that changes consistency depending on the season and weather. Rainy months lead to more groundwater, and that swells the clay. Dry months would cause the opposite. As you could imagine, it's difficult to build on ground that constantly changes density.

During construction, there were a number of cave-ins. Between the project's inception in 1875 and its completion six years later, at least ten men died while working in the tunnel. Even after it was opened, water had a tendency to seep in and cause problems, something that went on for decades.

Around 1901, though, alternative routes were created, and the Church Hill Tunnel was used less and less. But when the railroad wanted to increase capacity in 1925, they remembered the old tunnel and began work to bring it up to modern standards. Maybe now, they thought, they could do it right.

By the autumn of 1925, the tunnel was playing host to a crew of brave men, supported by a work train powered by steam. They were slowly making their way along the length of the tunnel, making repairs, improving the engineering, and hopefully making the tunnel safe for future use. But even after claiming so many lives decades before, the tunnel didn't seem to be done just yet.

On October 2, while doing what they had been doing for weeks, dozens of men were working inside the tunnel when the ceiling collapsed. Most escaped, but five men were trapped inside, buried alive. And to make matters worse, the steam engine exploded when the weight of the debris pressed down on it, filling the tunnel with steam and dust, and contributing to even further collapse.

According to the story as it's told today, something did in fact walk out of the tunnel, but it wasn't human. They say it was a hulking creature, covered in strips of decaying flesh, with sharp teeth and a crazed look in its eyes. And because witnesses reported that blood was flowing from its mouth, many have since referred to it as the Richmond Vampire.

No one could explain why the creature was there. Some suggested that it had been attracted to the carnage and had come to feed. They say that's why the early rescue attempts only found one of the five missing men, still seated at the controls of the work train. There was no sign of the other victims of the tragedy, though, so some suggest that perhaps the vampire had something to do with that.

Witnesses say that the creature fled out the eastern end of the tunnel, past the gathering crowd of workers, and then made its way south to Hollywood Cemetery. Some of the workmen who had managed to escape the collapse and witness the creature's getaway were able to give chase, following it through the graveyard for a distance. And then, they claimed, it slipped into one of the tombs, the final resting place of a man named W. W. Pool.

Pool, it turns out, was a relatively unknown accountant who had died just three years before. According to the local legend, this made sense. The blood on the mouth, the jagged teeth, the return to the mausoleum—all of it pointed to one undeniable fact. And the story quickly spread across the city, becoming one of the premier legends of Richmond.

Pool was a vampire, of course.

It's said that people returned to the cemetery for many nights, eagerly waiting to see if the vampire would emerge from his hiding place once more, but there are no other stories that tell us what happened next. If the Richmond Vampire had been active before the Church Hill Tunnel incident, it seemed he went into retirement immediately after it.

Like many tales of local lore, this story ends on an unsatisfying note. Just as the mysterious creature's trail from the collapsed tunnel finally ended in the shadowy doorway of a cold mausoleum, the story of what happened seems to end in shadows of its own.

Much like the tunnel itself, it was now nothing more than a dead end.

ALTERATIONS

A funny thing happens somewhere between real-life events in the past and the stories we tell each other around the campfire or dining room table. Much like the tried-and-true telephone game, where the message is passed from person to person through a long chain of possession, these old stories shift and change.

The change is never visible; the tales adapt to a new culture, or take on elements that are only relevant to a particular generation. But after decades, sometimes even centuries, these stories stand before us transformed. Which is the difference between history and folklore, after all. With history, there's a paper trail, a clear image of the original that time and distance have a more difficult time eroding. Folklore is like water, forever shifting to fit the crevice as the rock breaks down.

Richmond is an old city by the standards of most Americans. Yes, there are older places on the East Coast, but Richmond has a storied history that makes it feel almost timeless. Jamestown. The Revolutionary War. The Civil War and the Confederacy. American history would be lacking something essential without the role Richmond has played through it all.

Some of that history is unchanged, but some, it seems, has undergone deep transformation over the years. And the prime example of that is the story of the Richmond Vampire.

The collapsed tunnel and the train inside it are all fact. There've even been modern-day efforts to recover the train and clear the rubble, but the tunnel is now flooded with the same groundwater that made it unstable in the first place. The events of that dark October day in 1925 were real, though—at least, to a degree.

A lone survivor did crawl from the wreckage, as the story tells us. His teeth were sharp and his mouth was bloody. Even the condition of his skin, hanging from his body like wet linen bandages, is documented fact. But the survivor had a name: Benjamin Mosby.

He was a twenty-eight-year-old employee of the railroad and was described as big and strong. At the moment of the accident, he had been standing in front of the train's open coal door, shirt off, covered in sweat, and shoveling fuel into the fire. When the tunnel collapsed, the boiler burst under the pressure, washing Mosby in a flood of scalding water.

He somehow survived, crawled free from the rock and twisted metal, and walked to safety. He died the following day at the local hospital. And it was his appearance—with bloody, broken teeth and skin boiled from his body in ribbons—that fueled the story we still whisper today.

It's almost a cliché to say it, but it's true: sometimes the real-life events that birth a legend turn out to be more frightening and horrific than any folktale could ever be.

Everything Floats

$\mathcal{S}$OME TRAGEDY TAKES no effort at all to happen. One moment life is perfect and normal and everything we expect it to be. Then it changes in an instant. No warning. No chance to avoid it. It just happens.

Natural disaster is one of those agents of tragedy that seem to sneak up on us and bring ruin into our lives. Fire, flood, tropical storms. Just watching the news each night can give us a glimpse into yet one more episode of pain and suffering that no one saw coming.

Other tragedies, though, exist only because we have ushered them into our world. Sometimes that "we" has been humanity as a collective, and sometimes it's been just one broken individual. Genocide or patricide, school shootings or terrorism—regardless of the source, these are tragedies that couldn't have existed without human involvement. It doesn't make them any less painful, mind you. Sometimes it even makes them worse.

These moments of tragedy are, thankfully, very spread out. We have a chance to breathe and move on. But give a city enough time and those tragedies can start to pile up. The older the place, the deeper the pain. A murder here, a disaster there. Throw in a war or two for good measure. Soon its entire history can feel like one long nightmare.

Nowhere is that more true than in the city that most would call the Big Easy. Underneath its eclectic architectural mix of old Creole, French, Spanish, Victorian, and even Greek Revival, amidst the parties and lights and music that all seem to pulse through the streets like blood, there's something darker.

Because there's one thing that's hard for anyone to deny: if it was tragic, painful, or eerie, it probably happened in New Orleans.

A DARK PATINA

It's safe to say that New Orleans is one of those cities that just about everyone has an impression of, whether correct or incorrect. It's a cultural icon, and a showcase of just how textured and diverse America's history truly is.

We can blame much of that on the age of the city. The city, which celebrated its tricentennial in 2018, was founded by the French Mississippi Company in 1718. Other than the early settlements of New England, many of whom can claim incorporation in the early to mid-1600s, there are few places in the United States that are as old as New Orleans. And that age has brought the city more than its fair share of pain and tragedy.

It was land that had once been occupied by the local Chitimacha tribe of Native Americans, and the Europeans, of course, took it from them. From the outset, it was seen by everyone as a valuable territory. Sitting at the mouth of the mighty Mississippi River, it acted like a doorway into the heart of the continent, and for nearly fifty years the French controlled the gate.

When the French and Indian War came to a close in 1763, a treaty was signed between Great Britain, France, and Spain. One outcome of that document was that New Orleans fell under the control of Spain, which held on to the city until the French reclaimed it in 1800. Three years later, Napoleon sold it to the United States as part of the Louisiana Purchase.

The War of 1812 brought the first major dose of tragedy to New Orleans. In late summer of 1814 the British attacked Washington, D.C., and burned the White House, the Capitol, and much of the rest of the city. Then they turned their eyes to New Orleans, that doorway into the heart of America.

It was Andrew Jackson, future president of the United States, who was charged with defending the city as over eleven thousand British troops marched toward it. And he found help in one of the most unlikely places: two brothers known across the city as pirate outlaws.

Jean and Pierre Lafitte were smugglers who operated out of their blacksmith shop in New Orleans. In *Star Wars* terms, Jean was the Han Solo of the pair, the daring sailor and smuggler of illegal goods. Pierre, in contrast, was Lando Calrissian, managing the business and acting as the public face of the operation. But after American naval vessels captured their offshore hideout in the fall of 1814, the Lafitte brothers found themselves in legal hot water.

They found salvation, though, in a deal with Andrew Jackson. In return for gathering troops and supplies for the approaching battle—things like sorely needed gunpowder and flint—Jackson promised to pardon the brothers and turn them into heroes. The brothers delivered the supplies, the Americans won the battle, and Jackson made good on his word—although he had to become president to do so.

Today, Lafitte's Blacksmith Shop is a bar on Bourbon Street, and one of the oldest buildings in the French Quarter. And with a past as daring and dangerous as Lafitte's, it's no wonder that stories of ghosts still echo through the establishment. The most common sightings speak of a figure who sits at the bar near the fireplace, dressed in the attire of a late eighteenth-century sailor.

Ghosts aren't unique to old bars, though. Just outside the borders of the French Quarter sits the historic St. Louis Cemetery Number 1. Founded in 1789, it's the oldest and most iconic cemetery in the city. In some ways, it has an appearance and atmosphere similar to Highgate Cemetery in London. It's a maze of small aboveground vaults, many playing host to entire families. It's crowded, and old, and feels more than a bit creepy.

But it's not what's inside the tombs that gets talked about the most. Visitors to the cemetery have frequently encountered mysterious figures, ghosts who apparently haunt the narrow spaces between the tombs.

One common sighting is a man known as Henry Vignes. He's said to have been a young sailor who was scammed out of his family tomb by a dishonest landlady. When he died, his body was buried in an unmarked pauper's grave, and because of that, he still wanders the cemetery today, searching. Multiple visitors have claimed to see him approach, and after he asks where the Vignes tomb is, he's said to turn around and vanish from sight.

Another frequent sighting is the ghost of a young man known only as Alphonse. Witnesses claim that they've seen him floating toward them and asking for help finding his home. Others say they've seen him gathering flowers from random graves before walking off with them. Maybe he's lonely, or perhaps he's just looking for a little beauty in such a somber place. No one really knows.

St. Louis Cemetery Number 1 plays host to dozens of well-known figures from the early days of New Orleans. But the most famous resident, according to most, is someone that very few graveyards in the country can lay claim to: a real Voodoo queen.

SOCIAL AND POLITICAL MAGIC

When the Atlantic slave trade brought millions of people from Africa against their will and deposited them all over the New World, these people—Africans from dozens of distinct tribal groups, cultures, and languages—were forced to find a common ground. At home, they might have been rivals, or even enemies. In captivity, though, unity meant survival.

Today we call it the African diaspora, the dispersal of the continent's cultures and peoples and beliefs throughout the world. And everywhere the seeds landed, they sprouted into something slightly different. What was known as Vodu in Africa became Voodoo, Hoodoo, Vodun, and more. And each had its own character and uniqueness.

Voodoo is considered to be a religion, with its own core beliefs and leaders. The Voodoo of Louisiana has a distinct flavor thanks to what's called syncretism, the blending of its practices and beliefs with those of the Catholic Church. Much as the Church has priests, Voodoo honors practitioners called kings and queens.

A Voodoo queen was someone who conducted ceremonies and ritual dances, sometimes before crowds in the thousands. To earn a living, these queens would make talismans for others to purchase and use. Things like gris-gris bags, which were filled with all sorts of ingredients, then blessed with intention and meaning. These bags function similarly to crosses, and are even worn around the neck.

One Voodoo queen who is still mentioned throughout New Orleans is Julie White. She practiced in the late 1800s, and legend says that her cabin was near the edge of Manchac Swamp. She was more reclusive than most Voodoo queens, but visitors still came for her blessing and predictions. What she preferred to dole out, though, weren't kind words. Julie, they say, was cranky and threatened everyone.

Her favorite thing to do was to predict the destruction of local communities. In the Mississippi Delta, you never have to wait long for a flood or a storm, and Julie seemed to have an uncanny knack for prophesying some of them. If ever there was a shining example of a warm, inviting person, Julie White was probably not it.

The most famous Voodoo queen, though, hands down, lived a century before Julie White, and her name was Marie Laveau. She was born in the French Quarter sometime between 1795 and 1805 to Charles Laveau, the fifth mayor of New Orleans. She married in 1819, but her husband died just a year later. And with that, Marie was forced to find new ways to support herself. Local legend says that she worked for a time as a hairdresser, and there's some documentation that points to work as a liquor importer. But sometime after that Marie set in motion a legendary career as a practitioner of Voodoo.

Let's put this in perspective. In 1874, she held a St. John's Eve gathering on the shore of Lake Pontchartrain. Estimates place the total number of people in attendance at around twelve thousand.

Maybe it was the power of Voodoo at the time, or Marie's electric personality. It was probably a mixture of both. And people loved her for it.

She followed the same pattern as most Voodoo queens: she held rites and ceremonies, and crafted gris-gris bags for sale. Legend says that Marie learned the practice from an earlier Voodoo king, Doctor John, and quickly became his cultural successor.

She had the unique privilege of being able to host Voodoo rites inside the largest Catholic church in New Orleans, St. Louis Church, thanks to her friendship with the church's rector, known locally as Père Antoine. Most people have forgotten that that friendship was built on a very noble pursuit: Marie and Antoine worked together for years to free slaves in the New Orleans area.

Marie was also said to be quite well connected. Countless public figures came to her for advice, and it was rumored that she also employed a network of spies throughout the city. All of those connections earned her influence and power, things she wasn't afraid to use.

One story in particular about Marie Laveau stands out. According to local legend, the son of a wealthy businessman was arrested and charged with murder in the mid-1830s. The father, aware of the reputation Marie had for getting what she wanted, offered her a deal. If she could free his son, he would purchase her a house of her own.

Marie accepted the offer. It's said that she spent the weeks before the trial praying incessantly at St. Louis Church. And all the while, Marie held three hot Guinea peppers in her mouth. When the morning of the trial came, she used her influence to get access to the courtroom and placed the peppers beneath the judge's chair. Filled with her prayers, they were a talisman, designed to influence his mind.

In the end, the wealthy man's son was acquitted of all charges, and Marie received her reward. Whether it was her Voodoo powers that made it possible or simply her political clout and connections, we'll never really know. But in New Orleans, Voodoo always gets the vote.

Voodoo isn't the only cultural transplant in New Orleans,

though. In a melting pot that includes Creole, Spanish, French, and Native American influences, it probably won't come as a surprise to hear that there are even Turkish stories whispered in the city.

What's surprising, however, is just how *bloody* they are.

Stairway to Hell

The house that stands at the corner of Dauphine Street and Orleans Avenue was built by Jean Baptiste LePrete in 1836. LePrete was a plantation owner who wanted a city home, so he built the Greek Revival mansion as a retreat and as a symbol of his wealth.

But that wealth experienced hard times in the wake of the Civil War. Financial troubles forced LePrete to move out of the mansion and find someone to rent it from him. I'm sure he expected another wealthy business owner, or a government official. Imagine his shock, then, when it was a Turkish prince who arrived at the door.

The man told LePrete that he was Prince Suleyman, former sultan of an undisclosed country in the Middle East. Cash was exchanged, LePrete turned over the keys, and the sultan and his household moved in.

According to the story, that household fit the stereotype one might expect from a film adaptation of the Arabian tale *One Thousand and One Nights*. The sultan had many wives, a large extended family, and a whole team of servants. He brought with him furniture and decorations—enormous rugs and tapestries, paintings, and other symbols of his wealth and power.

After the sultan settled into the mansion, a pair of Turkish soldiers was assigned to stand guard outside the door, armed with scimitars. But the guards weren't able to keep the rumors from spreading, and the stories grew more and more elaborate. It was said that the house would be quiet during the day, but after darkness fell, it would come alive.

The mansion, locals said, had become a pleasure palace. Nights were filled with orgies and extravagant parties. Some whispered that young women, and even boys and girls, had gone missing in the neighborhood, and the blame was placed on the sultan's appetite for carnal pleasures. There was no proof, of course, but neighbors love to talk. Neighbors always love to talk, and they always will, I suppose.

Those who walked past the mansion would often comment on the smell of incense that drifted out of the windows. But that's not all the locals noticed. One morning, a neighbor was out for a walk, and as he passed by the sultan's mansion, he noticed something dark on the front steps. He stopped and took a second look, and then slowly backed away in horror.

Blood was everywhere. It covered the top step and had run in small rivers down the dark stairs, and all of it seemed to have come from the narrow space beneath the door. The neighbor quickly went to the police, and they arrived a short time later. After attempts to unlock the front door failed, they forced their way in. What they found inside, though, was far worse than they'd imagined.

Bodies lay all about the main hall. Some of them were complete, but most were torn apart. The floor was covered in blood, and it was easy to see how it could have managed to run all the way to the doorway and then down the stairs. Everywhere they looked, they saw death and gore.

According to the story, the police continued on into the house, and soon came upon the courtyard garden near the rear of the mansion. At first everything seemed normal there, but then one of the officers pointed to a spot on the ground. There, protruding from the wet soil, was a human hand.

It's said that the sultan himself was spared the dismemberment that the rest of his household experienced. Instead, the killer had buried the prince alive in the garden after wrapping the man in three white sheets and binding him with rope. He had somehow managed to get one hand free before suffocating to death.

To this day, no one knows who the killer was, but there are theories. One suggestion was, oddly enough, pirates. It's not likely, and not a popular theory, but it suggests that perhaps the wealth and possessions inside the house were not really the sultan's after all. Still, I have a hard time imagining pirates doing whatever it is they do on land, in the middle of a large city.

The more popular theory is that the sultan was actually on the run from his homeland. People whispered that he wasn't really a prince but the brother of one, and that he had somehow stolen a portion of his brother's wealth and escaped to America. As a result, the false sultan was hunted down, and his entire household was killed for his crimes.

Today, after decades of neglect, the mansion has been converted into luxury apartments. Tenants claim to have heard mysterious footsteps and the sounds of parties. Some have even heard the faint echo of unusual music, something that they say has a Middle Eastern flavor.

Others, though, have *seen* things. Some have witnessed groups of ghostly people passing from room to room, or body parts that vanish a moment later. Most significant, though, is the lone figure of a man who's been seen floating through the halls before mysteriously disappearing through locked doors.

Perhaps, even after all these years, the sultan is still looking for a way out.

Everything Floats

New Orleans is a big city with a deep past, and I fully admit that its history and lore are larger than the picture I've painted here. And maybe that's the power of it, the uniqueness of it, you know? There are very few places in America that can claim as much tragedy over so many centuries, and that legacy shows.

And the attraction of that legacy has never faded. Celebrities and tourists alike still flock to the city. Anne Rice gave it new life through her vampire novels, and in 2010 Nicolas Cage purchased a plot in St. Louis Cemetery No. 1. He plans to build a tomb shaped like a small pyramid because, well, why the heck not, right?

I think we would be missing the point to think of New Orleans as simply the place where Mardi Gras happens every year, or as just a center for jazz and Cajun cuisine. It's bigger than that, deeper than that. There's a darkness, you see, that floats just beneath the surface, and we'd be mistaken to ignore it. And some say that darkness still holds power.

Remember Julie White, the Voodoo queen who lived on the edge of Manchac Swamp? Like Marie Laveau, she was sought after by many in the community for her advice and oracle-like predictions. And because of that, she had quite a following. Still, her final prediction left people feeling unsettled. "One day I'm gonna die," she said, "and I'm gonna take all of you with me."

Julie did die, of course, in late September 1915. She was feared, yes, but she was also deeply loved, and so the locals gathered in large numbers to throw her the funeral they felt she deserved. And on the day of that gathering, September 21, a category 4 hurricane made landfall, ripping through New Orleans and the surrounding area.

Out of nowhere, 130-mile-per-hour winds and fifteen-foot waves ravaged the Delta region. Everyone at the funeral died—nearly two hundred of them, they say—and locals from the town of Frenier were left with the grim task of gathering their bodies and burying them in a mass grave in the swamp.

Even today, more than a century later, locals say that bodies will occasionally float to the surface of the water. Perhaps it's just a natural process for a swamp that's filled with hundreds of corpses. Or maybe Julie White, the oracle of Manchac Swamp, just wants us to never forget that she was right.

Downriver

THEY NAMED THE village after the Latin word for "serpent," *coluber*. Today though, so many centuries later, its name is rarely spoken by those who live in the Basilicata region of Italy. There's something about it that gives local Italians a feeling of dread, and they'd rather not speak its name.

Colobraro earned that reputation, though, if we're to believe the stories. It's said that in the early years of the twentieth century, the town was home to a very successful, but very disliked, lawyer named Biagio Virgilio. Virgilio was speaking in court one day, according to the story, when he pointed up toward the ceiling of the courthouse.

"If what I say is false," he shouted, "may this chandelier come down!"

And it did. It dropped right into the middle of the room and shattered into a thousand pieces. And while no one was injured, the town's reputation took on a dark hue. It was cursed, they said. Hexed. And later events only served to reinforce that belief. Landslides. Car accidents. There are even stories of babies born with two hearts or three lungs. And, of course, tales of witchcraft.

Locations take on a flavor over time. Whether it's our hometown or just an infamous spot in the area, we have a tendency to treat locations like people. They have a personality and a reputation. And some, if you listen to the locals, are even cursed.

When life doesn't go the way we'd hoped, we look for reasons. Claiming that our town is cursed is an easy way to make sense of the accidental, the unexpected, and the unfortunate. But sometimes the evidence is dark and deep, and includes suffering, death, even utter destruction.

FOR WHOM THE BELL TOLLS

There's this notion that's almost as old as time itself, that a city or nation that strays too far from its roots, or from its moral center, puts itself at risk of being cursed. Hebrew legend speaks of the Tower of Babel, which shows how the pride of one settlement brought about destruction and confusion.

The ancient stories of Atlantis spoke of the island civilization as technologically and socially advanced, but it was their greed and immorality that led the gods to destroy them. According to the interpretation of the ancient writers, they were cursed by their behavior.

Other ancient stories speak of a city that once stood in the southern sands of the Arabian Peninsula. It's mentioned in the Quran, the Christian Bible, even the Arabian Nights tales. It was known as Ubar, Iram, Wabar, or the city of Ad. And after serving as a trade center for over five millennia, it vanished roughly two thousand years ago. Satellite scans in the 1980s finally provided us with an answer. The city, it turns out, was built on an enormous subterranean cavern, and sometime in AD 300, it all collapsed.

There are so many other examples. Port Royal in the Caribbean. The ancient Greek city of Helike. Even Pompeii comes to mind. But these stories aren't limited to dusty cities spoken of in ancient texts. Even here in the United States, in a country that's relatively young compared to much of the world, we can find stories of cursed locations and horrible tragedy.

On November 1, 1886, tragedy came to Lafayette, Oregon. That was the day that David Corker, a fifty-seven-year-old shopkeeper, was found dead in his general store by a customer. The shop had been broken into overnight, and Corker had been killed while defending his store.

The suspect was a man named Richard Marple. He'd moved there with his wife, Julia, and mother, Anna, just the year before, and the rumor was that he'd chosen a life of crime over gainful employment. The man, they said, was a thief.

Add to that a handful of eyewitness reports about how Marple openly mocked the shopkeeper, and it was hard to ignore him as a suspect. The sheriff visited his home and found a bloody shirt, a scrap of paper in his pocket with bloodstains on it, and a collection of tools used for breaking into locked buildings.

Marple was convicted of murder on April 9, 1887. His wife and mother fought the charges. They provided a solid alibi, swearing as to his whereabouts that night. It didn't work, though. Marple was hanged on November 11, just a little over a year after Corker had been found dead. Thirty locals gathered to watch as the man strangled to death at the end of the rope for nearly eighteen minutes.

Marple's mother wasn't allowed to watch the execution, but she could be heard screaming from a distance. She cursed the town, they say, and predicted that three fires would burn Lafayette to the ground. It was easy to laugh it off, though. Predictions like that always are. So that's what the inhabitants did.

No one was suspicious when a blaze ripped through town in 1895. Towns—especially those built mostly out of wood—have a knack for catching fire. Six buildings were leveled by the flames. Two years later, another fire broke out, destroying four more. And then, in 1904, a fire destroyed sixteen buildings as it raged across town.

A random series of accidents, or the product of the curse of a very angry mother? For some, that isn't an easy question to answer.

Another location that's haunted by tales of a curse is the Dutch village of Saeftinghe. Well, it was, up until the late 1500s, that is. Let me explain what I mean.

In the Middle Ages Saeftinghe was a hub for the harvesting of peat. The village was situated in what is known as the polders, the floodplains that were separated from the ocean by man-made dikes and dams. And because peat was a popular source of fuel at the time, Saeftinghe was an important community in the region.

Peat was in such high demand that, according to some historians, the farmers of Saeftinghe were said to dress in fine silks. They even decorated their draft horses with gold and silver jewelry. Of course, this led to a reputation for greed and selfishness, which wasn't helped by the fact that the townsfolk would chase newcomers away with weapons and dogs. Basically, they weren't friendly people, and no one likes a jerk, right?

As the story goes, a farmer was fishing outside Saeftinghe one day when he reeled in a real-life mermaid. Apparently she could speak Dutch, and she warned the farmer that unless the town straightened up and stopped being greedy, something horrible was going to happen.

The farmer laughed at her, and decided that a pet mermaid would be nice to have, so he tied her up. Even when the mermaid's husband surfaced and begged for her release, the farmer refused. So the merman uttered a curse. "The lands of Saeftinghe will fall," he said. "Only its towers will continue to stand tall."

In 1570, a flood swept over the Dutch coast, inundating the land around the town. Fourteen years later, in 1584, the Dutch army was fighting the Eighty Years' War and destroyed one of the dikes that held back the ocean. The town of Saeftinghe was overcome by an enormous wave, and was never seen again.

Today the region is known as Verdronken Land, "Drowned Land." But locals say that not all of Saeftinghe is gone. Somewhere beneath the marsh and water, if the stories are to be believed, the old church tower still stands tall.

And on foggy days, they say, you can still hear the bell toll.

THE IN-BETWEEN PLACE

In the southwestern corner of Illinois is a city on the edge of the Mississippi. Now, it's easy to limit the history of a place to our

American experience, but Illinois is older than that. In fact, the entire area from the Arkansas River up to Green Bay was once controlled by the French. They explored the region in 1673, and then claimed it for the French crown shortly after.

They called it Upper Louisiana, and sometimes Illinois Country. Most of the settlers who moved into the area were French Canadians from the north, and the biggest draw for them, across this whole stretch of new territory, was fur trapping. The upper Mississippi valley was apparently a gold mine for trappers and hunters, and so they moved south to chase their fortunes.

They built six major settlements along the eastern edge of modern-day Illinois. One of those was established near a tribe of Native Americans who took their name from a small tributary that joined the larger Mississippi. There were a lot of variants—white Europeans were rarely ever good at taking a Native American name and carrying it over to French or English in a consistent way—but everyone there began to call the place Kaskaskia.

Before we move on, though, let me briefly explain the geography of this area. You see, Kaskaskia was a settlement built right on the tip of a small peninsula that stuck out into the Mississippi River. To the east, you could walk deeper into the Illinois territory. Looking west from the town would give you a spectacular view across the great river. That was the territory now known as the state of Missouri. Kaskaskia, in a lot of ways, was a place caught in between.

And not just geographically. On a social level, the settlement was a mixture of French Canadian fur trappers, Jesuit missionaries, and local Native Americans. The Jesuits brought the structure, the trappers brought the economy, and the indigenous people brought . . . well . . . they'd already been there. And as with so many other stories about the early days of this country, that meant the Native Americans weren't going to get a fair shake.

One story clearly highlights this disparity. In 1698, about twenty-five years after the settlement was founded, a Frenchman named Jean Benard immigrated to Kaskaskia, along with his wife and daughter, Marie. Like a lot of the people who moved there,

Benard was a fur trader, and the abundant resources of the area promised to make him a wealthy man.

He set up his trading post on the edge of town, where it would be easily accessible to the trappers moving up and down the western edge of Illinois. They brought in the fur, he purchased it from them, and then he sold it to buyers outside the wild frontier. It was simple and lucrative, and before long, he had a thriving business.

As the trading post grew, Benard brought on more help. It was common in those days of Kaskaskia for European business owners to hire local Native Americans to do the manual labor, and that was how one man in particular came to work for the Frenchman.

History doesn't remember his name, but the tale does describe how Jean Benard mistreated the man. He was cruel and unfair toward him, and always gave the worst of the labor to him and the other Native Americans who worked in the shop. But this man was different from most of the other Kaskaskians in the region.

It seems that the Jesuits had worked with his family decades before, and he himself was raised to speak both his native tongue and French, which made him a valuable helper. Benard took a liking to the young man, and they formed a good working relationship as a result.

But Jean Benard wasn't the only person to take a liking to the Kaskaskian. Apparently his daughter, Marie, fell in love with the man, something that her father was strongly opposed to. The legend says that he fired the young Native American, and then spread word around town that he wasn't to be hired by any of the other businesses. His goal was to drive the man to leave town in search of a job, and it apparently worked.

Marie, of course, was brokenhearted, but there was nothing she could do. And then, a year later, a group of traders rode into town, and among them was her lost lover. He'd returned to claim her hand and take her away, to end their separation and build a new life together elsewhere. Somehow he managed to pass a message to her, and they arranged to meet in secret later that night.

Once together, the couple left town, disappearing up the great Mississippi.

It's never that simple, though. Yes, they had a head start, and yes, they had love on their side. But Marie's father wouldn't be defied so easily.

DROWNED

The moment he learned of his daughter's escape, Benard gathered together a large group of men, and they rode out of town to hunt the couple down. I don't know how they knew to ride north, but that's what they did. Maybe they assumed her lover was looking for work in one of the bigger settlements. Maybe they knew he had friends or family north of Kaskaskia. Whatever their reason was, they followed the Mississippi northward.

It would have taken them hours, but eventually they tracked the young lovers down just outside of Cahokia. The town of Cahokia was another ancient Native American settlement that had become the site of a French outpost. Like Kaskaskia, it was home to a mix of French Canadians and Native Americans, and that made it a good hiding place for a couple like Marie and her true love.

When Benard's group found them, they immediately separated the couple. Marie was kept safe and watched over while the man she loved was beaten and bound with rope. They dragged him to the very edge of the river, and then began searching for a large branch or a fallen tree that they could manage. When they found one, they hauled it toward their prisoner.

The young man was tied to the log with yet more rope. We know he spoke French, and so did Benard and his men, so there was probably a lot of conversation. It's likely that he begged for his life, begged for Marie, begged for freedom. But the wrath of an angry father isn't something words can sway. Not for Jean Benard, at least. So the work continued.

When they were satisfied with their knots, the men pushed the log into the dark waters of the river. I imagine them wading out a bit, pushing it along, making sure it made it past all the debris and vegetation growing along the bank there. And then they let go, and watched as the young man drifted downriver with the current.

We don't know if Benard made his daughter watch it all. We don't know if she was whisked away back to Kaskaskia before she could see it all unfold. But we do know that the man she loved shouted out from the river as he drifted away. His words, they say, carried a powerful curse.

Benard would be dead within a year, he claimed, and he and Marie would be reunited forever. And then he added that the town of Kaskaskia itself would suffer. The French there would be destroyed, and even the dead would find no rest in their graves.

Later that year, Jean Benard got caught up in a bad business deal. He accused another man of cheating him and challenged him to a duel. Benard lost the duel and his life. Later that year, Marie herself died. They say she wasted away from a broken heart, but her death allowed her to reunite with her lover, and nothing would ever keep them apart again.

By the 1740s, the British were making moves to take over the territory controlled by the French. They bribed a number of neighboring Native American tribes to join them in a war against the settlers there, and by 1765, the French were run out of town. It seems Marie's true love was right about more than a few things.

Kaskaskia did its best to persevere, though. After the American Revolution, it became the capital of the Northwest Territory, and then in 1818 it became the first capital of the state of Illinois. But that only lasted for about a year. All along, the town kept growing, and by the mid-1800s it was home to roughly seven thousand people.

And then the Mississippi River got involved. In 1844, a flood nearly wiped the town off the map, and very few of the citizens stayed to rebuild. Instead, they went looking for a safer place to live. The Mississippi has always flooded. It still does. And that's made life difficult for anyone who lives along its banks. After 1844, a lot fewer people in Kaskaskia were willing to take that risk.

In the years that followed, the great river did something extraordinary: it moved. Slowly, it began to change course, shifting to pass by the town on the eastern side, rather than to the west. What was once a peninsula was slowly becoming an island instead, and after another major flood in 1881, the shift was complete.

Today, Kaskaskia is on the western shore of the Mississippi. Thanks to an act of Congress, it's a little pocket of Illinois on the edge of Missouri. Not that most people would notice, though. By 1950, there were only 112 people left to call the place their home.

WASHED AWAY

I think there are a couple of indisputable facts buried in these stories that we would be wrong to ignore. First, people love to curse their own town, or the town of their enemies, or whatever town they had a bad day in. We like to blame others for our own misfortune, or tell stories that explain away our bad luck and tragedy. It can't be our own fault, after all, so maybe the town itself is to blame, right?

Second, no place is safe from tragedy. At some point, whether it takes decades or centuries, every location is going to experience its own fair share of loss and misfortune. Fires. Floods. Natural disasters or human error. No matter what the cause is, every location will eventually receive a visit from adversity.

On their own, these are both sad truths. Together, though, they create a new world. One where cities are cursed, and the tragedies they experience are rooted in supernatural causes. Oftentimes the easiest thing to believe is also the most irrational.

Still, some locations *do* seem to have an unusual amount of tragedy heaped upon them, Kaskaskia being a prime example. And it didn't end in 1950. Even after that flood, the remaining citizens rebuilt the old Jesuit church and tried to move on. That's all they *could* do, I suppose. Still, they had to wonder.

And then, on April 4, 1973, the Mississippi rose nearly forty feet above normal levels. The north levees broke and the river rushed in, threatening much of the town. Hundreds of college students from nearby Southern Illinois University, along with residents of the mainland and dozens of prison inmates, all gathered there to lay sandbags and fight the flood as best as they could. But it was no use.

The new church and most of the town around it were washed away. And that includes the cemetery. Local legend says that the flood of 1973 caused a number of graves to burst open, washing hundreds of caskets—along with their occupants—into the depths of the river.

The dead, just as Marie's lover had predicted, had risen from their graves.

A Way Inside

IN 1897, BOSTON opened the Tremont Street Subway. It was a pioneer, setting the stage for the future of underground public transit. And as crazy as it might seem, it's still in use today, making it the oldest subway tunnel in North America, and the third-oldest in the world. Not too shabby for a dark hole in the ground.

It isn't a long tunnel system, but it helped people traveling around Boston Common, the massive public park in the middle of the city. Grab a map sometime, find the Common, and then trace your finger around the southeastern "chin" of the park where Boylston and Tremont Streets intersect. That's where the tunnel passes through.

Two years before it opened to the public, though, workers were digging furiously beneath that corner when they ran into something unexpected: skeletons. Hundreds and hundreds of human skeletons. Over nine hundred, in fact, and all of them right smack in the middle of their path.

Since the 1720s, thousands of people had been buried in what would later become known as the Central Burying Ground. But when Boylston Street was extended past there in 1836, the city engineers ran it right over a section of the graves. It's more than ironic, really: the Burying Ground, or at least part of it, got *bur-*

ied. After the skeletons were discovered in 1895, they were all moved to a mass grave, which is still nearby today.

This is what happens in old cities. When people have lived and died in one place for so long, things have a tendency to get buried and lost to time. Bodies, for sure, but also the lives those bodies represent. We end up burying our pain, our tragedy, our loss. And all those hidden memories have a way of popping back up when we least expect it.

Boston is one of those old cities. I know it's young by European standards, but it's one of the oldest in America. And all that age comes with a rich history. One that's full of conflict, and tragedy, and pain. Pain, some say, that can still be felt today.

LOW-HANGING FRUIT

The city of Boston probably requires no introduction. It's central to so many of the early ideas and emotions that fueled the birth of America, and it's one of the key stages upon which that conflict was played out. Boston was—and still is—an epicenter for rebellious spirit.

Most of us know it was the setting for the Boston Tea Party in 1773, which wasn't really a party, by the way. Three years before that, there was the Boston Massacre, which *was* really a massacre. These are well-known events with their own touch of darkness. But Boston's history is even darker than that.

Boston Common, that giant public park in the middle of the city that I mentioned earlier, is a good example. Sure, locals still used it for cattle grazing all the way up to 1830, but long before that, the Common was the popular place to execute criminals. Although *criminals* might be a misleading term. They hanged a good number of pirates and thieves, true, but they also killed Quakers for trespassing, and suspected witches for heresy.

And if tragedy leaves a painful shadow on a city, Boston has some dark spots. The Great Molasses Flood of 1919 is exactly what it sounds like. A company called Purity Distilling had a massive steel tank that contained 2.3 million gallons of molasses, which they used to make rum. In January 1919, that tank burst.

A wave of syrup twenty-five feet high rushed through the streets at thirty-five miles an hour. Buildings were pushed off their foundations. Children were swept away from their parents. At least twenty-one people were killed. Locals say that on hot summer days you can still smell the molasses. Simple chemistry, or the ghost of a tragic past reasserting itself?

There are other echoes, too. Back in the Central Burying Ground above the Tremont Street tunnel, many visitors have seen things they have trouble explaining logically. The most common sighting is of a little girl who has been seen standing among the gravestones, sometimes walking between them. This ghost, they say, is unique because of one key feature: she lacks a face.

Just north of the Common is another graveyard known as the Granary Burying Ground. It's one of the oldest cemeteries in town, dating back to 1660, and that means it holds a lot of history . . . and *story*.

The Granary is home to a number of well-known individuals, Paul Revere, Samuel Adams, John Hancock, and the parents of Benjamin Franklin among them. All of the Boston Massacre victims are interred there as well. But the graveyard is home to much more than burials. Some say it's full of restless spirits as well.

Ghost hunters love the graveyard for its abundance of orbs, those fuzzy white spots that sometimes appear in photos at night. They also claim to have recorded odd voices and unusual spikes in temperature and electromagnetic fields. If that's your cup of tea, the Granary offers a strong brew, for sure.

One of the common figures sighted in the Granary, though, is said to be a man named James Otis. He was a well-known lawyer prior to the American Revolution, and is famous for coining the main rallying cry of the rebellion, "No taxation without representation." But in 1769 he had an encounter with a British tax collector that ended in violence. During the struggle, the tax official struck Otis in the head with a blunt object, cutting him and, according to some, accelerating the symptoms of a mental illness he had struggled with for years. It's said that years later, Otis was so depressed over his illness that he wrote to his sister and expressed his desire to die quickly: "My dear sister, I hope, when God Almighty in his righteous providence shall take me out of time into eternity, that it will be by a flash."

On May 23, 1783, Otis was standing in the doorway of a friend's house in Andover when he dropped dead. The cause? A bolt of lightning.

But not all of Boston's haunted past is limited to outdoor spaces. Like James Otis, it stands on the doorstep, and if the stories are true, much of it has walked inside.

NO VACANCY

When John Pickering Putnam designed and built the Charlesgate Hotel in 1891, he was at the top of his game. As an architect, he was one of the leading designers of modern apartment buildings. As a builder, he was wildly creative, developing a number of new patents for building elements including ventilation systems and plumbing.

He was just forty-four when he finished the Charlesgate. It's a hulking Romanesque Revival structure at the corner of Beacon Street and Charlesgate East, and if you drive past, you can't miss it. And although it's been converted to condominiums today, it was originally designed to be a luxury hotel. In between, it's been a boardinghouse, a college dorm, and home to a few other less savory businesses.

But tragedy moved into the hotel early on. In 1908, just seventeen years after it was completed, a manufacturing executive named Westwood T. Windram ended a long struggle with depression and insomnia right there in the hotel. When a loud noise woke Windram's wife on March 14, she climbed out of bed, only to find her husband dead in the closet, gun still in hand.

Nine years later, architect John Putnam himself died at the age of seventy, right in the hotel he designed. And it's all that death and tragedy, some say, that helped give birth to a new type of resident in the building: ghosts.

Between 1947 and the 1990s, the hotel was converted into dorm space for Boston University and, later on, Emerson College. Many of the darker tales come from that era. In one encounter, a student opened his eyes in the middle of the night to see a stranger in his room. That's odd enough on its own, I know, but even more unusual was that this stranger was floating above the student's bed.

To make matters worse, the student discovered that he was unable to move. According to the story, the ghostly floating stranger attacked the student, who screamed in horror. A resident assistant and a handful of other students ran to help, and all of them claimed to see the same ghostly figure for a moment. And then it vanished.

Another student reported waking up to see a black cloud hovering near the ceiling of his dorm room. As he watched it, the dark mist moved across the room and vanished through the wall. There have been tales of unusual Ouija board encounters, unusual dreams, and strange sensations in places closest to the building's most tragic events. On their own, they are curious stories; together, though, they paint a haunting picture.

Another story-filled hotel in Boston is the Omni Parker House. It opened its doors in 1855, which makes it the oldest continuously operating hotel in the country. In the 1920s, most of the original building was torn down and replaced with a new, fourteen-story structure. But with all that history comes a lot of baggage.

The most frequent story told in the hotel is that of a ghostly older man seen walking the halls late at night. Those who have seen this figure describe him as bearded and dressed in Victorian-era clothing. Members of the hotel staff claim it's the spirit of Harvey Parker, the man who built the original hotel nearly two centuries ago.

If so, Mr. Parker gets around. Not only has he been seen in the halls of the ninth and tenth floors, but on at least one occasion a guest has witnessed him inside one of the rooms. One woman who stayed in Room 1012 awoke in the night to find the man standing at the foot of her bed. She locked eyes with the ghostly figure for a moment before he spoke. "Are you comfortable?" he reportedly asked. We can probably guess what her answer was.

Most stories, though, are focused on the third floor. Guests there have reported hearing sounds late at night that they identify as a rocking chair, slowly creaking back and forth. Other guests report that the elevator has an eerie tendency to stop on the third floor—with no one inside. The spirit they blame for that is Charlotte Cushman.

Cushman was born right there in Boston and quickly rose to become one of the most famous American actresses of the mid-1800s. She toured most of the English-speaking world with theater productions, selling out everywhere she went. But in 1876, she was at the end of her battle with breast cancer, and died of pneumonia at the Parker Hotel that February. Her ghost, some say, never checked out.

In the 1940s, a traveling liquor salesman apparently killed himself in Room 303, and that tragic event has left an indelible mark on the hotel. Guests in the past have complained about the constant smell of whiskey, while others claim they witnessed odd shadows in the room. Shadows, they say, that moved.

Other reports claim that the bathtub faucet would turn on all by itself. Guests have heard noises and felt cold spots, all of which create an environment that's a bit too unsettling for their tastes. Since then, the hotel has permanently closed the room, converting it into a storage space. The hauntings have reportedly stopped.

Clearly, these spaces have played host to the highs and lows of human life. Somewhere between the wealthy and celebrated and the tragic and painful, something has taken hold of them. Whether it's ghosts or just the echo of a dramatic story, that's ultimately up to the people who experience the effects.

But the story that just might be Boston's darkest is actually set seven miles to the east, in the middle of a busy harbor. It's easy to overlook it now, but 150 years ago, one island played host to an emotional tale filled with loss and misfortune.

And some say that story has never really ended.

SHADOWS

George's Island isn't large by any stretch of the imagination, but it was big enough for early settlers to use it for farming. In 1825, though, the government purchased it for another purpose: coastal defense.

This little island seemed like the perfect place to build a fort, which they did. But by the time they finished it in 1847, it was already outdated. They called it Fort Warren, after a local American Revolutionary War hero, and it remained in use for another century before closing its doors just after World War II.

Now, admittedly, there aren't any records that support the tale I'm about to tell you, and I know that makes for wobbly history. But the reality is that sometimes the only evidence of something historical is the folklore that it leaves behind. It's like a shadow, in a way; it hints that something bigger and more real is there, even if we can't see it. And in this case, it's a story that's worth repeating.

During the American Civil War, both sides of the conflict found themselves with a unique problem that none of them could have prepared for. Through the course of battle, prisoners were taken. And prisoners of war needed to be kept somewhere. Sometimes, as was the case in Richmond, Virginia, an out-of-the-way place was taken over and converted into a prison camp. Other times, old forts were used. And that's what happened in Boston.

In October 1861, about 750 Confederate prisoners arrived on the island. Some were political figures, like Confederate vice president Alexander Stephens. Most, though, were just soldiers, captured in battle. Thankfully, when compared to how prisoners were treated in places like Andersonville in Georgia or Belle Isle in Richmond, the Fort Warren prisoners were treated humanely and with dignity. But they were prisoners nonetheless.

One of those prisoners, according to the legend, was a man named Andrew Lanier. Shortly after his arrival, Lanier is said to have written a letter to his wife, Melanie, telling her what had happened and where he was. But when she received the letter, Andrew's wife didn't do what most of us would have done. Melanie didn't resign herself to waiting. She didn't weep and accept defeat. She took action.

When she got her husband's letter, Melanie saddled her horse and made the journey north to Massachusetts, eventually arriving in the town of Hull in late December 1861. Now, Hull is important because it's on the coast, and just about a mile across the water to the north is a fort. Fort Warren, in fact.

As the story goes, Melanie hacked off her long hair with a knife, dressed up in a man's clothing, and then tucked a pistol and hand axe into her belt. I can't think of anything more hardcore, honestly. This was a woman on a mission.

She climbed into a rowboat one night in January 1862 and made her way alone across the channel. When she arrived on the shore of George's Island, where Fort Warren sat waiting, Melanie hid the boat and threaded her way through the dark toward the prison. And then she whistled a song in hopes that her husband would hear it and recognize her. He did, and he whistled back.

Once she found the window where Andrew was standing, she managed to slip through. A grown man could never have done it, but she was smaller. And braver. Honestly, she traveled hundreds of miles from her safe home in the South just to willingly slip inside a northern prison. All for love.

What happened next is a bit of an action movie montage. It's that scene in *The A-Team* where they build the tank out of a bulldozer, some sheet metal, and leaf blowers equipped with artillery shells. The Laniers rallied the other prisoners, and together they began digging a tunnel. Their goal was to dig their way to the interior of the prison, overpower the handful of guards who were on duty, and then arm themselves for battle.

It was a solid plan, and they labored at the tunnel for weeks. All the while, the men worked together to hide Melanie from the guards. They each gave her a portion of their food. They kept her safe. And they dug. Each and every night, armed with that little hand axe, they dug. Until the night they made a mistake, and one of the guards heard the digging.

The alarm was instantly raised, the tunnel was discovered, and each of the prisoners was pulled out. When the last man was yanked free, Melanie jumped out of the darkness and drew her pistol, pointing it at one of the officers. Before she could pull the trigger, though, the man slapped the handgun aside, and it fired as it struck the stone floor.

There was silence for a moment. No one spoke. Not the guards, not the prisoners. It was as if the shot had silenced them all, and for a moment, there was no sound except for the slowly diminishing ring of the gunshot. And then Andrew Lanier toppled over, a red, bloody wound in his gut. The pistol had found a target after all.

Melanie would follow her husband soon enough, it turns out. For her crimes, she was sentenced to death, but before they executed her, she asked for more appropriate clothing. Something more feminine. Something befitting a lady. All they could find, though, was a large black robe.

Melanie Lanier was hanged in that black robe. After all she'd been through, after all she'd done, she was finally reunited with her husband. Death, as is so often the case, turned out to be the Great Connector, bringing the lost and separated back together in the end.

Of course, it could all be fantasy. The tale of Melanie Lanier is one that defies historical research, only appearing for the first time in a 1944 book about the fort. There's no record of a woman ever being hanged in the prison. No record of a tunnel. Nothing that can definitively prove the legend's accuracy.

But stories have a way of pointing toward the truth. And while that truth might or might not be the tale of one woman's love for her husband and how she gave everything to set him free, it might be something else. Maybe the story, like so much of folklore, was born out of a need to explain things.

You see, ever since the 1860s, people on the island have frequently reported odd sightings. Shapes that seemed to slip past the corner of their eye. Police have seen things there, as have tourists, and historians, and even researchers from MIT. Dark shapes outside the fort, moving against the walls. As if something were trying to find a way inside.

Shapes, according to the reports, that resemble a figure . . . dressed in a long black robe.

MAKING A HOUSE A HOME

Admittedly, there are a lot of cities around the United States with histories full of tragedy and suffering. But few have seen so much across such a broad space of time. Boston is unique in its dark, unfortunate beauty.

Every city has a ghost story, though. Or a collection of them. They're as common as the people who tell them. People who believe, deep down, that something darker is going on beneath the surface of the place they live.

Think of it this way: our houses are really nothing more than walls and floors enclosing a space. But that's not what makes a house a home. It's the people inside, the personal touches, the familiar objects. They transform a building into a home.

And that's what folklore does. It finds a way inside. It dresses up a sterile place and gives it life. True or not, it's essential. I have to wonder: without folklore, can anyplace ever really feel like home?

One of the things I find fascinating is just how many important figures called the Omni Parker House home, if only for a while. The hotel has experienced a nearly endless parade of history right through its hallways. Ho Chi Minh worked there for a year in 1912. And before Malcolm X stopped calling himself Malcolm Little, he worked as a busboy there in the 1940s.

The hotel has had countless famous guests . . . and some that were more *infamous*. John Wilkes Booth stayed there just eight days before he killed Abraham Lincoln. He came to Boston to visit his brother, also an actor, but while he was at the Parker Hotel he slipped over to a nearby firing range to practice using his pistol.

The most famous guest at the Parker House, though, might just be Charles Dickens. He'd been to Boston before, way back in 1842. But he was a struggling author back then, and so when he arrived in 1867, things were very different. He was a literary superstar.

He lived at the Parker for over five months beginning in the fall of 1867. While there, he performed his novella *A Christmas Carol* for sellout crowds. And all that performance meant he needed to practice. According to the hotel, Dickens would stand in front of his mirror for hours on end, working through his performance and trying to get it just right.

Two years later, Dickens died back home in England, but some say that Boston, and specifically the Parker, always had a special place in his heart. Perhaps he left a bit of himself there. Because that would explain another of the hotel's odd stories.

The mirror Dickens rehearsed in front of has long since been moved to another location in the hotel, out in a public area. And because of that, it requires regular cleaning. A few years ago, one of the hotel workmen was walking through the hall when he noticed that the mirror had condensation on it. The sort you might expect if someone had leaned in and breathed really heavily on the glass.

So he stopped, pulled a cloth out of his pocket, and proceeded to clean the mirror. When he was done, he turned around and looked to see if anyone was nearby, someone who might have done it. But the hall was empty.

When he looked back at the mirror, the fog had returned. He cleaned it a second time, and then watched in horror as it appeared once more, just a few inches from the first spot. It was as if someone were standing at the mirror with him, breathing on the glass. But there was no one else there.

As you might imagine, the man refused to ever clean the mirror again.

Behind Closed Doors

WHEN JOSEPH ASCH opened his new Asch Building in 1901, it was hailed as a modern marvel. It was a massive ten-story block of stone and iron, and it was said to be every bit as solid as it looked. But it was inside the building that the true break-throughs could be found.

It had freight elevators, wide-open floors, and fire exits. In fact, Joseph Asch was so proud of his modern building that he called it "fireproof." And for a city in desperate need of more factory space for its massive garment-making industry, it was perfect. So business partners Max Blanck and Isaac Harris signed a lease for the eighth floor.

And business was good. Soon they expanded upward, taking over the top three stories of the building. Their shop, the Triangle Shirtwaist Company, became the premier manufacturer of the most popular type of shirt in the country. But they also became sloppy.

On March 25, 1911, a fire broke out in a pile of scrap cloth. The building might have been billed as fireproof, but inside it was overcrowded and full of flammable materials—perfect conditions for a horrible tragedy. Less than an hour later, it was over. Some workers had burned to death. Others had fallen ten stories to es-cape the flames. All told, 146 people had lost their lives.

Today, the building is part of the New York University campus, but its tragic past hasn't completely evaporated. For years, witnesses have reported the telltale scent of smoke throughout the halls. Others have heard voices. Sometimes it's just a faint whisper, while other times it's a frightening cry for help. Most people, though, just sense an overwhelming air of darkness.

Whether it's the tragic past of countless historic buildings or the personal darkness of the people who lived inside them, New York—it seems—is a city overpopulated by ghosts.

And if you know where to look, the stories they tell will leave you feeling haunted.

OVERCROWDED

New York City is a monster. There's no better way to say it. It's so large and unwieldy that it operates more like a country than a metropolis. Yes, it's beautiful. It's full of life and culture and a depth of social awareness that few other cities in the world can match. But it's also a beast. In a lot of ways, New York City is like an Olympic athlete: mortal like us, yes, but there's very little about it that we'd consider *average*.

And it's old, too. Europeans have been in the area for over four hundred years, a century and a half longer than America has been a country. It's played host to everything from rebellion and war to epidemics and terrorism. And all of that death and violence leaves a veneer of darkness on New York, like soot from a wildfire.

The trouble with a city so large, though, is that it's easy to live inside it and be completely unaware of the stories you're standing on top of. Take Washington Square Park, in Greenwich Village. It was established in 1827 as a public space, kicking off the construction of all the beautiful things you see there today. The arch, the fountain, all those amazing flowers and trees . . . and twenty thousand dead bodies.

That's because prior to being a public space, Washington Square was a potter's field, a graveyard for the poor and unidentified. Then, in the early nineteenth century, as yellow fever rolled across the city like a tidal wave, thousands of victims were added to the burial ground there. The graves are shallow, sometimes just a foot or two below the surface. And because of the sheer number of them all, they've never been removed.

Just three blocks north of Washington Square Arch, there's an innocent-looking brownstone with a story of its own. You see, sometimes we bury the dead and they stay there, in the ground below our feet. Other times they refuse to go away, becoming dark roommates in an already overcrowded city. That was the experience of actress Jan Bryant Bartell, who moved into 14 West 10th Street way back in 1957.

For sixteen years Bartell lived in the building while suffering through what she claimed was intense paranormal activity: shadows that moved, sounds that echoed from empty rooms, even objects that levitated. She claimed it was all a result of the dozens of deaths that had occurred in the building since the 1850s, and she wasn't alone in that theory.

Decades earlier, in the 1930s, a woman and her mother both reported seeing a white-haired man in a white suit. He turned to the women and reportedly spoke to them. "My name is Clemens," he said, "and I has a problem here I gotta settle." And then he vanished.

It turns out that the man looked a lot like Mark Twain, who had lived there for a year in 1901. Twain's real name, of course, was Samuel Clemens. All of this was too much for Bartell, though, who committed suicide in 1973, just before publishing a book of her experiences there. Today, many New Yorkers refer to the old brownstone as the House of Death.

But death happens all over the city. It always has, but more often than not, the reason is more human than supernatural. In fact, one of the first highly public murder trials in New York City happened way back in 1799, although it still haunts the area to this day. That was the year a twenty-one-year-old woman named Elma Sands was killed and dumped into a well on Spring Street in Manhattan.

Her killer, according to the prosecution, was her wealthy fiancé, Levi Weeks. While much of the witness testimony and evidence pointed to Weeks as the true killer, his wealth brought a team of powerful attorneys to the courtroom: Aaron Burr and Alexander Hamilton.

Oh, and if any of that sounds even the least bit familiar, go ahead and assume you're the smartest in the room.

Weeks got off the hook, but Elma Sands has apparently refused to slip away. The well was covered by a building in the 1820s, and for decades the site played host to a restaurant. Reports of unusual activity in the building have been nonstop ever since, including plates and silverware that have been seen floating. Some have even claimed to see the ghost of Elma herself crawling out of the well, now located in the basement.

There's also the small matter of the curse. According to legend, as Burr and Hamilton were exiting the courtroom after their victory, Elma Sands's cousin Catherine Ring blocked their path and shouted a prediction to the room. "If you die a natural death," she cried, "I will think there is no justice in heaven." Then she pointed at Hamilton, who would be killed just four years later by Burr.

But you don't have to take part in a murder trial to attract the attention of the dead. In fact, if you believe the stories, life is full of moments with the potential to leave us feeling haunted. And few locations in New York City can compare to one historic neighborhood near Prospect Park.

But the story that lies dormant beneath the ground there is far worse than a shallow graveyard or body in the well. It's a tale of secret rooms, violent politics, and a love that refused to die.

HIDDEN AWAY

The area of Brooklyn known today as Flatbush began life as a Dutch colony in 1651. The name comes from the original appearance of the landscape, which was described as a flat, wooded plain. It's difficult to imagine, given the urban sprawl of modern New York, but for a while Flatbush was a wide-open collection of forests and farms.

Roughly a century later, the city was under British rule, and that meant the old Dutch architecture was slowly giving way to English manors. And one of those newer homes was built in 1749 by an Englishman by the name of Lane. He came from a wealthy family that didn't care for his drunken parties and new lower-class wife, and so New York became his home in exile.

Life didn't change much for him in the colonies, though. The parties continued unchecked, and his grand manor, which he called Melrose Hall, became the centerpiece of local gossip. And then, some years later, he stepped outside during one of his celebrations and never returned. As far as I can tell, no one knows what happened to Mr. Lane after that.

But Melrose Hall remained, and from the descriptions that survive, it was quite the home. It was two and a half stories tall, with a gabled roof that created numerous small spaces—something Lane had apparently taken advantage of. The right-side wing of the house held the dining room and library, while the left wing contained a large banquet hall. But it wasn't this collection of traditional rooms that gave the house its flavor. No, the true personality came from its hidden parts.

According to one writer in 1888, the fireplace in the banquet hall was flanked by two closets. And it was inside one of them that a secret door could be found. It only unlocked from the outside, but once unlocked it revealed a narrow staircase that led to a hidden bedroom above the hall.

Across the house in the dining room, another secret passage was hidden behind a piece of furniture. One writer claims that the whole thing swung outward like a door, and that walking through it would take you into the slave quarters. And as if that weren't enough, the home even had a small vaulted dungeon beneath the main house.

At the same time, a few miles to the north, in lower Manhattan, a man named William Axtell was growing restless. He was a merchant who'd spent most of his life in Jamaica as part of the business, but had moved to New York in the 1750s. But the city was expanding around him, and it was time to find more space and solitude.

So when a home as textured and unique as Melrose Hall suddenly became available for purchase, Axtell didn't blink. But before he and his family arrived to move in, he sent someone ahead of them: his mistress, Isabell.

Now, history is a bit foggy on who she really was. Some say she was his wife's sister, while others claim she was a woman he met in Jamaica. She was described as tall and dark, with long black hair and a kind, beautiful smile. And when she showed up at the house ahead of Axtell and his wife, it was Miranda—one of the Axtells' most trusted slaves—who welcomed her inside and guided her to the secret bedroom above the banquet hall.

Miranda would, in fact, become Isabell's lifeline. Since she couldn't open the door in the closet from her side, it was up to Miranda to bring her food and care for her needs. It was also a responsibility that Miranda kept entirely to herself, at the request of William Axtell.

Once the family had moved in, the lovers fell into a new, clandestine routine. Once a week at midnight, William would creep downstairs to the banquet hall and sit by the fire. Then Miranda would appear and open the closet beside the fireplace, unlock the secret door, and release Isabell from her hidden chamber. Then the lovers would . . . well, whatever lovers do. You get the idea.

All of this went on for years. By day, Axtell ran his merchant business and worked for the English crown as a member of the Governor's Council. At night, though, he secretly met with his mistress. It wasn't honest, but you could certainly call him busy, I suppose.

But life was about to change dramatically in Melrose Hall. Those midnight trysts would continue, of course, but daily life for William Axtell was about to slip into chaos and danger. You see, war had arrived. Not in some far-off land, or even a few miles away. No, when the Battle of Brooklyn took place on August 27, 1776, it happened in the worst possible location.

Right in Axtell's backyard.

All of this was bad news for William Axtell. He was an English loyalist who stood to lose everything—power, money, land, all of it—if the Americans managed to succeed. And in 1776, the Battle of Brooklyn showed just how close to home this new war for independence could get.

As a member of the Governor's Council, he had a duty to perform. So it was common for rebel leaders to be captured and transferred to his personal dungeon below Melrose Hall. But it wasn't enough to hide them away from the watchful eye of the rebels; Axtell was being pushed toward action by the king.

He was told to gather five hundred men and get ready to march. It wasn't clear if he would be gone for weeks or months, but he would be out of the house and away from his lover, Isabell. And that's when a problem occurred to him: Miranda, the slave woman who cared for Isabell and kept their secret from the rest of the household, was getting along in years.

In fact, she was old enough that Axtell feared she might be close to death. Which, as we all know, would be a very bad thing. Because without Axtell around, Miranda was the only access that Isabell had to food and water. That secret door in the closet only opened from Miranda's side, and if she were to die . . . well, that hidden bedroom would slowly transform, first into a prison, and then into a tomb.

So the night before his departure, Axtell went to the banquet hall at their appointed time and waited for Miranda to open the door and lead Isabell to his side. When she arrived, he made his case. Leave, he told her. Run away and find safety someplace else. He even handed her a bag of gold and told her to use it to take care of herself while he was gone.

But Isabell didn't take the news well. She felt as though William was trying to abandon her, that he was essentially breaking up with her and using his impending military tour as an excuse. She screamed and threw the coins back at him and ranted about his motives. And then she ran back to the secret staircase inside the open closet, closed the door, and vanished from sight.

They say that he was gone for a full year, far longer than he'd expected. In his absence, the very thing he had feared might happen *did*. Miranda, the only keeper of his secret, became sick and died. Legend says that on her deathbed she tried to tell the others about Isabell, but everyone thought it was just the madness of a dying woman.

Weeks later, William Axtell rode up the path to his beautiful estate and entered his home for the first time in a year. His wife welcomed him home. His adopted niece, Eliza Shipton, did the same. And then they led him into the banquet hall, where a gathering of his friends waited for him. The moment he walked through that door, the party began.

But it wasn't all laughter and joy. Axtell kept glancing at the closet door beside the fireplace. He longed to hold Isabell, to kiss her and hear her voice. But something was troubling him: he had seen no sign of Miranda since arriving.

The legend tells us that Axtell got up from his seat at one point in the night and ran across the house to the slave quarters. There he was greeted with the terrifying news that Miranda had passed away weeks before. And that's when panic fully gripped his heart.

He staggered back into the banquet hall and wandered slowly through the gathering of people. They were laughing and singing and talking joyfully, but he couldn't hear their voices anymore. All he could think about was Isabell and the secret room that had become her prison. That's when the impossible happened: every single candle in the room went out.

At first everything was dark, but then a subtle glow began to illuminate the edges of the room. One newspaper from 1886 described it as a "sickly glowworm light." Then the sounds began. They were soft at first, low and distant, as if they were coming from a great distance. And then, just as they exploded in volume, the closet burst open and the secret door swung outward.

That 1886 article described the woman who stepped out as "ashen pale, each vein strongly defined on the emaciated features, her long black hair hung drooping over her shoulders to the floor, and she seemed clad in airy gossamer." She didn't walk so much as glide, and she headed straight toward William Axtell.

The room was silent. Every eye was on this strange new visitor. Maybe they were frightened. Perhaps they were waiting to see if this macabre performance would end in applause. Or maybe they were under some sort of spell. Whatever the reason, not a single sound could be heard as the pale shape came to a stop just inches from their host.

The woman lifted her hand, a single finger extended, and aimed it at Axtell's face. And then she opened her mouth and uttered a single, chilling word.

"Betrayer," she said.

And then the glow vanished, leaving all of them in pitch darkness.

When candles were brought in and lit, the guests found no sign of the pale woman, but they did see something else: Axtell was sprawled out on the floor, eyes closed and body motionless. He was moved to his bedroom almost immediately, and a doctor was called to the house. But the legend tells us that it was all futile.

Colonel William Axtell, they say, died that very night.

BURIED TRUTH

In places as old and sprawling as New York City, history is bound to get buried beneath the bustle of everyday life. The tragedy of the Triangle Shirtwaist fire evolved into a watershed moment for labor reform and working conditions. The burial vaults and shallow graves of Washington Square Park have given way to beauty and art and culture, making the park a place that practically pulses with life.

History slips away. It fades into the backs of our minds much the same way it sinks beneath our feet. Humans are good at a lot of things, but forgetting is one of our crowning achievements. But there are always clues . . . if you know where to look for them.

Colonel William Axtell was a real person. In fact, if you visit the Metropolitan Museum of Art, you can see him. There's a painting of him hanging in Gallery 747. He commissioned it in the 1750s just before moving into Melrose Hall, and it hung there for years.

But as it turns out, William Axtell didn't die that night in the banquet hall of his home. The tides of war turned against the British, and by 1782 Axtell had packed up his family and returned to England. He died there in 1795, and there were no reports of ghosts at his deathbed.

Stories can be tricky, it seems. Sometimes they're rooted in fantasy, in events that never happened at all. Other times they sprout from truth like a sapling sprouts from a seed, and take on a shape and life of their own. Stories grow. They evolve and shift with the passing of time. But the truth is always there, even if it's buried beneath centuries of hearsay.

Melrose Hall passed from hand to hand over the years that followed. In a bit of irony, the first couple to take ownership after the Axtells left was their own adopted niece, Eliza Shipton, and her new husband, an American military officer named Aquila Giles.

In 1880, the house was purchased by Dr. Homer Bartlett, and he felt it was time for some changes. An entire neighborhood had grown up around the property in the century since the Axtells' departure. So he had the main house lifted up and moved four hundred feet farther back from the road. It was a change that came with casualties.

All of the external buildings were demolished, and a number of ancient trees were cut down. The biggest loss of all, though, was the left wing of the house, which Bartlett decided was no longer necessary. But right before they moved it, Melrose Hall gave up one final secret.

While searching the structure for valuables worth saving, someone discovered a secret chamber. After grabbing a light and venturing inside, they made a grisly discovery. It was a skeleton, many decades old and covered in dust.

The skeleton, they say, was of a woman.

 INSIDE THESE WALLS

Echoes

THE SETTING OF a story is everything. It creates mood and atmosphere. It triggers memories and helps our minds fill in the blanks, adding tension and suspense where there were only words and images.

What would *The Shining* be like without the long hallways of the Overlook Hotel? Or *The Legend of Hell House* without the dusty bones of the old Belasco House? And can anyone ever look at an old cabin in the woods without a chill running down their spine? Not me, that's for sure.

One of the most iconic and most visceral settings for any horror story, without question, has always been the insane asylum. These days, we refer to the institutions that treat mental disorders as psychiatric hospitals. They're hard places to work—I know this firsthand thanks to a colorful college internship during which I met a double amputee who enjoyed streaking down the hallway on his knees. Mental health professionals do amazing work.

But a lot more than just the name has changed for these hospitals of the mind. In the late 1800s and through to the 1950s, asylums were a very different place. They were filled with sick people in need of help, but frequently patients were offered only pain and suffering.

When H. P. Lovecraft wrote "The Thing on the Doorstep" in 1933, he imagined a place that he called the Arkham Sanitarium.

Arkham is the seed; it's the first of its kind. Through it, Lovecraft brought the asylum into the horror genre, and others quickly caught on. The famous super-prison and mental hospital of the Batman universe, Arkham Asylum, is a direct descendant of Lovecraft's invention.

Arkham was a real place, though, known as the Danvers State Hospital. In fact, the remains of it stand just eight miles from my front door. And even before construction began in 1874, the hospital's story was already one of fear and suffering, a theme that continued unchecked well into the twentieth century.

BEGINNINGS

Before the days of institutional care for the mentally ill, the job was left largely to independent contractors, people who were hired by the state to look after others. But that was a system with far too many opportunities for failure.

Patients were routinely placed in cages or stalls, and they were chained and beaten into submission. Violence, rape, and death were everyday occurrences. Thankfully, people began to look for a better, more humane way of caring for these individuals, and those conversations led to the establishment of a new, state-of-the-art mental hospital.

Plans started off on the wrong foot, though. The site that was chosen for the construction was the former homestead of John Hathorne, one of the nine magistrates who oversaw the witch trials of Salem in 1692. Hathorne was known for his vicious, harsh attitude toward those who were accused of witchcraft, and he pushed hard for their execution.

He was so well known for his violent, hateful personality that his great-great-grandson, the author Nathaniel Hawthorne, changed the spelling of his last name—adding the w—to distance himself from that reputation.

It was there, on Hathorne Hill, that the foundations of the hospital were laid. The chances are pretty high that no one made the comparison at the time, but hindsight is always 20/20, and looking back over the last century and a half, it's clear that Hathorne's legacy lived on atop that hill.

The Danvers State Hospital was actually intended to be a beacon of hope. There was a specific plan behind its design, one that was based on the work of Dr. Thomas Kirkbride. He designed the building with four radiating wings emanating from a central structure. His reason was simple: with more sunlight coming into the rooms, and proper ventilation, more patients would experience recovery.

All told, the hospital was designed to house five hundred patients, covering a wide spectrum of mental illness, who were served by a team of roughly a dozen staff. When the doors finally opened in 1878, it was called the State Lunatic Hospital, and there was no other place like it in the country. It was set up to be a leader in the humane treatment of patients, and became the model for countless other facilities like it.

Rightly so; this place was amazing. The ornate interiors, private rooms, and sunny corridors all connected to the central Kirkbride Building. The patients were encouraged to exercise and participate in the community gardens. The small farm there even produced enough food for the hospital kitchen to feed the patients home-grown meals.

Over time, though, the hospital expanded. There were separate tuberculosis buildings, housing for staff, a machine shop, a medical building, and a pump house to pull water from the reservoir. All of these locations were connected underground by a network of dark, brick-lined tunnels arranged in the shape of a wagon wheel to allow for easy movement during harsh New England winters.

But the hospital campus wasn't the only thing that was expanding.

BREAKDOWN

As with all good things, the bright days of the Danvers State Hospital didn't last long. More and more patients were admitted each year, and the staff struggled to keep up. Decreased state funding prevented them from hiring more help.

By the 1920s, the population had grown to over two thousand patients, four times what the facility was designed to hold. One eyewitness reported that in November 1945 the evening shift of the entire hospital consisted of nine people, and they were expected to care for the needs of more than twenty-three hundred patients.

You'll have to pardon the expression, but things at the Danvers State Hospital had begun to get crazy. Patients were frequently sick and filthy. It was not uncommon for some to die unnoticed, only to be found days later. It was nearly impossible for the staff to manage so many patients, and so they turned to the accepted tools of their time.

Straitjackets, solitary confinement, and even restraints, however barbaric they might seem to us today, were mild compared to some of the other methods used by the staff. Patients were regularly subjected to hydrotherapy and electroshock therapy. And yet it somehow still managed to get worse.

That's where the lobotomy enters this story.

First pioneered by Dr. Walter Freeman in 1936, the lobotomy was a complicated procedure. The surgeon would literally cut into the patient's brain, severing the connection between the frontal lobes and the thalamus. The goal was to reduce symptoms and make the patient more manageable, but the results were mixed. Some patients died as a result of the procedure, while others would commit suicide later.

Freeman, though, quickly grew tired of how long it took to complete the procedure. He had heard of a doctor in Italy who was operating on his patients' brains through their eye sockets. Working without drilling or cutting presented an opportunity that Freeman simply couldn't pass up.

He called his new technique the transorbital lobotomy. It's fairly easy to describe, but it's not for the faint of heart. Freeman discovered that the only surgical tool he really needed was an ice-pick. According to his son Franklin Freeman in a PBS interview in

2008, those first icepicks came right out of their kitchen icebox, and "they worked like a charm."

By inserting the icepick into the inner corner of a patient's eye, Freeman could punch through the skull to reach the brain. Then he would essentially—um—*stir* the frontal lobe until it was no longer functional.

Oh, and one more thing: he did all of this without anesthetic.

And he got good at it. So good, in fact, that he took his show on the road. He literally toured the nation in a van that he called the Lobotomobile, stopping at mental institutions where he would train the staff in his technique. While he was there, he would perform as many lobotomies as they needed for the low, low cost of just $25 per patient.

It sounds like Freeman was delivering the solution to a desperate industry, but that was pretty far from the truth. His patients often lost the ability to feed themselves or use a bathroom unassisted, and those skills would have to be retaught, if indeed it was even possible. And about 15 percent died from the procedure. Also, relapses were common, and sometimes the lobotomy would have to be reattempted.

Once, in 1951 at Iowa's Cherokee Mental Health Institute, Freeman stopped in the middle of a lobotomy, icepick clutched in his hand, so that he could pose for a photograph. The instrument penetrated a bit too far, and the patient died.

He never wore gloves. Or a mask. And he apparently had no limits. In fact, of the thirty-five hundred lobotomies that he performed in twenty-three states, nineteen of those patients were minors—one of them a four-year-old child.

Ironically, some people still don't believe in monsters.

EMPTY NEST

The horror of institutional lobotomy ended in 1954 when a new drug was brought to the market. Thorazine was marketed as a "chemical lobotomy," and the need for the surgical procedure dropped dramatically. The drug worked as promised, and by the 1960s there was less and less need for massive facilities like the Danvers State Hospital.

Massive budget cuts, building closings, and structural damage had all conspired to slowly push the institution's doors closed. By 1985, nearly every building on the campus was abandoned, and the Kirkbride administrative building itself closed down in 1989. The last remaining patients were moved to the medical building on the site, but were all eventually transferred to other facilities with the help of the National Guard and eighty ambulances.

The hospital was officially abandoned in the summer of 1992 and stood vacant and derelict for nearly a decade. The rooms that once played host to victims of Dr. Freeman and his icepick became shelter for homeless squatters. They built their lives around the decaying medical equipment, wheelchairs, and bed frames. It was probably the healthiest inmate population the building had known for decades.

In 2005 the property was purchased by a developer, and much of the campus was demolished to make way for a sprawling apartment complex. But they left the front façade of the Kirkbride Building, with its soaring gothic towers and intricate brickwork. The hospital didn't go quietly, though.

In April 2007, four of the apartment buildings, as well as a handful of construction trailers, mysteriously burned down. It was a fire so big that it was visible from Boston, seventeen miles to the south. There was an investigation, but it turned up no evidence other than webcam footage of the construction site, which inexplicably cut out just before the fire began.

ALL THAT REMAINS

The image of an asylum will forever hold a place in our hearts as something to be feared and avoided. Whether new and sunny or ancient and decaying, the asylum is a setting that causes people to back away, a knot of terror in their stomachs.

But why? On a rational level, these were places of hope for

many people. Still, the very concept of a residential hospital for the mentally ill, complete with nineteenth-century decor and equipment, is the stuff of nightmares.

Perhaps what we really fear is losing control over ourselves. Restraints, locked rooms, medication, and irreversible medical procedures represent, for many of us, the opposite of freedom. We fear losing our dignity, losing our well-being, losing our very minds.

Death, however, is chasing all of us. The curse of mortality is that we are already handing those things over, day by day, until the time when there is nothing left to give. Perhaps the stereotypical asylum simply reminds us of the inevitable truth that is our own death.

The Danvers State Hospital is nearly gone today, but reminders still linger of its presence. There is the brick façade of the Kirkbride Building, and one of the roads there is called Kirkbride Drive. The reservoir that provided the facility with its water can be found behind the apartment buildings. And that vast network of ancient tunnels is still there as well, snaking its way beneath the modern structures and the people who live inside them.

One final reminder awaits people who come for a visit, though: the old asylum cemetery. It's where the staff buried patients who died and went unclaimed by family. There are no tall tombstones, though. Instead, each grave is marked by a small square stone with a number engraved on it. And there are hundreds of them.

Anyone looking for the cemetery will know they've found it when they see the large boulder that marks the entrance. It was placed there in the recent past to explain why all those small square stones are there. But it's the message engraved on it, and not the grave markers themselves, that communicates everything we need to know.

It simply reads: THE ECHOES THEY LEFT BEHIND.

Southern Drama

ASK ANYONE WHO'S explored the world of haunted houses for a list of their top ten, and almost all of them will include a plantation in St. Francisville, Louisiana, known as the Myrtles. And rightly so, because the stories that surround the place are among the most detailed and enthralling on record.

The property—all six hundred acres of it—was first purchased in 1796 by David Bradford. He was one of the typical colonial American success stories. Born in the colonies to Irish immigrants, he climbed the social ladder quickly, working his way from simple independent attorney to deputy attorney general of his county in Pennsylvania.

But when he got on the wrong side of the Whiskey Rebellion in 1794, he had to flee. The fledgling U.S. government didn't take kindly to people who encouraged tax evasion and arson—ironic, considering the roots of the new nation—and as a result, Bradford found himself in need of a new home.

Leaving his family behind, he traveled down the Mississippi and purchased land there. Four years later, when President John Adams pardoned him, he was able to return to Pennsylvania and pack up his family to come join him. After bringing them back to the Baton Rouge area, he set up shop as a teacher, offering classes in law.

One of his students, a man from Maine named Clark Woodruff,

eventually married Bradford's daughter, and over time the young couple assumed management of the huge estate. Like many plantation owners across the South, the Woodruffs used slave labor, and it was the intersection of those two social groups that brought on much of the legend of the Myrtles.

According to the stories that have been told for decades, Clark Woodruff had an affair with one of the slaves, a woman named Chloe. Some say it was mutual, while others describe how Woodruff coerced her into the arrangement. Either way, it put Chloe into a difficult position.

Eventually, though, the affair ended. In one version of the legend, it was because Chloe was caught listening at the door while Woodruff conducted business. Because of this, he had one of her ears cut off as punishment, and it is said that she wore a green turban to hide the injury.

Out of spite, Chloe brewed a syrup from oleander leaves, which are highly toxic, and included it in a birthday cake with the intent of poisoning Clark Woodruff. The plan backfired, though, and rather than killing him, it killed his wife, Sarah, and two of their young children.

When the other slaves found out what she had done, they took action before Woodruff himself could punish them all. Their justice was harsh, and it was swift. They waited until night and kidnapped Chloe while she slept. Then, under the cover of darkness, they dragged her outside, where she was hanged from one of the large oak trees on the property.

According to the story, her body was then cut down, weighted with stones, and thrown into the nearby Mississippi River. It's said that her ghost haunts the property to this day, and that she's even been captured in photographs. But what most people don't know is that all of it—from the affair to the hanging—is one long string of lies.

Historians researching the plantation and events of the last two centuries have been able to prove that the Woodruffs never owned a slave named Chloe (or even Cleo, as her name is sometimes mistakenly given). And although Clark Woodruff's wife, son, and daughter did all die tragically within months of each other, it was yellow fever that ended their lives, not birthday cake laced with oleander poison.

The root of these tall tales, according to researchers, was Marjorie Munson, a woman who owned the property in the 1950s. She apparently noticed strange things—such as the vision of a black woman in a green turban—and the stories were created to help explain what she saw.

That hasn't stopped visitors from reporting strange phenomena, though, no matter what the underlying truth might be. From Robert Stack and the *Unsolved Mysteries* production crew to modern tourists who wander through the property, the Myrtles have left an impression that something supernatural is at work there.

Some have reported seeing children playing out on the wide veranda, or in the halls and rooms of the house itself. The children are described as being a small boy and a similarly young girl. Perhaps these visions are of the Woodruff children—lives ended too short by illness, not poison, mind you.

Others have seen a young girl with curly blond hair who floats outside the window that looks into the game room. Witnesses say she cups her hands and peers inside, all while hovering in the air in a pale dress. Who she might be, though, is difficult to guess.

There's even a grand piano that has been known to play music on its own. Sometimes it happens in the light of day, and other times during the dead of night. Those who have entered the room to check have found only an empty room, with nothing but the echo of the last notes still lingering in the air.

Nothing matches the eerie tale told by one former gatekeeper of the house. While manning his post at the main gate one day, this man claimed that a woman in a pale, old-fashioned dress walked past him and through the open gate without speaking a word. He watched her pass, struck mute by the impression that all was not as it seemed. After traveling up the drive, this woman approached the front door of the house and then stepped inside.

The door, however, never opened.

Behind the Door

Guests who visited 1140 Royal Street in the 1830s dined off the most exquisite china available. They sat next to social elites from all across the city. There was polite laughter, and the gentle ring of sterling silver flatware as it tapped against the delicate plates. But nothing could top the hostess herself, who presided over these gatherings.

Delphine LaLaurie was beautiful, intelligent, successful, and powerful. Her daughters wore only the best dresses from European cities like Paris. Dresses that had been carefully packaged up and placed on a ship, and then brought across the Atlantic, around the coast of Florida, and up to the Mississippi Delta.

Delphine's husband was a prominent surgeon, and she had wealthy French family roots. They had arrived in New Orleans to an almost immediate show of respect, awe, and power. And we shouldn't forget that this couple was among the wealthy elite in the pre–Civil War South. Their social gatherings, their extravagant meals, and the operations of their stately mansion were all powered by slaves. Dozens and dozens of them, forced to work against their will.

It was a beautiful façade hiding a darker truth, and sometime shortly after their arrival in New Orleans, that façade showed its first crack. According to the local legend, Madame LaLaurie was having her hair brushed one evening by a young slave girl named

Leah. Everything was going well enough, the story goes, until Leah hit a tangle in the woman's hair.

Delphine let out a cry of pain, and then spun around on the girl. She beat her right there in the room, they say, so viciously that Leah, despite her upbringing as a slave, turned and dashed out the door. Delphine gave chase, some say with a whip, and the girl ran all the way to the third floor of the mansion. Cornered in a room, the girl climbed out onto the balcony, slipped, and plummeted to her death on the pavement below.

That sort of tragedy attracts attention, but Madame LaLaurie managed to talk her way out of the situation with nothing more than a $300 fine. Her reputation, though, was stained.

In April 1834, just two years after their spectacular arrival in New Orleans, a fire broke out in the mansion. Neighbors called the firefighters, who entered the house to battle the blaze. Searching for the source of the smoke, they entered the kitchen and then stopped. There was a woman chained to the stove.

She was bloody, with cuts all over her body, and she was slumped on the floor as if dead or unconscious. When they released her from the chains, she told them her story. She had upset the LaLauries that morning, and after brutally beating her, they had locked her to the stove. Out of desperation, the slave woman had lit the house on fire in the hopes of killing herself and destroying the mansion. But she'd failed.

Not entirely, though. In fact, she still managed to bring the mansion down around her owners, if only in a figurative way. She told the firemen of a room on the third floor where other slaves had been taken after disagreements with the LaLauries—slaves who had never returned.

The men went looking for this room, but when they found it, the door was locked, bolted shut from the outside. Beyond the door, though, they could hear sounds. Cries for help. Moans of pain. The rattle of chains.

Armed with axes and pry bars, they tore the lock off the door and pulled it open. I'm not sure what they had expected to find. I think we tend to hope for the best, in general, and maybe that's what they had done. But when the overwhelming smell of decay and rot and death washed over them from the open doorway, they stumbled back. Some of them vomited right there in the hall. Others muttered prayers or curses.

Inside the room, there were bodies. Some were dead on the floor, flies buzzing around their decaying limbs, and some were still alive and hanging from the ceiling by chains. All of them, though, had been tortured. Bones had been broken and reset. Flesh had been cut and stitched. Fingers and limbs had been removed.

It seems that the LaLauries had been experimenting on their slaves. Anyone who defied them, disobeyed them, or failed to serve in an appropriate manner would be brought to this room and punished. And none who entered the room had ever returned alive.

Local legend goes into horrible detail about the extent of those experiments, although there's little documentation to support the claims. One story tells of how the firemen found a young woman in the room whose limbs had been broken and reset at odd angles, causing her to walk like a crab on all fours. Another story mentions a man, still living when they found him, with a hole in his skull that was full of maggots.

But even without the sensational stories, the core truth was horrifying enough. The LaLauries possessed such a low regard for the lives of their slaves that they treated them like laboratory animals. No sane, caring person would have been capable of what these two social elites had done. And when the city caught wind of it, the public was outraged.

The LaLauries hadn't been home when the room was discovered, and somehow they managed to slip out of town before the consequences could catch up with them. Stories tell of how the family fled to Paris. Others say they changed their names and blended into a community outside New Orleans. But while the criminals might have escaped, the scene of the crime remained behind. And it kept telling its story, over and over.

Bodies continued to be found under the floors and inside the walls of the house for nearly a century. Some historians put the death toll in the neighborhood of three hundred slaves, although that seems like a bit of a stretch for a highly public mansion in the middle of the busy French Quarter. But death did take place there, and it left its mark.

Today, there are still reports of sounds from inside the house. Some have heard pained moaning, while others claimed to have heard cries for help. Those who have lived there speak of the sound of chains and the smell of fire. And some have seen things.

Specifically, people inside and outside the house have seen the same ghostly image over and over throughout the past century and a half. It's the vision of a girl dressed in the rags of a slave, falling to her death from the third floor. Over and over again.

A Bad Spirit

SOMETIMES, NO MATTER how hard you try to move on, the past manages to stay right behind you, chasing you like a shadow.

It's not that all of Mary Gray's life was difficult, but a lot of it certainly was. She and her husband, Andrew, had been part of that early wave of settlers in central Illinois who tried to make a life for themselves in newly formed Peoria County. Peoria was the name of a local tribe of Native Americans, and most likely meant something along the lines of "dreaming with the help of a bad spirit."

But this frontier life wasn't for everyone. It was hard work, each and every day. The trade-off, though, was the beauty of the countryside. So despite the challenges, life seemed to be all right for Mary and Andrew Gray. And then Mary's brother died.

He had lived in the area, so his grown son was able to travel to Peoria and move in with the Grays. That's not the sad part; family should always stick together, I think, so there was the potential here for a good change. But the nephew brought a laundry list of problems with him.

He was lazy and had a knack for getting into trouble. He also loved to drink, and was drunk so often that sobriety was the less common state for the young man. Which of course led to all sorts of bad relationships and troubles with the law. Mary Gray's nephew, it seems, made a hobby out of getting arrested.

It's easy to look at someone like that young man and say, "That's a quick way to ruin your life, son." And I can agree. But behavior like that has a way of damaging the people around a person. For the Grays, that damage was financial. Every arrest led to a court date and a lawyer. And lawyers need to be paid. So as the arrests added up, what little money Andrew and Mary Gray had managed to save slowly began to vanish. But it was clear their nephew wasn't going to stop just because they ran out of money, so Mary made a foolish decision.

A young lawyer had recently moved to the area and set up shop in a small shack at the edge of town. His name was David Davis, and while he lacked a lot of experience, he was friendly, bright, and eager. Mary approached Davis with a proposal: take on the criminal defense of her nephew, and if she failed to pay the fees, her house and property would be his.

Davis wrote up the necessary paperwork for the agreement, and they signed it on November 10, 1847. And then they crossed their fingers. Which never works, by the way. The Grays' nephew was soon arrested again, the Grays failed to pay the fees, and the attorney took possession of the house and land.

Rather than admit defeat, Mary played dumb. "What agreement?" she said. I don't know what her strategy was here. Maybe she thought she had the only copy of the agreement. Perhaps she had failed to tell her husband about the shady deal and didn't want to admit guilt in front of him.

Whatever the reason for protesting it, though, she lost, and the Grays were asked to move out of their home there on Monroe Street. That's when things got even worse. Mary told her nephew to leave and never come back. A few days later, his body was found floating facedown in the Illinois River.

That was enough for the Grays. They packed up what little they still possessed and left town forever. But not before Mary stepped outside of the home she no longer owned and raised an angry hand to the sky. "May this land turn to thorns and thistles," she screamed, "with ill luck, sickness, and death to everyone who lives here."

TENANTS OF DARKNESS

Davis tried renting the house out for a while, and soon after the Grays left, a new couple moved in. Legend says that the husband was Thomas Ford, who had recently finished a four-year term as governor of Illinois. Legend also says that Thomas and his wife, Frances, died of grief, but in reality it was cancer that took her life in 1850, and her husband followed her three weeks later, a victim of tuberculosis.

Neighbors were quick to notice their ominous deaths. Mary had called for "ill luck, sickness, and death" for anyone in the house, and the Fords certainly seemed to fit the bill.

After the Fords died, Davis decided that life as a landlord was a lot of work, and he was already a busy man. He left the house empty, and it eventually became overgrown and run-down. The legend says that the yard was filled with thistle bushes, fulfilling another element of Mary Gray's curse.

It's hard to believe, but it seemed as if Mary's words had a deathly grip on the place. Sadly, the curse wasn't ready to let go just yet.

Davis soon abandoned his claim and moved out of town. In 1865, a local business owner bought the property from the township and then gifted it to one of his former slaves, a man named Tom Lindsey. Lindsey worked hard to improve the house and property, but after lightning struck the home and the resulting fire burned it to the ground, neighbors approached him and told him of the curse.

When he rebuilt the house, it's said that he buried a charm beneath the front doorstep and hung horseshoes throughout the home, which seems to have worked. For the next twenty-five years, no new tragedy fell on the house there on Monroe Street.

After Lindsey passed away, a local banker bought the property and immediately tore down the modest home, the horseshoes with it. He wanted something grand, and so he built a large Victorian mansion there. He married a younger woman and they settled into life, completely unaware of the words that old Mary Gray had uttered fifty years before.

Eighteen months later, the man's wife and newborn child tragically died. He mourned them, then lived alone for a time before eventually marrying again. Soon after, he and his new wife welcomed a son, but when the child died of illness, the banker's wife became so sick with grief that she was sent to a hospital to recover. She never came home.

The house became a boardinghouse for a while, but after a number of deaths there, it was eventually abandoned. Finally, in 1895, the property was bought by the town for the construction of a new public library. The banker's mansion, along with all of those dark memories and the echoes of his tragic loss, was torn down and covered with earth.

But remember, that was *cursed* earth. Mary had uttered powerful words that day in 1847. In a town whose name literally meant "dreaming with the help of a bad spirit." It's hard to ignore the connection. But you would think that all those decades had put some space between the curse and the people who chose to live there.

Sadly, that doesn't seem to be the case.

By 1924, the library had lost three directors to tragedy. The first, E. S. Wilcox, was killed when he fell in front of a moving streetcar in 1915. His successor died of a heart attack right inside the library during a board meeting. After him, Dr. Edward Wiley took over, but he died in 1924 after intentionally swallowing arsenic.

Not everyone suffered so much, though. That young attorney, David Davis, went on to become a U.S. senator, and then became an associate justice on the U.S. Supreme Court. He even worked for a time as campaign manager for Abraham Lincoln.

Today, the original Peoria Public Library is gone. It was replaced in 1966 with a more modern structure. Still, even with all that glass and steel, some echoes of the curse remain. No one else has died, but past employees have reported hearing voices after the doors are closed, cold drafts when none of the windows are open, and the occasional appearance of a man—dressed in turn-of-the-century clothing—staring back at them from a basement doorway.

As I said before, no matter how hard we try to move on, sometimes the past manages to stick around, following us like a shadow. And for the people who have lived and worked on Mary Gray's Monroe Street lot for the last century and a half, it seems there will be no escape.

Steam and Gas

A<small>SK ANY GROUP</small> of people where they feel the safest, and the answer is almost universal: their own house. It's a place they know well, where they have built a life and crafted wonderful memories—home sweet home.

But what happens when we leave the safety of our homes and travel? Once outside our comfortable safe haven, we often find ourselves exposed to whatever awaits us. Some people are more courageous than others, of course, but travel can be a source of fear for many.

Hodophobia is the fear of travel, and while the vast majority of people don't necessarily suffer from a clinical fear of being away from home, many do struggle with strange places. And no place can feel more foreign and strange to a traveler, in my opinion at least, than the places where thousands upon thousands of guests have stayed.

Perhaps it's the well-worn carpets that make us feel uneasy, or the imperfect walls and ceilings. Noisy plumbing, finicky lights, and the sounds of a settling structure can leave even the best of us feeling a bit out of our element.

No other place in the United States can cause that uneasy feeling more than an often-forgotten mountain lodge built over a century ago in the shadows of the Rocky Mountains. Despite its classic architecture and lavish decor, there is very little inside that feels safe.

And I'd like to take you there.

A STEAM-POWERED FORTUNE

They were twin wonders. Freelan and Francis Stanley were born in Maine in 1849. They had five other siblings, two of whom were also twins. But something was different about Freelan and his brother. They were exceptional students, quick learners, and gifted with an unusual mechanical aptitude.

As nine-year-olds, they were using their father's lathe to craft wooden tops, which they sold to their classmates. At the age of ten, they were taught how to make violins by their paternal grandfather. It was said that their instruments were concert-quality. Those early experiments helped fuel a lifelong passion for building things.

After a short career as a teacher and principal, Freelan Stanley went into business with his brother, refining and marketing a photographic process known as dry plating. It was a revolutionary change, allowing even amateur photographers to take quality images. So revolutionary, in fact, that the Eastman Kodak company purchased the technology in the late 1800s, making the brothers very, very wealthy.

From there, the wonder twins moved into the world of motor cars. Their first automobile was built in 1897, and by 1899 it was the best-selling motor car in the country. Because of its unique steam-powered engine, the automobile was called the Stanley Steamer. It was the Steamer, along with a few other smaller businesses, that helped turn the twins into tycoons in their own right.

In 1903, Freelan was diagnosed with tuberculosis, sometimes referred to as the "wasting sickness." At the age of fifty-three, he had dropped to just 118 pounds, and his doctors told him that he had six months to live, at the most. So like many people of that era, Stanley traveled west, to the clean mountain air of Colorado. And that's where he discovered Estes Park.

Freelan and his wife, Flora, instantly fell in love with the setting. They built a home there almost immediately, and after Freelan somehow shook the tuberculosis, the couple returned every summer thereafter, he in his tailored suits and pointy gray beard, she in her high-collared floral gowns.

But it was another building they constructed there—a massive, grand hotel—that has left the most lasting mark. Built at the cost of nearly half a million dollars, the Stanley Hotel opened its doors in 1909 and has been serving guests ever since.

The Stanley Hotel was a modern marvel in its day. It featured a hydraulic elevator, electricity throughout, running water, telephones, and even a fleet of Stanley's own steam-powered Mountain Wagons to ferry guests straight from the train station to the front door of the hotel. It had nearly three hundred rooms, 466 windows, a music room with a grand piano, a billiard room, a restaurant, a ballroom, and three floors of guest rooms.

And that's just inside the hotel. Outside, scattered around the property, were staff dormitories, a concert hall, the ice house, a carriage house, the manager's home, and many others. A private airstrip was even built on the property at some point, although it's been abandoned for decades.

Over the years, the Stanley Hotel has played host to a number of famous guests. John Philip Sousa not only stayed there frequently but would tune the piano in the music room and record the dates inside the lid. Other guests have checked in there, including *Titanic* survivor Molly Brown, President Theodore Roosevelt, Bob Dylan, Johnny Cash, and Barbra Streisand.

And Freelan Stanley? The tuberculosis never got him. He died in 1940 at the age of ninety-one, just a year after his wife, Flora, passed away. But while the couple was no longer there to oversee the hotel's day-to-day business, one thing has been very clear to those who work there today: the Stanleys, it seems, never checked out.

ECHOES OF MUSIC

In July 2009, a tourist in the lobby of the hotel approached her friends with complete shock. She had been shopping for postcards in the gift shop and had exited the shop while reading the backs of the ones she bought. According to her story, she still had her head down when a pair of pant legs came into view.

She did the polite thing and stepped to the side to allow the man to pass, but when she did, she claimed, the legs moved to block her new path. Taken aback, she raised her head to scold the man for his rudeness, but stopped when a wave of cold air washed over her. The man, according to the woman, was dressed in clothing that seemed out of place, and his pointy beard had an old-fashioned look to it. She then watched as the man walked away toward the lobby fireplace, where he vanished out of sight.

After rushing over to her friends to tell them what had happened, she was approached by another woman who had happened to overhear the conversation. This woman led the tourist toward the antique Stanley Steamer automobile that sits in the hotel lobby and pointed toward the photo of Freelan Stanley on the wall behind it.

The tourist was astonished. The man she had just seen with her own eyes had been dead for over sixty years.

Mr. Stanley has also been seen in the billiard room, a favorite location of his during his time at the hotel. According to one report, a group of tourists were once being led through that room when a vision of Stanley appeared behind one of the tourists.

Mr. Stanley also seems to have a soft spot for his beloved rocking chair on the front porch. Visible from the front desk through the large lobby windows, it has been witnessed by many to be rocking of its own volition. But if Mr. Stanley really has remained behind in the hotel after death, then he is apparently not alone.

In February 1984, the night bellman was working the front desk when he heard footsteps coming from the direction of the hotel bar, known as the Cascades. The bellman leaned over the counter to peer around the corner, and in the reflection of the lobby windows he was able to see the figure of a woman. She wore a pale gown that he described as off-the-shoulder, in a southern belle style.

The bellman quickly exited the front desk area through the back doorway, but when he arrived in the side hall near the windows, no one was there.

During an overnight shift in 1976, the clerk at the front desk reported hearing piano music. She left the desk and entered the music room, where the sound was coming from, but found it empty. According to her, however, the piano keys were still moving on their own.

In 1994, a guest heard similar music from the direction of the music room, and stepped inside. He claimed to have seen a young woman sitting at the piano, and he approached so he could watch and listen as she played. As he walked across the room, though, the girl transformed into an elderly woman before disappearing completely.

The Stanleys have frequently been sighted on the main staircase in formal attire, and even in the elevator. The encounters are never violent or malevolent, but they frighten guests and staff nonetheless. Bartenders there in the Cascades claim they have even seen the deceased owner strolling through the bar. Some have given chase, only to lose sight of the ghost as it vanished into one of the walls.

Whether or not you believe in ghosts, the frequency of the reports is enough to make you wonder. From glowing orbs caught on film to the faint sound of piano music drifting into the lobby, there seems to be no lack of fuel for the legends that fill those halls.

But it's not just the Stanleys who haunt the hotel. Sightings have been reported throughout the structure's four stories, with the vast majority of them occurring in the most unwelcome of places: the guest rooms.

JUST PASSING THROUGH

In the early 1900s, many visitors to the Stanley Hotel would stay for more than a weekend. In many cases, guests would stay

through the summer, and that meant arriving equipped for months of living away from home.

Those of us who have spent the past few years watching the British television show *Downton Abbey* might be very familiar with the process: the gentlemen and ladies would arrive by carriage—in this case, steam-powered, of course—along with a caravan of servants and luggage. And while the wealthy guests had access to the many finely appointed rooms of the hotel, the servants and children were relegated to the fourth floor.

This was an era when children were expected to be seen but not heard, and so they played in the rooms and halls far above the heads of the guests. They slept there, played there, and even ate there in a small windowless corner of the upstairs kitchen.

These days, the fourth floor is just one more level of guest rooms. According to many accounts, however, that doesn't mean the children are gone. Many of these stories center around Room 418.

There have been reports of the sound of balls bouncing in the dark, of high, childlike voices laughing and talking in the hall outside the room, of the clink of metal jacks on wooden flooring, and the pounding of little feet. Guests have been startled out of their sleep by voices and sounds, some of which have been captured on video.

Even the staff have had experiences. The cleaning staff always enter the room with a bit of fear due to the many odd things that they have witnessed inside Room 418. The television has been known to turn on and off on its own, and on at least one occasion a housekeeper has turned to see that the bed she has just made up now has the deep impression of a body in the bedspread.

The room with the most activity, though, is on the second floor, and there are legends as to why. It is said that in 1911 a thunderstorm caused a power outage in the hotel, sending the building into complete darkness. It was dinnertime, and most of the guests were downstairs in the MacGregor ballroom, but the staff still needed to provide a temporary fix for the lack of light.

Because the Stanley Hotel was built at a time of transition between gas and electric lamps, the fixtures throughout the hotel were equipped for both. With the building in darkness, staff were sent from room to room with candles to light each acetylene gas lamp. But when one of the chambermaids, a woman named Elizabeth Wilson, entered Room 217, something happened.

It should be said that this room was the Presidential Suite. It was enormous and elegantly decorated in the style most beloved by Flora Stanley herself. Bright floral wallpaper, with reds and pinks and greens, covered the walls, and the carpet was the color of grass, with accents of red and blue. It was the jewel of the hotel.

According to the legend, the light fixture in that room had a hidden leak, and the room had filled with gas. When Mrs. Wilson opened the door with her lit candle in hand, the gas ignited, setting off an explosion that destroyed nearly 10 percent of the hotel along the western wing.

Part of the floor gave way, and several steel girders fell on tables in the ballroom below, thankfully missing the guests. Mrs. Wilson, though, was not so lucky. She fell through the floor, breaking both of her ankles when she landed.

It's a good story, but there are many versions of it. Five separate Colorado newspapers carried the story, but details varied wildly. One paper listed the chambermaid as Eva Colbern and said that she was thrown through a wall onto the porch with no injuries. In another, she was Elizabeth Lambert, who died in the fall. Still another report claimed the chambermaid was a woman named Lizzie Leitzenbergher. All of the stories *did* agree that the explosion happened at 8:00 p.m., but none mentioned the thunderstorm.

There are other glitches in the story. No employee records exist from this period in the hotel's history. Among the many photographs of hotel staff over the past century, there are no pictures of anyone named Elizabeth Wilson, or Lambert, or Leitzenbergher. All of it has the smell of window dressing, designed to lend some credibility to the odd experiences that guests have had in Room 217.

Just what experiences am I referring to? Well, according to firsthand accounts, the ghost of Mrs. Wilson has been known to unpack the suitcases of guests, toss their clothing on the floor, and rearrange the bed linens. Another common report is that some guests and staff have seen a mysterious black hole in the floor, said to be the location of her fall after the explosion. The faucet in the bathtub has been known to turn on and off on its own, and maids have seen doors in the room open and close.

In 1974, a man and woman arrived at the hotel at the end of the season. According to his story, they were the only guests in the entire hotel. After dinner that first night, the couple retired to bed, where the husband had a horrible nightmare.

"I dreamed of my three-year-old son running through the corridors," he later said. The boy was "looking back over his shoulder, eyes wide, screaming. He was being chased by a firehose. I woke up with a tremendous jerk, sweating all over, within an inch of falling out of bed. I got up, lit a cigarette, sat in a chair looking out the window at the Rockies, and by the time the cigarette was done, I had the bones of the book firmly set in my mind."

The man was Stephen King, and the book, of course, would later become *The Shining*.

WORKING BACKWARD

Some folklore is historical. We tell the tales because they happened— at least to some degree. There's a grain of truth at the core of many myths and legends, a real-life event or fear that caused people to remember, to retell, and to eventually immortalize.

Other legends, however, lack that core truth. They work backward instead, creating a unique story to explain the unexplainable. Oftentimes these stories lean on the past and mine it for hints of validity, but in the end, we're still left with stories that have no roots.

The reason people do that isn't really a mystery. Story, you see, helps keep us grounded. It helps provide us with bearings as we navigate life, like a landmark we can all point toward. And when something odd or unexplainable happens, I think it's only human nature to look for those landmarks. When we can't find them, oftentimes we simply invent our own.

Perhaps the original events that led to the unusual activity at the Stanley Hotel have simply been lost in the past. It would be reasonable to assume that at least *some* of the stories have a foundation in reality, rather than just the narrative of a hotel with a supernatural reputation to keep. That's not my decision to make; I'll leave that up to you.

But sometimes we're reminded that stories can evolve, that the unknown can suddenly become a bit more knowable. In 2014, while doing maintenance in a service tunnel beneath the hotel, workers found debris. Specifically, they found pieces of drywall covered in pink and green wallpaper. Carpet fragments were also discovered, still pale green with red and blue details.

It turns out the explosion really did happen. And if we can find truth at the center of one of the stories, even a century later, how much more truth is out there to be found?

I'll leave you with one last story from Room 217. According to a previous guest who was preparing to go to bed, he opened one of the windows to let in some of the cool Colorado air. Later, after having been asleep for some time, he felt his wife climb out of bed and quietly walk across the room toward the window.

The man said that he opened his eyes, and after glancing at the glowing face of the alarm clock, he looked to find her standing at the window, face pressed against the screen.

"You have to see this," she whispered to him. "There's a family of elk outside."

The guest didn't move. He just smiled and watched his wife for a long time, noticing how her hair moved in the breeze. It's hard to blame him, after all. She'd been dead for over five years.

DREADFUL PLACES

99

Steam and Gas

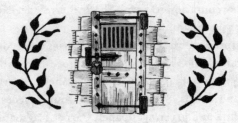

In the Bag

EVERYONE HAS AN opinion. Whether it's politics, religion, popular culture, or brand of coffee, everyone has a preference. For most people, their opinion is set in stone. It's an emotional choice. It's rooted in habit. It's safe and comforting.

But some opinions are darker. For example, ask anyone you know what their greatest fear is, and you'll get a five-minute answer. Their pulse will race. Heck, they might even shudder in front of you. No one wants to die, and no one likes to feel unsafe. And that means everyone has one big fear.

Maybe it's the thought of being buried alive, trapped inside a confining space while hundreds of pounds of dirt are shoveled on top of the only exit. Maybe it's the thought of drowning, or being kidnapped. But here's the secret: most big fears are really just all about the same thing. Nearly all of them are about losing control.

There are few places in modern culture that represent the loss of choice, the loss of freedom, and the loss of safety more than prison. It's a setting that fills us with dread and inspires hopelessness, but somehow also remains oddly attractive. Films like *The Shawshank Redemption* and *The Green Mile* and small-screen hits like *Oz* and *60 Days In* stand as testament to that obsession. And rightly so.

Prison, to many, is a dark collection of pain, despair, guilt, and hatred. And while it might not be the same as physically being buried alive, it never fails to strike fear into even the strongest of hearts. But our modern prison system didn't start out that way. Instead, it was built on hope, opportunity, and change.

Like all good intentions, though, those goals have been worn down over time by the worst of human nature. Whatever hope and light they might have tried to bring into the world has been washed away by horrible darkness. And no prison represents that evolution more accurately than Eastern State Penitentiary.

HISTORY IN CHAINS

The idea of prison has been around since the dawn of written language. Early legal codes, dating back as far as four thousand years, listed punishment for illegal behavior. Back then, it was all about retaliation for wrongdoing, but imprisonment was on the horizon.

The ancient Greeks dabbled with the notion of captivity. In Athens, the prison there was known as the *desmoterion,* which meant "place of chains." You get the idea, I'm sure. It was the Romans, though, who took the concept of prison and turned it into an art form, and trust me, they pulled no punches.

The Romans built prisons in the worst places imaginable. If it was unpleasant or nasty, it was perfect for holding criminals. They used basements, abandoned stone quarries, and even metal cages. The infamous Mamertine Prison in ancient Rome was literally built into the city's sewer system. Prisoners ate and slept among piles of wet, rancid human waste.

With the advent of the castle in Europe, captivity moved inside the fortresses, becoming an extension of the crown. It was a display of power, in a sense. In order to encourage people to obey and respect the ruler of the land, they were taught to fear the power those rulers wielded. But even then, prison was only a sort of purgatory, a waiting room for the final verdict. It was rarely the end itself.

For centuries, prison was where criminals would await their trial, and the waiting was oftentimes the least unpleasant part of the process. After their sentence was handed down, the punishment was intensely harsh. Painful whipping, physical mutilation, branding with hot irons, and even public execution were all waiting for them outside the walls of their cell.

But all of that changed in the eighteenth century. The Age of Enlightenment brought with it a new focus on rational thought, which led to public outcry against violent punishment. Instead, people called for a new type of prison, one that would inspire moral reform and help criminals become better people. It sounded good on paper, and so many countries got behind the idea.

The British Parliament passed the Penitentiary Act in 1779, introducing the concept of state prisons. Inmate populations in England had multiplied following the loss of their North American colonies, the prisons filling up quickly with traitors and rebels. It's ironic, when you think about it; our own declaration of independence led to an increase of captivity and imprisonment back home across the Atlantic.

One of the strongest voices for prison reform in the newly formed United States of America was, of all people, Benjamin Franklin. In 1787, while the Constitution was being crafted in Philadelphia, Franklin was gathering others in his home nearby to discuss the poor conditions of the local prison known as Walnut Street Jail.

Rather than individual cells, prisoners there were gathered into groups inside large pens. There was no segregation, so men and women, along with young children, were all living in the same space. Inmates ran the spectrum, from simple thieves to cold-blooded killers. It wasn't safe, and it was common for rape and violence to take place unchecked in there.

Those being held for trial were forced to buy their own food and water. Jailers would even sell heat in the winter, that's how bad it'd become. So Franklin and his fellow reformers demanded change. There were immediate effects that changed much of the system there, but the biggest impact wouldn't be seen for another forty years.

After decades of campaigning, funding was finally approved for a new prison. But this building would have a different sort of name. Today when we hear the word *penitentiary*, we think of it as a generic term for a prison, but in the early 1800s, it carried a specific meaning. The root of the word is *penitent,* which means "to be repentant, to seek change." And that's the attitude that this new prison was meant to embody: a building full of inmates who were no longer awaiting a violent end to their lives but instead were improving themselves.

On the outside, Eastern State was designed to look like a gothic castle: intimidating, imposing, and impenetrable. One look at the exterior and most people would give up their life of crime. At least, that was the theory. Inside, though, it was different.

When inmate number 1 entered the building on October 25, 1829, he was ushered into a state-of-the-art facility. Criminals were housed in private cells with shower baths and toilets. Central heating pipes ran throughout the building and into each cell, keeping the inmates warm in the winter. The original cellblocks even included skylights.

This was a huge change. President Andrew Jackson, sitting in his office in the White House, didn't even have those luxuries. But that lack of modern amenities was offset by the freedom he enjoyed, which is more than we can say for the inmates at Eastern State.

And it was only downhill from there.

Pipes and Bags

Central heating and individual toilets sounded like a fantastic idea, but there were problems with them from the start. The plumbing that carried the hot water to each of the cells ran through tunnels that also housed the sewer pipes. As you can imagine, applying heat on a 24/7 basis to pipes that carried human waste is never a good idea. Because of this, the first few cellblocks that were constructed suffered from some odors that were . . . *offensive.*

Early doorways in the building were tiny, requiring inmates to stoop low to pass through. And those doors didn't even open up into the hall inside the building. Instead, cell doors opened outward into tiny outdoor courtyards, where each prisoner was encouraged to be active, to garden, or to meditate quietly. Separating each courtyard were ten-foot walls, meant to discourage communication between the prisoners.

All of this complexity was designed to create an atmosphere of isolation. The toilet system was built the way it was because the prison staff needed to be able to remotely flush the toilets twice a week, rather than give the inmates control over that. Flushing, you see, could be used as a method of communication.

And for those rare moments when a prisoner was being moved through a cellblock and could possibly be seen by other inmates, the prisoner always had a cloth bag over his head. Walking in on his first day, being moved from one block to another, even going out into his private yard; each prisoner wore a cloth bag, sometimes with eye holes cut into it, to engender a deep feeling of isolation. And for a while it worked.

True to the stereotypes that we've come to expect from prison movies over the years, Eastern State Penitentiary was no stranger to attempted breakouts. This became possible, in part, because of changes to the layout and flow of the prison itself. Doors were enlarged, access to the internal hallways was opened up, and overcrowding put more than one inmate in each cell.

The first escape attempt was by inmate number 94, William Hamilton. He climbed out a window in the warden's office, but was caught a short time later. In 1927, William Bishie —an inmate of fifteen years—escaped with a friend. They managed to push a guard off one of the towers and then climb down the side before making a run for freedom.

Bishie was pretty bold. He stayed on the run for seven years, and eventually got a job in Syracuse, New York. What was the job, you might ask? He worked as a crossing guard. For the police department. Like I said, the man had guts.

The most famous prison break, though, was Willie Sutton. He was probably the second-most-famous inmate in Eastern State's entire history. I'll get to number one in a bit. But Willie, he was sort of a criminal celebrity. He'd been a bank robber before his time in Eastern State. They called him the Babe Ruth of bank robbing. Slick Willie. The Gentleman Bandit. But he got caught, didn't he?

He checked into Eastern State in 1934. During his eleven-year stay there, he tried escaping five times. But it was his last attempt that was an affair to remember. Sutton, along with eleven other men, dug a tunnel twelve feet down from cell 68, then another hundred feet straight out to breach the wall. They removed the dirt from their excavations just like *The Shawshank Redemption* showed us: hiding it in their pockets and then dropping it in the yard. The tunnels had ventilation and support beams. It was a production like none other.

It took them months, but on April 3, 1945, all twelve men slipped into the tunnel and crawled to freedom. Some of the men actually evaded the authorities for a couple of months. Slick Willie, though, was caught within three minutes. There's a joke in there somewhere, I think.

Over the century and a half that Eastern State Penitentiary was in operation, more than one hundred prisoners managed to break out. Only one of them managed to never be recaptured. I think we get it: people want to escape prison. It happens all over the world. Certainly there are prisons with higher escape numbers, even here in the United States. But why the rush to leave?

Eastern State, it turns out, was originally designed to house a maximum of three hundred criminals. But that was the 1830s, and society was changing. In the beginning, most of the inmates were horse thieves. By the 1920s, though, inmates were being sent in with darker crimes. Rape, violence, even murder. As a result, numbers swelled to an astounding two thousand. That's nearly seven times the original capacity.

With the shift in prisoner population came adjustments to the philosophy behind the penitentiary itself. Gone were the notions of hard work, solitude, and meditation. In the minds of those who ran the overcrowded prison, only one corrective method would actually work: torture.

CREATURE COMFORTS

Aside from the straitjacket, which was used often as a way of containing unruly prisoners, one of the more frightening methods of punishment was a seat called, affectionately, the "mad chair." It resembled an old dentist's chair, and prisoners would be strapped into it as tightly as possible and left for days without food. There are rumors that extended time spent in the chair resulted in amputations.

Some inmates found themselves placed in "the hole," a small, confining cell that had been dug out of the foundation of the building. With only a tiny slot for food and air, prisoners in the hole would share their space with rats and insects for weeks at a time. There was no bathroom there, no contact with other humans, and no light to see by.

Then there was the room where inmates were taken during the winter. They would be stripped naked, plunged into a bath of cold water, and then strapped to the wall to freeze throughout the night. Oftentimes the guards would return to find a layer of ice on the skin of the man being punished.

None of those methods could hold a candle to what was known as the "iron gag." To reinforce the no-talking policy in the prison, this punishment brought the consequences directly to the offender's mouth. It's hard to describe with words, but stick with me and I'll do my best.

An inmate's wrists would be locked behind his back with crude manacles, and then a short chain would be connected to the wrists. On the other end of that chain would be a small iron clamp.

And that clamp was fastened to the tongue. Talking, movement, or struggling would all result in the tongue being torn, and it was said that extreme blood loss even led to death in some cases.

But as hard as it is to believe, some prisoners even managed to rise above all of that. Some, in fact, managed to enjoy a fairly luxurious life inside Eastern State. Inside one of the seven cellblocks that radiated off the central hub was a string of cells known as "Park Avenue." The inmates there enjoyed a bit more freedom. And none took advantage of that more than Al Capone.

Today Capone is remembered as a mob boss of near mythic proportions, and Eastern State was his first experience with prison life. Just months after his men brutally murdered members of a rival gang in an event now referred to as the St. Valentine's Day

Massacre, Capone was picked up in Philadelphia and convicted for carrying a concealed weapon. For the eight months that spanned the summer of 1929 to the spring of 1930, Capone called Park Avenue his home.

Here's what an August 1929 article in a Philadelphia newspaper had to say:

> *The whole room was suffused in the glow of a desk lamp which stood on a polished desk.... On the once-grim walls of the penal chamber hung tasteful paintings, and the strains of a waltz were being emitted by a powerful cabinet radio receiver of handsome design and fine finish.*

Even with his better-than-average accommodations, Capone still complained. But it wasn't about the food or room temperature. No, Capone—bold and brazen mob boss that he was—appears to have been haunted by ghosts of his past. Literally.

One night shortly after arriving at Eastern State, Capone was heard screaming in his cell. It wasn't anger or disobedience that drove him to it, though; Capone was apparently scared. When asked, he told the guards that he just wanted Jimmy to leave him alone and go away. Jimmy was attacking him, it seems, and he wanted it to stop.

At first, the guards and other inmates were confused. There was no one else in Capone's cell, and no Jimmy on the cellblock. But then the dots were connected. Jimmy, they guessed, was really James Clark, one of the men killed on Capone's orders in the St. Valentine's Day Massacre. And if that was true, then Capone was screaming because he felt that Jimmy had followed him into the prison, just to torment him.

Eastern State closed down in 1970 but was reopened in 1991 as a museum. Even without the inmates, something dark seems to have remained behind, and many who have stepped inside for a tour have come away with an experience that's hard to forget.

The most common sightings occur in one of the guard towers that watches over the building and its perimeter, where a ghostly figure has been seen by many people. Others have reported the sounds of footsteps in the prison hallways and laughter that echoes down through the cellblocks. Soft, mournful wails have been heard there as well.

In cellblock 12, a shadowy figure has been seen darting from cell to cell, always noticed at the corner of the eye. Some have seen it rush away from a dark corner as a group of tourists pass by, while others have seen it moving up or down a wall like an enormous, shadowy spider.

A few years ago, a locksmith was called in to remove the lock on one of the original doors in cellblock 4—after 140 years, it was understandably stubborn, and so they needed the services of a professional. While there, though, he experienced something that haunts him to this day.

The locksmith said that moments after he unlocked the cell, an unseen force rushed out and pressed him against the wall of the hallway. For what felt like an eternity, he was pinned there and couldn't move. Staring into the now-open cell, his heart froze. The walls inside, he said, were covered with faces. Dozens and dozens of faces, their expressions writhing with agony and horror.

Once free, the locksmith left, referring to the prison as a "giant haunted house." He never returned.

SILENT GUILT

There's a lot to be debated in the world of prison reform: how inmates deserve to be treated, what role imprisonment should play in the overall realm of consequences and due process. We could even explore how motives and methods transform over time, under pressure, and through human brokenness. It's a can of worms, and I don't have all the answers.

But there's an overwhelming feeling of guilt in all of this. The prison reform that Eastern State represented—at least originally—was born out of guilt about earlier, more barbaric methods. And each inmate, in their own way, was caught in a prison of their own personal guilt. It's easy to see how anyone trapped inside might feel remorse and want desperately to escape.

Maybe Eastern State Penitentiary really *is* haunted. Maybe there are real ghosts that drift through the dark halls, and shadows that move at the corner of our vision. Considering all of the horrific things that have taken place there over the years, it seems only natural for there to be some sort of an echo still present.

Or maybe it's nothing more than madness. Some think it's crazy to believe there are spirits roaming the halls of a prison, or any building for that matter. It defies logic. It's unprovable. Jimmy never really haunted Al Capone, they say. The man was haunted by guilt, nothing more.

It's interesting to note that even after his release from Eastern State, Capone still complained of Jimmy's presence. Back in Chicago and living at the Lexington Hotel, he still screamed for Jimmy to leave him alone. The screams would always bring his bodyguards running, and they would always find the man alone.

Even though everyone else thought he was losing his mind, that his guilt was the only real ghost haunting him night and day, Capone looked for help elsewhere. He hired a psychic named Alice Britt to conduct a séance for him, and she begged Jimmy—on Capone's behalf—to leave the mob boss alone. And that, they hoped, was the end of it.

One day, a few weeks after the séance, Capone's personal attendant, a man named Hymie Cornish, stepped into Capone's quarters to retrieve something. When he entered the room, he immediately noticed a stranger standing near the window, facing out to look down on the street.

He glanced around the room for other visitors. No one was supposed to be in Mr. Capone's room, after all, and the intruder would need to be dealt with. Turning back to the man, Cornish called out for his attention—and then stopped.

The man, whoever he was, had disappeared.

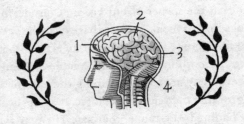

If Walls Could Talk

IN THE MIDDLE AGES, most people would go their entire life without ever experiencing surgery. Today we live in the age of preventative medical procedures and things like cosmetic surgery, but six hundred years ago, no one ever thought of going under the knife without a very good reason.

Why? Because it was difficult to manage the pain. Anesthetics were incredibly primitive in the early days of the Middle Ages. No, people didn't undergo invasive procedures completely without pain relief, but the options available were limited and . . . well . . . potentially deadly.

In England, a common method for pain relief was a potion called *dwale* (pronounced DWALL-uh), which the patient drank prior to surgery. Dwale was a solution of wine mixed with a number of other ingredients. Some were pretty mild, like lettuce and boar bile. But the recipe also called for hemlock and belladonna, both known to be highly poisonous.

Everyone wanted *dwale* for their pain, but it was always a gamble. If it was prepared correctly, it worked. If it wasn't, though—if you used a flawed recipe or bought your potion from a less savory individual—you ran the risk of horrible pain, even death.

Sometimes even the most honorable goals can lead to horrible results. As the old cliché says, the road to hell is paved with good intentions. It's a powerful glimpse into the core of the human mind: we're really good at breaking the things we try to fix.

And in no other field has that been more true than the early days of the mental health profession. While there might not have been bottles of *dwale* lying around, the early practitioners of mental health had their own fair share of misguided intentions and flawed recipes.

They tried to help, but in the end they did more harm than good. And while most of the people who suffered through that pain are long gone, the aftereffects remain. And the stories they tell are more than horrifying.

BUILDING REFORM

The early decades of the nineteenth century were filled with reform movements. Abolitionism, education, women's rights, and voting rights all featured prominently in the early 1800s. American culture was maturing, becoming more aware of what it was and what its flaws were.

And as it did, champions rose up to move those issues forward. Leaders like Sojourner Truth, Elizabeth Cady Stanton, Susan B. Anthony. Progressive women. Persistent women. We wouldn't have the culture we have today without them. And right there beside them was Dorothea Dix.

Dorothea's area of passion was for the mentally ill. Inspired by the lunacy reform movement in England, she threw herself into an investigation of American methods for mental health care, and what she found was appalling. Many who suffered from mental illness were kept in cages or stalls. They were often restrained with chains and beaten into submission. The sick were treated as prisoners, not patients, and that needed to change.

Through the 1840s, she pushed state after state to do better, calling for humane treatment and housing. And that resulted in a new crop of facilities specifically designed to care for the mentally ill. Building a better home for these patients required a fresh approach, and the man who helped with that was Dr. Thomas Kirk-bride.

As we discussed earlier, Kirkbride was a physician, but his passion for modern mental health care also led to a whole new architectural style. Buildings shouldn't be large, square structures. They should stretch out and provide as much sunlight and fresh air as possible.

Two decades before his work in Danvers—in the mid-1850s, in fact—Kirkbride was consulting on a similar project in Westin, Virginia. It would be a modern, conscious approach to caring for the mentally ill, where people would be patients, not prisoners. And they would call it the Trans-Allegheny Lunatic Asylum.

After some hiccups caused by the outbreak of the American Civil War, the facility opened its doors in October 1864. By then, though, Westin was a city in the newly minted state of West Virginia, and so the asylum was renamed the West Virginia Hospital for the Insane. New building. New name. It was like a beacon fire had been ignited, and people flocked to it from far and wide.

Like a lot of the early mental health facilities in America, the West Virginia Hospital was built on a foundation of naiveté and hope. It was only designed to hold about 250 patients at a time, which should have been enough, but as we all know, expectations are meant to be broken, right? As you can imagine, things quickly got out of hand.

See, the problem was the mid-nineteenth-century view of mental illness. It was a massive catchall category, so patients suffering from all manner of "disorders" were sent there. And I'm using large, exaggerated air quotes when I say "disorders" because, well . . . just listen to some of these.

You could be committed to the asylum for superstition, for sexual deviance, for deserting your husband, for having fits of anger, or for being lazy. Women were routinely admitted because of what people then called "menstrual derangement." It's well beyond the limits of irony, isn't it? In the pursuit of caring for the insane, the caretakers went crazy.

Within sixteen years, the facility was caring for over seven hundred patients in a space designed for 250, so new wings were added to the original structure. One was devoted solely to the elderly and those suffering from dementia. Another was set up for tuberculosis patients, giving them plenty of fresh air and sunlight—and, of course, keeping them isolated from the rest of the patients.

Other facilities were built nearby on the property. Things like a large home for patients whom the courts declared to be criminally insane. They even built their own morgue, but because many of the patients would become upset when the hearse pulled up to the front door, they built a new entrance at the back, away from prying eyes.

The hospital grew from seven hundred to sixteen hundred patients by the 1930s. A decade later, there were eighteen hundred people there, and by the early 1950s there were twenty-six hundred. The West Virginia Hospital for the Insane was growing like a weed, but inside such a cramped facility, all of that growth was beginning to choke off the lives they were trying to save.

It was a time bomb, quietly ticking away behind a hauntingly beautiful Gothic Revival façade. And that bomb was about to explode.

PEELING BACK THE SKIN

If you grab a tomato and squeeze it slowly, the insides will eventually start to leak out—and that's what began to happen to the Westin State Hospital, as it was called in the late 1940s. Reports of overcrowding began to spread, and people were alarmed by what they heard.

In January 1949, a newspaper in Charleston, West Virginia, the *Gazette*, ran an investigative series on the facility. What it discovered was horrifying. One reporter described how disabled children were left naked and alone, chained to their chairs for hours.

When he visited, there was a portion of the cafeteria ceiling that had begun to collapse in on itself because of a septic problem with the toilets on the floor above. Rather than fix it, they had simply propped up the collapsed area with spare lumber.

Some of the rooms were so crowded with beds that you couldn't access the floor or run a hand between the mattresses. Another report noted how poorly the facility was heated in the winter, and how little light there was.

And darkness, as we all know, can be a breeding ground for terrible things.

Looking back, some historians and mental health professionals blame the conditions on how poorly the staff was treated. They worked incredibly long hours for very little money, which contributed to a high turnover rate. And it's hard to offer consistency and quality in care when the people managing the patients are constantly changing and have varying levels of experience.

So with limited, unskilled staff and very few resources to make it better, the facility did the only thing it could—it tightened its grip. Patients rarely had contact with the outside world. Even letters in and out were prohibited. Once you stepped through the door of the Westin State Hospital, you would never see the outside world again.

One effort to control the patients came in the form of the lobotomy. The man who pioneered the transorbital lobotomy, Dr. Walter Freeman, spent a good amount of time in Westin, traveling there in his van, which he lovingly referred to as the Lobotomobile. Conservative estimates place the number of lobotomies performed there by Freeman at around seventy, while other reports go as high as a few hundred.

And with each one, the goal was the same: subdue the patient. To physically sever the portion of the brain that controlled their psychotic behavior, cutting it off from the rest of their mind. According to one historian, only one-third of those procedures were effective, which left a lot of patients physically disabled or, worse yet, dead.

But it was clear why they were trying, however desperate those attempts had become. Some of the patients were horribly violent. Once a nurse went missing during her work shift, and the administration just assumed she had quit in frustration and gone home without telling anyone. Her body was found two months later, lying under a disused staircase.

Much of the violence was due to the mixing of patients. Children were kept in the same place as adults. Patients with a history of violent behavior lived on wards with other, more vulnerable people. Physical assault, rape, and murder were common occurrences because of this.

One powerful story tells of three men who shared one bedroom. One of the men reportedly snored, which bothered the other two. So one night they dragged the snoring man out of bed, pulled his sheets off, and tied them into a noose. Then they hanged the noisy roommate from a pipe overhead in an effort to silence him.

It didn't work, though. When they untied him, he fell to the floor and began to struggle to get up. So the others lifted the man's bed, placed one of the bedposts on his head, and then jumped on the bed.

When they were later asked about what happened, one of the men responded with a simple answer. "The ghosts did it."

The hospital had come full circle. Created as a solution to the horrible conditions found by Dorothea Dix over a century before, it had somehow become just as dark, and just as horrifying, as before. There were efforts to fix it, to right the ship and save the mission, but it was too little, too late. The damage had already been done.

The hospital's doors finally shut for good in 1994. Like the patients who once lived there, the Westin State Hospital was abandoned to the ravages of time, a shell of its former self.

But the story wasn't over yet.

IF WALLS COULD TALK

Like a lot of abandoned buildings, the old hospital became the centerpiece of a number of new schemes. The governor of West Virginia at the time wanted to convert the facility into a prison, which speaks volumes about the perception of the place. When the most logical use for an old mental hospital is a place to lock up criminals . . . well, it's revealing.

Over a decade later, in 2007, the facility came under new ownership, and the name was changed back to the original Trans-Allegheny Lunatic Asylum. As a whole, the old hospital is a massive complex of ancient buildings, but portions of it have been opened up to the public for historical tours. Which, as you might imagine, drives a good number of people through those old hallways—hallways that have seen the worst of human behavior.

And that's a lot of watchful eyes, so it's no surprise to learn that visitors have *seen* things. Things that are difficult to explain. Things that leave a chill in the air. As the old saying goes, if walls could talk, right? And if you believe the stories, the walls of Westin State Hospital do much more than that.

The morgue building—that separate structure near the main complex where dead patients were examined and prepared for burial—is one of the many places that have sparked tales. Visitors there have seen shadows moving in and around the back entrance, as well as in the exam room.

Most of the shadows seem to be centered around the large wall of metal racks used to hold bodies. And witnesses have said that these shadows are unnaturally large and evoke a deep feeling of sadness and oppression.

Inside the main building, though, is where the experiences have been the most unnerving. After serving strictly as the female ward of the hospital, Ward F transitioned in the early 1900s to the home of the most violent of Westin's patients. Later, patients disabled by lobotomies were also moved there.

Visitors have seen more of the same shadow figures, sometimes appearing from around corners. The sound of footsteps has often been heard there, as well as the distant echo of laughter, and even knocking on some of the doors.

Speaking of doors, there is apparently a set of doors on the top floor of the hospital that have behaved in a rather unusual way. That's the area that began life as an onsite residence for some of the staff before transitioning into the ward for drug and alcohol recovery patients.

These doors are never locked, and there is nothing blocking

them on either side. But one historian reports being in the hallway one day and reaching out to try and open them. She gripped the handle of one of the doors and tugged, but nothing happened. She tried the other, and got the same result. So she pulled harder.

And that's when something on the other side pounded on the door, rattling it in the frame. Whatever was waiting on the other side of that doorway, it didn't want anyone coming through.

Ward 4 is home to a particularly chilling story. One tour guide reported coming into work early one morning, only to discover wet footprints in the hallway there. Wet *human* footprints. One set was apparently adult-sized, while the other was smaller, like a child's.

The tour guide followed the prints down the hall until they ended at a chair, where it seemed as if they turned around and took a seat. They faded away a short time later, of course, because that's what water does. But according to some of the tour guides, if the weather is damp enough outside, those prints mysteriously reappear.

The most popular story, however, involves a particular room in Ward R, up on the fourth floor. There are a number of slightly different stories, but the core legend is that a pregnant female patient was admitted long ago. When the child was born—a daughter— that child remained in the hospital, where she was raised by the staff and other patients.

This little girl, called Lily by some of the people who tell her tale, was said to have died at the age of nine from pneumonia. And while her body was most likely taken across the yard to the morgue, her spirit is rumored to have remained behind. Trapped in death, just as she had been in life, within the walls of Westin.

Her room is still there, too. Or at least that's what visitors believe. There *is* a room. Its walls, once a calming shade of pale green, are peeling and spotty. Those who have stepped inside have reported incredibly odd experiences: the feeling of a child reaching out and holding their hand, the faint sound of giggling, objects that move on their own.

And scattered all across the filthy tile floor are tributes, left for Lily by her many visitors: dozens and dozens of toys.

Humans are, by and large, a well-intentioned species. We try. We really do. We see brokenness and need, and we step into the gap to help out. A lot of the time, that turns out really well. Sometimes, though, we fail. Miserably, in fact.

The world of mental health has come a long way since the days of Dorothea Dix and her reform mission. True, there are those who still put an unnecessary stigma on mental illness, while others simply ignore it, as if it doesn't exist at all. But for the most part, it's viewed today as a legitimate struggle for millions of people around the world, and we're slowly getting better at caring for them.

Buildings like the old Trans-Allegheny Lunatic Asylum stand as a reminder of how far we've come. The chains and hydrotherapy tanks and surgical theaters for icepick lobotomies are still there, abandoned by time and enlightenment. They were brutal and inhumane when they were new, but somehow in their decay they've grown even more horrifying.

We've all seen photos of abandoned hospitals, with rusted wheelchairs and medical implements tossed in a corner. The peeling walls, the water damage, the makeshift nests where something—maybe human, maybe not—has taken up residence in the dark. These are clearly not friendly, inviting places. But it's just a building, right? Thankfully, the old cliché is far from true: walls can't really talk.

Or can they?

One historian who visited Westin State Hospital claims to have had a very unusual experience. She toured the facility with a friend, walking down those long, dark hallways and peeking inside its countless rooms. There's a lot to see there, after all. And all the while they captured their experience on a voice recorder.

When she reached the room where the stories say the little girl named Lily had lived and died, she decided to have a snack, and pulled a box of crackers from her bag. After setting it down on the floor, she wrote some notes down in her notebook, and then stopped.

The box of crackers was moving. In fact, she claimed that it was actually *levitating*. It moved through the air a foot or two, and then returned to where it had been. A moment later, she heard the distinct, unmistakable sound of crunching. As you might imagine, it was an unsettling experience, and she left feeling oddly disturbed.

Later, after returning home, she began to listen to the audio recordings of her experience there at the old hospital. After listening for a while, she finally came to the portion of the recording that had taken place in Lily's room.

She heard herself set down her bag, and the noise from the box of crackers being taken out and opened. To her surprise, she also heard the crunching that she assumed she had imagined. And then she heard something else. Something unexpected that sent a shiver down her spine.

It was a voice. A fragile, tiny voice, barely more than a whisper. But as soft as it was, she could clearly make out the words the voice spoke. Someone—or some*thing*—in the room had spoken five chilling words.

"Thank you for the snacks."

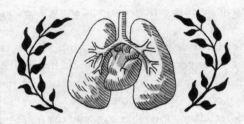

Withering Heights

WHEN THE MUMMIFIED body of a prehistoric man was discovered encased in ice in the Alps of northern Italy back in 1991, it was like stumbling upon a five-thousand-year-old time capsule. Along with his remarkably well-preserved body, the Iceman, as he came to be known, also introduced researchers to well-preserved examples of prehistoric clothing, weapons, and tools. And something else.

It was a lump of organic matter about the size of a walnut that had been strung onto a leather strap to keep it safe. After getting the unusual object under a microscope, microbiologists realized what it was: a fungus known as *Piptoporus betulinus*.

This fungus has an amazing property: it contains substances that kill off harmful bacteria and parasites. For a prehistoric hunter, traveling through all sorts of harsh environments and eating anything he could find, this fungus would have acted as a sort of antibiotic.

Humans, it seems, have been medicating themselves for millennia. And while the reasons have always been the same—to relieve the symptoms of illness and disease—those tools of medicine have varied greatly over the years. Every new wave of sickness has driven us to find better solutions, fresh cures, and powerful weapons with which to fight back.

So when a fresh wave of disease swept across America in the

late 1800s, one community decided to use every tool at their disposal. The solution they proposed would lean heavily on both social compassion and the power of nineteenth-century medicine. It was their last stand against a disease that was killing so many people.

That desperation meant that no option was left off the table, however drastic it might be. And honestly, it's hard to blame them. But when the experiment ended five decades later, it was far from a success. In fact, while countless lives were saved, they were paid for with blood.

Fighting back, it seems, can often lead to *horrific* results.

DEATH AND HOPE

They called it the "white plague." It can be found in historical records dating back thousands of years, from the ancient Near East and India to China and Africa. Classical writers such as the Greek physician Hippocrates and the historian Herodotus all mentioned it within their body of work. Every culture had a name for it, and all of them meant roughly the same thing: death from within.

When European culture moved into the nineteenth century, the illness became a sort of romantic focal point, and took on the poetic name "white plague." But it was easy for those who remained untouched by its effects to paint it so lovingly. To many, it was just another disease, one they called consumption.

Today, in the modern age of information, we refer to it by its scientific name, tuberculosis. But you can dress a disease up in any clothing you want—be it romantic or gothic or utterly modern—and it still won't change how powerful it is. Whatever people were calling it, tuberculosis was devastating, and as urban populations exploded across England and America in the mid-nineteenth century, this silent killer expanded with them.

But consumption did more than make people sick and kill them; it consumed *hope*. There was a palpable fear in the air, spreading as fast as any infectious disease, and people were desperate for a solution. So with an eye toward just how contagious this sickness was, they proposed a new idea: humane isolation.

It was an idea that had been proposed by an English physician named George Bodington in 1840, but while his own proposed facility never came to fruition, the idea spread, quickly reaching America. And one of the first places it was put into action was a location in Kentucky known as Mammoth Cave.

The cave happened to be owned by a physician named Dr. John Croghan, and he saw it as a perfect setting for healing. Caves have a tendency to maintain a constant internal temperature, and with the wide opening supplying the interior with fresh air, Croghan felt that tuberculosis patients could only benefit.

In late October 1842, he transported fifteen patients to the cave and set each of them up in small stone huts. Those who were able would share meals together, while the rest stayed in their little homes, resting and hoping. It was rustic living with the goal of recovery.

The experiment didn't last very long, though. By early February, two of the fifteen patients had died from the disease. The remaining thirteen packed up and went home, and over the following three weeks, the rest of them died as well. Even the project's mastermind himself, Dr. Croghan, couldn't escape the grasping hands of tuberculosis, dying six years later at his home ninety miles to the north in Louisville.

It would take another sixty years, but eventually someone else in Louisville tried implementing the idea of an entire facility devoted to the care of tuberculosis patients. With the city positioned right in the wetlands of the Ohio River, it was in a sort of horrible sweet spot for the spread of the disease. Which is why, in 1910, a fresh outbreak began to take lives.

In response, an open-air hospital was built with the goal of caring for the sick. But a year later plans changed and the location was moved south of the city, into the hills of the Kentucky countryside. It was there that the hospital planners purchased the land that had long been known as Waverley Hills, named by a young schoolteacher in the 1880s after a series of novels by Sir Walter Scott.

When the first Waverly Hills Sanatorium opened its doors in December 1912, the physicians had a lot of hope. With open-air environments and room for over forty patients, it was the perfect location to care for the sick. Two years later, another fifty beds were added. But as the years went by, that initial hope began giving way to creeping despair. There simply wasn't enough room for everyone who needed help.

So funds were raised and construction began on a new, larger, more modern facility. It would take them nearly three years to complete it, but when it was finished in 1926, the new Waverly Hills Sanatorium was an impressive beacon of hope. At five stories tall, the new facility boasted room for over 400 patients. Surely that would be enough, right?

Sadly, that wouldn't be the case. As the years went by, more and more buildings were added to the original, expanding the hospital's capacity and ability to help. But while their intentions were good, some of the methods they used in the service of that goal were much less humane than we might imagine.

Modern medicine was offering the doctors there a fresh batch of new treatments. And just as humans have done for thousands of years, Waverly Hills was quick to put those new tools to the test. Still, no one fully expected just how many tools would need testing. And with all that experimenting came *pain*.

Pain . . . and so much blood.

LAST RESORT

In the 1920s, our understanding of tuberculosis was far from complete. People understood it correctly as an infectious disease, and that it focused on the lungs in most patients. But as far as treating it went . . . well, the medical profession was still in the dark. What they were fully aware of, though, was the destructive path the disease carved through each new victim.

The infection would set off a chain reaction inside the body of each patient. Breathing would become difficult, even painful, and this would often be accompanied by violent fits of coughing. And it was common for those fits to produce blood. As you might expect from any sort of infection in the body, fever was common, as were digestive issues.

It was the weight loss and fatigue that earned the disease the common name of consumption. And it was also the most visible sign that caretakers could see. Tuberculosis was clearly gaining ground if the sick person was withering away day after day. In the age before X-rays and MRIs, it was hard to argue with proof you could see with your own two eyes.

And this, of course, was at the root of the New England vampire panic, which spanned the century between the 1790s and 1890s. It was built on the unusual belief that families and communities plagued by this wasting disease were actually victims of dark forces, feeding on them from the grave. Stop and think about that for a moment: tuberculosis was such a devastating disease that supernatural folklore was a natural lens to view it through.

Thankfully, as the twentieth century picked up steam, so too did modern medical science. There were new ideas about what caused the sickness to spread, and with them came possible new solutions for those infected. For the first time, people had ways of fighting back.

At the ground level, the spread of the disease needed to be stopped, so patients were isolated in places like Waverly Hills Sanatorium. No matter the person's age or place in life, once they were diagnosed with the disease, they were removed from society. Families were often pulled apart, with a parent or child taken away from the rest of their loved ones and kept in isolation.

It was also believed that fresh air and sunlight could be effective against the disease. After all, that's why Waverly Hills—and so many other sanatoriums like it—was built on an elevated site. Because of this, patients would be left to sit for hours inside open-air sunrooms. Admittedly, this sounds great if the weather is 75° and breezy, but this practice was maintained even in the dead of winter.

The Waverly Hills physicians weren't content to let the fresh air of the Kentucky hillside do all the work for them, though. Patients who didn't recover fast enough were often at the mercy of new, experimental techniques that were born out of noble intentions but carried horrible prices. And almost all of them began with the lungs.

One of the ideas wasn't actually new. Developed in 1891 by a French surgeon, the technique known as plombage thoracoplasty was a surgical attempt to intentionally collapse a lung with the hopes that it would force the body to heal faster. To do this, surgeons would cut away a piece of a rib, deflate the lung, and then fill the space with . . . well, *stuff*. While lead bullets were the original filler, time led to other materials, such as animal fat, pieces of bone, wax, silk, and even plastic balls.

Another object often inserted into the lungs of patients at Waverly Hills was a balloon. In this technique, known as balloon dilation, surgeons would open up a patient's chest and place inflatable bags into the infected areas. It was meant to relieve the pain and pressure associated with breathing, but often it came with complications.

Instead, another practice was implemented to get rid of the tight-chested feeling that tuberculosis created. Surgeons at the hospital would literally remove the muscles and ribs that protected the infected lung. In theory, this gave the patient a bit more room to breathe, but it was a horribly destructive procedure, and it was used only as a last resort.

No matter what treatments were employed, though, there was always one common element underlying almost every aspect of life inside Waverly Hills: death. Whether it was brought on solely by the disease itself or as a result of complications from the various treatments used, death was in the cards for a good percentage of the patients.

As always, the march of modern medicine rarely misses a beat. In 1943, while patients were being locked away inside the walls of Waverly Hills and experiencing the worst of experimental procedures, something miraculous happened. An antibacterial treatment was discovered with the potential to cure a number of bacterial infections. And one of those was tuberculosis.

As a result, the number of new TB cases began to dwindle year after year. By 1961, the total population of sick patients had dropped so low that it simply didn't make sense to house them in a massive facility like Waverly Hills, and so the patients were moved and the doors closed.

Like a lot of very large buildings, the facility experienced a second life. Waverly Hills became Woodhaven Geriatric Center, but that closed two decades later. Since then, the property has bounced around from owner to owner like a sort of real estate version of a hot potato.

But if the stories are true, the building is far from empty.

ACTIVE RESIDENTS

The past is like a shadow, following us wherever we go, and that was no less true for John Louis Griggs. He was a fifty-two-year-old ex-con who had been released in January 1954 from the Kentucky State Reformatory in nearby La Grange, and Waverly Hills was his chance at a fresh start. He'd found religion in prison, he said, and he wanted to leave the past behind him.

He had worked there for weeks as an orderly when the darkness caught up with him. Another orderly, a man named Edwin Bareis, apparently took offense at the former convict's presence. On the afternoon of March 1, Bareis approached Griggs with the smell of alcohol on his breath and threatened to kill the ex-con with a knife.

Griggs, to his credit, shrugged it off. He told Bareis that he was a new man and just wanted to live a good life. And even though Bareis slapped him to provoke a fight, Griggs ignored it. Instead, he went to his quarters to take a nap—and that's when Bareis made his move.

Sometime shortly before 7:00 p.m., Bareis and an accomplice entered Griggs's room and began to beat the sleeping man. Something snapped inside of Griggs, who jumped from his bed and fought back. He tossed Bareis into the hallway like a rag doll, and when the younger man got back up, Griggs leveled him with a punch to the jaw.

Rather than walk away, though, Griggs reportedly stomped on

Bareis as he lay on the floor. Then he stood on the man's chest and began to jump up and down, sometimes landing on his ribs, other times landing on his face. When he was finished, a pool of blood covered the hallway floor, and Bareis was dead.

Somehow, the darkness that Griggs had tried so hard to run away from had managed to catch back up with him. Maybe it was just a classic case of old habits dying hard, or perhaps the shadows of Waverly Hills held some sway over him. If the stories are true, those shadows still roam the halls today.

There are almost as many stories about unusual experiences inside the walls of Waverly Hills as there are hallways and half-open doors. Some have come down to us over the years from teenagers and adventure seekers who have stepped inside looking for a thrill, while others come from individuals who have been taken by surprise. Either way, they've become part of the common folklore surrounding the building itself.

Visitors to Waverly Hills have reported things that might sound at home inside any other supposedly haunted location. Doors that seem to swing shut on their own. The echo of voices from distant parts of the hospital. The sound of children on the playground, screaming with laughter . . . or something else.

Others have seen figures throughout the facility. One common sighting is a man in a white lab coat, often referred to as the Doctor. He's been seen in the dining hall, and is sometimes accompanied by the smell of freshly baked bread or other food. And as with many other abandoned hospitals, there are tales of a ghostly child who wanders from room to room.

The visions have been more disturbing than sounds and smells, though. Many visitors claim to have witnessed the spirit of an elderly woman walking the halls. Her wrists are said to be chained together, with blood dripping from her hands. And she calls out to them, begging for help.

But the most frightening visions, by far, have been the ones with the least amount of detail. Many visitors have seen what can only be described as shadow people, dark clouds that move like humans across open doorways and around the corners at the end of the hall. These shadowy figures almost seem to crawl, sometimes on the walls, sometimes on the ceiling. And while they might not have distinguishable features, they always leave witnesses with an overwhelming feeling of dread and fear.

However spread out across the facility these sightings might be, it's still a lot to take in. Which is why one room in particular is such a powerful location. Because it's there that so many of these elements all seem to come together. Countless stories paint it as the central hot spot at Waverly Hills, and it's hard to argue. From shadowy figures and visions of a dead woman to otherworldly voices and cries of anguish, Room 502 has it all.

There may be a good reason why. Legend says that a nurse took her own life in that very same room way back in 1928. There are a variety of stories about the reasons behind her death, ranging from hopelessness over an unwanted pregnancy to murder at the hands of one of the doctors. Whatever the cause might have been, her story came to an end right there, in Room 502.

Even the staff, it seems, could not escape the darkness of Waverly Hills.

The Darkness Beneath

Today we've pushed tuberculosis into the corner, along with other infectious diseases, but it's not gone, and we would be foolish to assume so. In fact, TB is still an active killer in places like sub-Saharan Africa, India, and Asia. And thanks to nearly a century of exposure to antibiotics, the TB bacterium has started to mutate, becoming even harder to treat.

To most, though, tuberculosis is a distant memory, something much of the Western world never really stops to consider, let alone fear. And yet its effects have altered history. For example, some people have made the case that without tuberculosis, we most likely wouldn't have the darkness of Edgar Allan Poe, whose mother and wife were both taken from him by the disease. It was his pain that fueled his art.

Heck, without an outbreak of tuberculosis in Exeter, Rhode Island, back in the 1890s, we might not even have Bram Stoker's

Dracula. Tragedy has always inspired people to rise above the shadows and aim for something higher. Maybe that's the silver lining beneath the dark cloud of TB.

But it also took countless lives.

At Waverly Hills alone, some people have proposed that the total number of deaths exceeded sixty thousand, but there are no records to back up that claim. We do know that hundreds died each year; some from the treatments they voluntarily underwent, and others from the illness itself. People suffering from the illness were taken up to the heights of the Kentucky countryside, and then . . . they just withered away.

One more detail. There's a large tunnel that runs from the foot of the hill to the facility up top. When it was constructed in 1926, the tunnel's original purpose was to serve as a ventilation shaft for the boilers down below. There was even a small track system installed to allow for supplies to be transported up the shaft, rather than forcing delivery people to make the trek on foot.

Hospital staff also found the tunnel to be useful, though, especially in the winter, when the snow was deep and the winds were cold and piercing. The warm, steady climb up the cement tunnel was the perfect alternative to hiking a small mountain in the snow each day. One side even had stairs. Honestly, it was practically built for pedestrian traffic.

But as the years wore on and the death toll ticked higher and higher, the hospital staff found another use for that underground passageway. You see, along with fresh air and sunlight, the physicians at Waverly Hills believed their patients needed hope and positive attitudes to truly heal. The last thing a patient needed to see from their window was the corpse of a friend being carried away.

So the ventilation tunnel took on new life as a highway for the dead. Rather than carry the corpses of TB victims out the front or back door, where the still-living might happen to see them, each new corpse was wrapped up and taken deep beneath the facility. Then it was placed on a cart and lowered secretly to the bottom of the hill. As a result, that old ventilation shaft took on a less optimistic name: the "Body Chute."

The real story of Waverly Hills isn't one of haunted hallways and paranormal investigation. It's a tale of suffering, death, isolation, and hopelessness. And that's what makes it a place of darkness more than anything else. Yes, over the years the facility has played host to countless sightings and unexplainable events. I get it; it's attractive in a dark and gloomy sort of way.

But in the end, whether or not we believe those stories takes a backseat to a much larger truth: we, as human beings, are very good at creating darkness.

And then we have to find a way to live with it.

Aaron Mahnke

Locked Away

THEY HAD BEEN searching for it for nearly fifteen years. So when they uncovered a set of steps on November 2, 1922, you can imagine how elated they must have felt. Word was sent to the man who had financed the entire project, and by November 26, the entire team found themselves standing in front of a sealed tomb door.

Today, most of the world knows what they found. As archaeologist Howard Carter led his team inside, they stepped into the three-thousand-year-old tomb of the Egyptian pharaoh Tutankhamen. It was the discovery of a lifetime, and it was everything they'd hoped for.

Things didn't go so well after that, though. Lord Carnarvon, the man who had paid for all fifteen years of digging and searching, died less than two months later from an infected mosquito bite. It's said that at the very same moment he took his last breath, all the lights in Cairo mysteriously went out. At the same time, his faithful dog howled mournfully, staggered on its feet, and then fell over dead.

And while Carter himself seems to have escaped the wave of death that followed the opening of the tomb, others weren't so lucky. George Jay Gould, another investor, visited the tomb shortly after it was opened, and died just two months later. Carter's secretary, Richard Bethell, died young a few years later himself. One other archaeologist on the project, Hugh Evelyn-White, is said to have committed suicide after leaving a message. "I have succumbed to a curse," he wrote with his own blood.

Whether the stories are rooted in fact or fiction, one thing is clear: people are convinced that their past can haunt them. That whether we like it or not, sometimes the things we've done follow us through life, waiting for that moment when they can take revenge. And as one story shows, it doesn't matter how far you run, or how high you build your walls.

Our past, like a dark and twisted shadow, has a way of following us wherever we go.

A SHOOTING STAR

They grew up near each other and didn't even know it. It was only for a couple of years, from 1850 to 1852, but later in life it would become one of those happy memories they pulled out at social gatherings to get a laugh. And that's fine; Sallie was going to need all the happy memories she could get.

She was born in New Haven, Connecticut, back in 1839. Hers was a large family, with Sallie being the fifth-born, and another after her, and for a while there, I think, that was a challenge for her parents, Sarah and Leonard. Finally, though, around the time of Sallie's eighth birthday, her father's carpentry business began to take off. They eventually bought a house over on Court Street.

In 1852, with business booming and the money pouring in, Sallie's parents purchased a six-acre estate in a different part of town. I have a feeling they all exhaled a collective sigh of relief. They'd made it. They were climbing the ladder to join the well-to-do and influential. Things were looking up.

New Haven in the mid-1800s was a fantastic place to grow up if you loved education. Yale University, known then as Yale College, was the centerpiece of the city, with a network of other schools surrounding it. Students in New Haven couldn't help but learn from the best minds, soaking in modern sciences and ideas.

There was more, though. As the 1850s faded into the 1860s,

other movements were spreading. Spiritualism had extended beyond its birthplace in upstate New York and was transforming the way many people viewed the natural world. In the South, rebellious tremors were shaking the structure of America, due to a growing interest in banning slavery. I'd be putting it far too lightly to say that 1860 was a year of change.

In 1861, everything fell apart. Under Confederate orders, General Beauregard attacked the Union-held Fort Sumter in Charleston, South Carolina, and effectively set a match to the dry and flammable mountain of tension between both sides. The American Civil War began that day, and the world was never the same.

A little over a year later, though, in September 1862, Sallie walked down the aisle on her wedding day. The man who would become her husband was the very same boy she'd lived near during those two years on Court Street. Even though her family had moved out of the neighborhood, they hadn't left the same social circles, which most likely led to this joyful moment.

William was born in June 1837. His father, Oliver, was a clothing manufacturer with a knack for improving the machines that did the work, and that ingenuity paid off. Business was profitable and brisk, and as Sallie's parents were climbing that social ladder, they were doing so right alongside William's family.

There's a good chance they knew each other for most of their childhood, too. We know that while she studied at the Young Ladies' Collegiate Institute, Sallie took classes with William's sister Annie. And both families attended the First Baptist Church of New Haven. They might have stopped being neighbors in 1852, but they were never really far apart.

If the families were to compare balance sheets, William's parents were vastly more wealthy than Sallie's, but that didn't matter. The couple was in love, and Sallie more than held her own in their relationship. She had a brilliant mind, having excelled in subjects like literature and music, and she spoke fluent French. Which was a good thing; she was going to need every advantage she could get, because life was about to climb to a whole new level very soon.

You see, a few years before the young couple's wedding, William's father had acquired another business through some, well, shall we say *aggressive* methods. The result was his complete ownership and control of what he called the New Haven Arms Company. If the name of the business isn't a big enough clue, it's important to point out that they made a very specific type of item: firearms.

In October 1860, one of the plant managers filed a patent for a new type of rifle. This new rifle would hold sixteen shots, and it didn't need to be loaded by inserting gunpowder and a bullet down the muzzle. In an era when a well-trained soldier might be able to fire three shots per minute, this new rifle was a game-changer.

It was officially known as the Henry Rifle, named after Benjamin Tyler Henry, the employee who patented it. Although it wasn't the most common rifle used in the Civil War, it was certainly the most sought-after. Infantry would save up their salaries for them or use their reenlistment bonuses, believing that its greater firepower might just save their lives.

It's hard to tell if that hypothesis really played out in reality. What we do know is that by the time the war was over in 1865, the firearm had been so popular that William's father went all in, putting his last name right there on the company and the star weapon it produced.

In doing so, he gave it a name that nearly everyone today has heard of: the Winchester Rifle.

RUNNING

What did Oliver Winchester name his new 1866 model? Creatively, the Winchester Model 1866. I know, not the sexiest name in the world, but it got the point across in a way that even Apple could be proud of. This firearm was new. It was better. While the Henry had been a hit, this new Winchester model came with a few improvements, and that only served to increase demand.

France would later buy six thousand of them, along with over four million cartridges. That's roughly the same number of Henry rifles that sold during the whole span of the Civil War, all in one transaction. But it got better: when the Ottoman Empire needed weapons for war against the Russian Empire, they purchased forty-five thousand.

All of this success brought an explosion of prosperity to the Winchester family, but there were still moments of darkness. In order to put his name on the rifle and take full control of its financial destiny, Oliver Winchester had had to wrestle the weapon out of the hands of its creator, Benjamin Henry, who spent the rest of his life working alone.

The Model 1866 wasn't the only Winchester born that year. Sallie—who at this point had dropped her childhood nickname in favor of her given name, Sarah—spent the first half of the year pregnant. In July 1866, she and William became parents to a baby girl. They named her Annie, after William's sister.

But that was a joy they barely had time to soak in. Just nine days after she was born, Annie Winchester passed away, leaving her parents in utter and absolute grief. Most new mothers struggle with some level of postpartum depression—and many fathers do as well—but this was something darker. After months of anticipation, they'd lost their child.

Sarah fell into a deep depression. By some accounts, the loss of Annie was a blow that would take her years to recover from, although I'm not sure you ever fully come back from something like that. So when I tell you that the Winchesters had a new home built just outside of New Haven and moved into it a couple of years later, we have to see that move through the lens of her pain.

She was running. Starting fresh, in a way, offered her hope.

I imagine the next decade was a bit of a blur for Sarah and William. He worked as the treasurer of his father's empire, watching the company coffers fill at a mind-boggling rate. The Winchester Model 1866 gave way to the Model 1873, which was even more successful, if you can believe it. It would become known as "the gun that won the West," and it would stay in production for fifty years.

Sarah and William would never have another child. Maybe they just didn't have the courage to risk more heartbreak. But that's the trouble with grief; you can build yourself a world without risk, but nothing will stop pain from breaking in on its own. And in 1880, that's just what happened. That's when William's father, Oliver, passed away.

If there was a bright side to this new wave of grief, it was William's inheritance. The Winchester company, those overflowing bank accounts, and that incessant demand for more of their rifles—all of it translated into a massive windfall. In modern currency, William inherited close to half a billion dollars from his father.

He wouldn't have a chance to enjoy it. Less than three months later, William Winchester died at the age of forty-three. Like a lot of tragic deaths in the nineteenth century, his killer was tuberculosis. The disease moved quickly, and when it was over, Sarah was alone. Alone, and looking for answers, because she'd lost her only child, her father-in-law, and her husband in a span of just fifteen years. Maybe that was normal in the late 1800s, but to Sarah, it felt unusual. In fact, it felt intentional.

We're told that her deep grief in the spring of 1881 led her to seek out answers. The growth of Spiritualism had put mediums— those individuals who claimed to speak for and with the spirits of the dead—firmly in the public eye, and so Sarah talked to a number of them. Finally, it was a man from Boston, Adam Coons, who delivered an answer she believed.

Those rifles that had made her family incredibly wealthy had accomplished something else, something more horrifying; they had led to tens of thousands of deaths. And according to William's spirit, with whom Coons claimed to be speaking, those deaths had cursed their family. But there was a way out, if she was willing to try.

William told her, through Coons of course, that she needed to follow the sun west. When she had traveled far enough, he would tell her to stop. She was being invited to do something she'd become so very good at: she needed to run away. So she did.

After selling her estate in New Haven, Sarah Winchester packed up everything and began her long westward journey, always listening for the voice of her dead husband to tell her she'd gone far enough. She crossed the Midwest and the Mississippi, the Rockies and the Sierra Nevada. We don't know how long it took her, but in the 1880s it was a journey that was far from comfortable and easy. Still, she did it.

When she finally stopped in 1886, she'd traveled all the way to California's Santa Clara Valley. Once there, she purchased a small farmhouse on a large piece of property and then began to build a new life for herself.

But as you might have guessed, that's not all she would build.

CONTAINMENT ISSUES

If Sarah Winchester's goal was to escape the past, California was a great destination. It was new and fresh and so full of possibilities, and that made it ideal for someone starting over. The state itself had only become part of the Union less than four decades earlier, and the pain and conflict of the Civil War had barely left a scratch on the culture there. It was a brand-new world.

But you can't run away from everything. By the early 1880s, the press had begun to look more compassionately on the Native Americans who had suffered under the march of westward expansion, and one of the things they pinned the blame on was the Winchester rifle. Without it, they said, countless lives might have been saved.

That's not to say she rejected the wealth that came with her ownership of the company. The entire fortune her husband had inherited from his father was now hers, along with a large monthly income of $1,000, roughly $25,000 in modern currency. That's monthly, not yearly. But don't worry; Sarah had a plan for how she was going to spend it all.

The house she bought was a simple eight-room farmhouse. I doubt it was the structure itself that interested her. No, it had to be the 162 acres of land that surrounded it. That represented a lot of space between herself and the rest of the world. It was a wall made of distance, designed to keep the public out.

Her demons, though, were another story, and she was going to have to do something even more dramatic to keep them at bay.

Back when she had visited the medium in Boston, the man had passed along another set of instructions from her dead husband. Build a house, he told her. Build a house that can hold all the spirits, and if you do it right, you'll find peace.

Now, I'll be the first to admit that much of what we know about her meetings with that medium comes down to guesswork. We don't have transcripts, and Sarah herself never went on record with a detailed account of those conversations. This is the place where legend pokes its head into the story, like Kramer sliding into Jerry Seinfeld's apartment. It's there, uninvited, and now we have to deal with it. That's how a lot of stories go.

What we do know is that Sarah Winchester started remodeling her new house as soon as she bought it. She had a bottomless pit of money, all the space she needed, and a whole lot of self-inflicted guilt, all of which powered the construction project. More and more rooms were added on, eventually expanding the original eight to a massive twenty-six. But she was far from finished.

A railroad line was added so that building materials could be brought closer to the house. Legend says that a team of construction workers toiled on the house every hour of the day, seven days a week. And she lived there, in the middle of all that chaos, managing the foreman and drawing up new plans herself.

Over the years, that house exploded with new rooms and features. The structure itself grew to become seven stories tall. And with no architect guiding the process with skill and logic, the results were more than a bit unusual. I don't mean that things were crooked or poorly made; I mean that the house began to look more and more like an M. C. Escher drawing come to life.

For example, there are staircases in the house that lead nowhere, literally ending at a blank wall or a ledge that a person could easily fall off. There are chimneys that you can see from the exterior, but when you look for their corresponding fireplaces or stoves inside, they just aren't there. You might come upon a massive door and open it, only to find a tiny closet. Or, because opposites are fun, you could open a small door and discover an enormous room. All told, the house has roughly fifty fireplaces, ten thousand windows, forty staircases, and two thousand doors.

Some people have speculated that Sarah Winchester was simply trying to confuse the spirits that haunted her. That somehow, if the home was illogical and unpredictable enough, those spirits wouldn't be able to get out. They see the house as one giant puzzle box, designed to trap things inside. To prove it, they point to the near lack of mirrors, and the overwhelming abundance of objects with thirteen parts, like steps or window panes.

In 1906, nearly two decades after construction began, San Francisco suffered a massive earthquake. The entire front portion of the Winchester house, along with the top three stories, all collapsed, leaving portions of the house in ruin. Sarah found herself trapped in her bedroom, and when she was finally rescued, she ordered the collapsed parts of the house—a section with at least thirty rooms—to be boarded up and ignored.

The work finally came to an end on September 4, 1922, thirty-six years after it all began. According to one legend, Sarah held a séance that evening and spoke with the spirits in the house. Then she went to bed and never woke up. She was eighty-three years old.

Sarah Winchester had finally achieved her goal—she got away.

TRAPPED INSIDE

Sarah Winchester spent her life running from pain. That's not something I'm faulting her for, believe me. Each and every one of us carries a bag that's overflowing with regret or guilt or suffering. We're all just too busy managing our own to notice everyone else is doing the same thing.

So Sarah ran. Maybe her story is powerful and unique because she took running to a new level. She literally got on a train and headed west, and then built walls around her inner struggles. Perhaps her story is attractive because she built a crazy house, or maybe because it feels familiar. She did what many of us wish we could.

What she left us with is a monument to forgetting. That eight-room farmhouse she purchased in 1886 grew into a complex maze of stairs and halls and room after room of space. Heck, it's so confusing that there's no official room count. I've seen estimates ranging anywhere from 148 to 161. If the stories are true, even the staff who worked for her had to use a map to get around.

There's a colorful rumor that Sarah hid a treasure somewhere in the house, locking away a piece of her vast fortune for some intrepid explorer to discover later. But of course, no one has ever tracked it down, if it even exists at all. The truth is probably a lot more simple: most of her fortune was poured into the very building itself.

There are other stories, too. Legends without a lot of proof, but they're threads that add color to the tapestry of Sarah's story. They say that the moment the workers learned of her death, they just stopped and walked away, leaving nails sticking out of the wood. Visitors to the house today have noticed doors that shut on their own, cold spots, floating lights, and the distant sound of breaking glass.

Trust me, I get it. A lot of people view the Winchester House as one of those ultra-cool, *can-you-believe-it's-true* sort of places. It's fascinating and eerie and so very rebellious and insane. But when we simply stare at the house and marvel at its eccentricities, we risk missing the pain inside those walls. After all, a person built that house, however broken the reasons.

Today, the house exists as something more inspiring. Legendary author Shirley Jackson, who grew up nearby, makes mention of it at the beginning of her 1959 novel, *The Haunting of Hill House*. When Disneyland built their Haunted Mansion, they took their inspiration from the Winchester House. And of course, the building is a state landmark and tourist attraction, open to the public for guided viewings.

In the fall of 2016, the preservation team at the Winchester House made a discovery. It was a new room, one that had been boarded up and hidden away for over a century. Their best guess is that the room was one of many that were closed up and abandoned following the 1906 earthquake.

It wasn't empty, either, but rather than finding that lost, hidden treasure everyone seems to whisper about, they found a snapshot of everyday life: a Victorian couch, a dress form, a sewing machine, and even a couple of paintings. It was a time capsule, locked away and forgotten.

Exactly as Sarah would have wanted it.

EPILOGUE

Sarah Winchester built her mansion as a way of confusing and tricking the spirits that she felt were chasing her. Some say that's why there are only two mirrors in the entire house, while others point to the symbolic number 13 that pops up in almost every room in one shape or another, a number that was considered evil and acted like a ward, fighting off the ghosts of her past.

But did it work? Well, if the stories that have been told about the house since her death are any indication . . . it's hard to tell. What's certain is that even though the house is empty now, there has been a lot of activity reported inside it.

One tour guide once reported hearing an audible sigh as she led a group of tourists into one of the bedrooms. When she paused to listen closer, she claims that a small, dark shape drifted in through one door and then vanished around a corner. No one was able to identify the source of the sound, or find the mysterious shape.

Over the years that people have been visiting the mansion and its surrounding grounds, multiple witnesses have reported the sensation of being watched. Some have even seen a figure of a dark-haired man watching over them, sometimes from inside the house and sometimes outside. And while the witnesses and locations are always different, the descriptions of the ghostly figure are always the same.

One more revealing tale comes from a few years ago, when a contractor was doing some restoration work on a fireplace inside the house. According to his story, he was up on a ladder in a room all by himself when he felt a tap on his shoulder. He turned to look, more out of reflex than any sort of expectation that someone might actually be there, but saw nothing.

A moment later, it happened again. Only this time the tap was a shove, and he almost lost his balance and fell off the ladder. Frightened for his safety, he said that he stopped his work, climbed back down, and didn't return to that room for the rest of the day.

And honestly, it's hard to blame him. With so many rooms in a place like the Winchester Mansion, they can't all be empty, can they?

 DISTANT SHORES

Bite Marks

IN 1890, THE tiny Greek village of Messaria, on the island of Kythnos, was plagued by something otherworldly. Whatever it was, the villagers claimed that it would enter their homes, eat their food, break their dishes, and then move on to repeat itself elsewhere.

They named this creature Andilaveris, and they claimed it was a vrykolakas, a close cousin to the traditional European vampire. Andilaveris drank their wine and smashed their belongings, howling like a wolf and making a horrible mess.

But the most interesting feature of this story is that no one actually saw Andilaveris do these things. The villagers claimed to witness it all, of course, but they said he was invisible. He was, in essence, a noisy spirit, but the only cultural lens they were able to view him through was as a vampire. And they weren't the first. Between 1591 and 1923, people across Europe told similar stories of an invisible monster that raided their homes and destroyed their belongings.

Today we see events like these play out across the screens of our local movie theater. Hollywood has been fascinated with invisible, violent forces since the early 1980s, when it brought us *Poltergeist*. What once was looked on as overly spiritual and easily disproven is now attracting the attention of popular culture.

But poltergeists have a history that runs far deeper than just the

1980s. From first-century Roman accounts to modern newspapers, stories of humans interacting with angry ghosts have been told for a very, very long time.

Some are clearly hoaxes. Some are misinterpretations of natural events. Oftentimes they are a grab for attention, or a cry for help. But sometimes—on very rare occasions—a story comes along that is nothing short of haunting.

HISTORICAL HAUNTINGS

The word *poltergeist* evokes a number of ideas for most people. Most think of the movie. Some picture objects being thrown around a room by an invisible hand. They might even envision the sound of chains rattling and doors creaking open in the night.

And they wouldn't be too far off from the truth. The word *poltergeist* is German, and it literally means "noisy spirit." The idea is that while the typical ghost story only uses one of our five senses, our sight, stories of poltergeists can oftentimes tap all five.

Most poltergeist accounts reference the same types of activity. Objects are mysteriously moved or broken, noises are heard in and around the house, and there are physical attacks such as biting, pinching, hitting, and even tripping. Some people even claim to have seen objects or other people levitated by an unseen force.

And unlike some folklore, stories of noisy spirits are nearly universal. Similar manifestations have been reported by witnesses in dozens of cultures for centuries, from Japan and Brazil to Australia and the United States. For those who view widespread distribution as a major sign of proof, the poltergeist has become an indisputable fact.

One of the earliest records of a poltergeist encounter comes from the first-century Jewish historian Flavius Josephus. He recorded an exorcism in AD 94 that sounds eerily similar to those of us familiar with modern exorcism tales. In his report, he describes how, as the spirit was being driven from the person, a bowl of water all the way across the room was suddenly overturned by an invisible force.

Jacob Grimm, one-half of the famous Grimm brothers, who recorded many of the stories we remember from our childhood, also wrote more scholarly books. In his book *Deutsche Mythologie*, Grimm recorded a story from the German town of Bingen-am-Rhein that took place in the fourth century.

According to the story, people were pulled out of their beds by an unseen force. Loud noises could be heard, as if someone were knocking on the walls or floor. Stones were even thrown, but the person—or spirit—who did the throwing was never found.

Gerald of Wales, the famous clergyman and chronicler, wrote in 1191 of a house in Pembrokeshire that was filled with poltergeist activity. Here, the unseen spirit was said to have thrown handfuls of dirt, as well as tearing clothing and breaking objects in the house. Most frightening to those who experienced it, though, was the fact that this spirit was also said to vocalize all of the secrets of the people in the room.

Similar stories have been recorded countless times in the centuries since Gerald's day. In one story from the early 1700s, one family encountered unusual activity in the church rectory in Epworth, Lincolnshire. Rev. Samuel Wesley and his wife, Susanna, had ten children, and had lived in the house since it had been built shortly after the previous rectory burned to the ground in 1709.

During the winter of 1716–17, the family began to experience regular noises. They would hear knocking on the walls and doors, or the sounds of people running up and down the stairs. The house was searched from top to bottom in the hope of finding the person responsible, but no cause was found. They even named the noisy spirit Old Jeffrey, and it was said that the spirit made himself visible on Christmas Day that winter. Shortly after, the noises stopped, never to happen again.

In more modern times, one well-known story is that of the Black Monk of Pontefract. There, in the growing community just outside the city of Wakefield in West Yorkshire, England, reports began to circulate about the most violent poltergeist in European history.

Joe and Jean Pritchard lived at 30 East Drive in 1970, along with their son, Philip, and daughter, Diane. According to their report, they were plagued by problems in the house from the start. Objects were thrown, the temperature in rooms would suddenly drop, and they would even find puddles on the floor.

They named the spirit Fred, and soon learned that Fred was not just mischievous but also violent. Not only did the spirit throw eggs and take bites out of their sandwiches, but it also dragged their twelve-year-old, Diane, up the stairs by her neck, leaving handprints on her skin. After Fred attempted to strangle Diane a second time—this time with an electrical cord—the family asked for help.

The police were brought in, as were a number of psychics and paranormal researchers. Even the mayor came by for a visit, but nothing seemed to help. Eventually, the Pritchards moved away, and the noises inside number 30 stopped.

But according to the woman who lives next door in the house that's connected to number 30, Fred the ghost hasn't gone anywhere. He still makes frequent visits to her side of the wall, and although he's usually very quiet, she claims that he sometimes stands in the room and glares at her with menacing eyes.

Under the scrutiny of historical research, though, most recorded poltergeist stories have been shown to be frauds. Oftentimes they were nothing more than pranks put on by the homeowner, or the person who stood the most to gain from the attention. But every now and then, a story comes along that defies explanation.

And when that story involves violent physical attacks and a serious threat to human lives, it becomes downright chilling.

A Dark and Stormy Night

In 1999, a homeless man broke into a large tomb in a prominent cemetery known as Greyfriars, in Edinburgh, Scotland. It was a cold and rainy night, and the man was looking for shelter. I might have gone elsewhere to find a warm, dry place to sleep, but when you're down and out, anything will do, I suppose.

This man wandered through the graveyard in the dark until he found a large mausoleum, something that looked large enough to allow him to get out of the elements and sleep in relative comfort. This one was known as the Black Mausoleum, and it was enormous. It resembled a large rotunda, with the spaces between the pillars filled in with cut stone.

When the homeless man stumbled upon this tomb, it was exactly what he had been looking for. It had plenty of room to stretch out and sleep in, and it was dry. So he did what anyone desperate for shelter would do: he broke in.

Because it's rare to find a tomb with windows, the interior of the vault was completely black. Thankfully, the man had a lighter or some other form of illumination, and he used it to explore. In the center of the floor was a large iron grate, similar to what you might find over a sewer drain or in the sidewalk over a subway tunnel in New York City.

Beneath the grate was a staircase that curved and twisted its way down to a lower level. I know this sounds like something out of an Indiana Jones movie, but it's real. And it gets worse. Because beneath the first level, at the bottom of the stairs, this homeless man discovered four wooden coffins.

They were, of course, very old, and the man probably assumed that because of this, they would contain valuables that he could sell. I imagine he set down whatever it was that he was using as a light on one of the nearby coffins, and then began to try and open another of them. When it didn't open, he resorted to smashing the lid to break the lock. And that's when he took a step backward.

The boards in the floor must have been very old. The man must have put his full weight in *just* the right spot. All of the possibilities must have lined up *perfectly* in that moment. A brief groan from the wooden floor was followed by a loud crash, and the man tumbled backward into a long-forgotten pit, some part of an even lower level that dated back centuries.

The best guess that historians can make is that the pit had actually been used for the illegal dumping of bodies in the wake of the plague in 1645. What they *do* know, however, is that the pit was sealed *very* well. So sealed, in fact, that when this homeless man landed on the pile of 350-year-old corpses, they were surprisingly well preserved.

They weren't skeletal and dry, like you might expect. No, these bodies were wet with something that resembled green slime. Their clothing was intact, albeit ragged and torn, and their hair was matted to their shriveled heads. And of course, there was an overwhelming stench in the air.

The man bolted, and I don't think there's a single one of us who could blame him. Fearing for his life, the man climbed out of the pit, up the stone stairs to the main vault, and out the door. He was in such a hurry that he even fell and cut his head on the doorway to the mausoleum.

Outside, a security guard was patrolling the area with his canine partner when the homeless man burst out of the tomb. Maybe it was the blood running down the man's face. Maybe it was the white dust that covered him from head to toe because of his adventures below the tomb. Or maybe it was simply the sight of a pale, shrieking figure charging out from the dark crypt.

Whatever it was, when the guard saw the man, he turned tail and ran just as fast as he could, away from the darkness of the cemetery and into the city beyond.

RUDE AWAKENINGS

As difficult as it is to imagine, the frightening events of that night in 1999 were just the beginning. Like a tiny spark igniting an entire barn, the break-in at the Black Mausoleum set in motion something that no one has since been able to adequately explain.

It turns out the mausoleum belonged to none other than Sir George Mackenzie, a man who had died in 1690. Along with being a lawyer and lord advocate to the crown of Scotland, Mackenzie had been instrumental in sending hundreds of Presbyterian Covenanters to their deaths in the late seventeenth century. Today he is known as Bloody Mackenzie, and according to the local reports, this invasion of his resting place set off a series of events that can only be blamed on a *very* angry spirit. And it didn't wait very long.

The day after the break-in, a woman was taking a walk through the cemetery. It's unclear whether she was a tourist interested in seeing the Covenanters' Prison area of the graveyard or a local just out for a walk. But when she drew near to the mausoleum, she decided to peer through one of the two small grates in the tomb door. As she stood there, a gust of cold wind rushed out of the tomb with such force that, she claimed, it knocked her backward and off the stone steps, onto her back.

A few days later, another woman was found unconscious on the sidewalk outside the tomb, sprawled out on her back as if she had fallen. She claimed that invisible hands had grabbed her around the throat and attempted to strangle her. When she pulled back the collar of her shirt, her neck was ringed by a series of dark bruises, as if fingertips had dug into her skin.

Soon after, another tourist—this time a young man—experienced something eerily similar. For others, though, the consequences of visiting the tomb were more physical and lasting. Some people have found scratches on their arms, neck, or chest, while others have discovered burn marks. Many of these injuries disappeared almost as quickly and mysteriously as they appeared. Some, though, claim to have been permanently scarred.

All told, people have broken fingers, felt their hair pulled, and been pushed or struck, all by an unseen force. People have even felt nauseous or numb, or both. And not just one or two people, but hundreds. Sometimes these attacks happen near the tomb, and sometimes they happen later.

One story in particular stands out. A former police officer reported participating in a tour of the cemetery a few years ago. After returning to his hotel room that night, he picked up the book he had been given on the tour that covered the details of the hauntings. As he did, he felt a sharp pain, as if someone were trying to burn him. When he ran to the mirror to check, he found five deep scratches on his neck beneath his chin.

The following morning, the officer visited his mother and told her what happened. He also gave her the book. According to him, he couldn't stand to have it around any longer, and so he left it at her house.

When he called her later and asked about the book, he caught her in the bathroom. She was standing in front of a mirror, examining five long scratches on her throat.

All told, nearly four hundred people have claimed to have been attacked by something otherworldly around the tomb. Almost two hundred of those are people who have actually passed out during a ghost tour. Sometimes every person in the tour will feel the exact same thing. Oftentimes complete strangers will independently report the exact same experience.

But the odd experiences extend beyond the tours. An unusually high number of dead animals have been found in the area around Mackenzie's tomb. Unexplainable fires have broken out in nearby buildings. People have reported cold spots, and the usual photographic and electronic malfunctions have occurred as well.

Some have gone looking for an explanation for such a large number of unusual reports, but the theories are as varied as the types of attacks. One idea tries to connect the dots between nearby Edinburgh University's Artificial Intelligence Unit—which uses high-voltage machinery—and the sandstone deep underground beneath the ancient cemetery. The porous stone, they say, absorbs the energy and releases it later, causing the odd experiences.

But this is a difficult theory to swallow, especially for the people who have been physically assaulted by whatever it is that haunts the tomb. The company that conducts the tours through the graveyard is just as interested in finding the cause, though, and that's why they've spent years collecting photographs of injuries, firsthand accounts, letters from witnesses, and other documentation.

Unfortunately, most of those records were destroyed in 2003, when a fire swept through their office. Everything inside the tour company's space was incinerated, but nothing more. Every single nearby building remained untouched.

The insurance company never found the cause.

The Unseen

Outside of places with frequent earthquake activity, most people don't think it's normal for photographs to fall off their wall, or for a chair to slide across the floor, or to find themselves knocked down by an unseen force. For some, these events are equal parts unusual and inconvenient. For others, though, they are frightening.

It's difficult to say what's really going on in these stories. Some events can be chalked up to natural causes, or the human tendency to misinterpret the things we see.

We are very good at finding patterns, after all. It's called pareidolia, that moment when we see patterns where they don't really exist. We do this when we look up at clouds and see the shape of a turtle, but it also happens subconsciously. Our minds are always searching for patterns.

Or perhaps there's something more to the stories. What if there really *are* sinister, violent spirits that can attack us if provoked? In many stories, priests are brought in to bless the homes or perform exorcisms, a solution that certainly assumed there's a supernatural source. And sometimes it's worked.

In the years since the break-in at the Black Mausoleum, there have been two attempts at exorcism. The second of those took place in 2000, just a year after the activity began.

Colin Grant, minister of a spiritualist church and professional exorcist, was brought to Greyfriars Cemetery. Standing in front of the Black Mausoleum, he performed his ceremony. While doing so, he claimed to feel overwhelmed by the sensation of oppression, that hundreds of tormented souls were swirling around him, trying to break through into our world. He said he had feared for his life, and quickly left before he could finish.

Just a few weeks later, Colin Grant was found dead, victim of a sudden heart attack.

The Cave

Dᴜʀɪɴɢ ʜɪꜱ ʜɪꜱᴛᴏʀɪᴄ journey aboard the HMS *Beagle*, Charles Darwin spent over a month on a small island off the coast of Chile known as Chiloé. It wasn't his final destination, but he still managed to work and collect information and specimens, including a small endangered fox now known as Darwin's zorro.

He also witnessed the aftereffects of an earthquake, and made note of a rainbow that transitioned from the typical semicircle to a full circle right before his eyes. But it was the people he encountered that seemed to impact him the most.

He later wrote, "They are a humble, quiet, industrious set of men. Although with plenty to eat, the people are very poor . . . and . . . the lower orders cannot scrape together money sufficient to purchase even the smallest luxuries."

He also noted seeing a pair of black-necked swans, but thankfully Darwin didn't have the same view of birds that the local people did. And still do, actually. One local historian recalls how, when he was a boy, a hunchbacked heron flew low over his fishing boat. When he told his father, the older man grabbed his shotgun and waited for the bird to return.

Why? Because for as long as anyone could remember, the people of Chiloé have believed that some birds are more than they appear. Some people, it seems, believe they are warlocks. Seeing one was a bad omen, hinting that someone close to you would soon die.

All of us are ruled by authority to some degree, whether it's through our government, our religion, or our family ties. Often it's all three. But there's another governing body, one that's as old as time itself, and on Chiloé, it controlled people for centuries.

Sometimes, you see, people are ruled by fear.

BEYOND THE EDGE OF THE WORLD

The Incas called it the Place of the Seagulls. They stayed away from the area, believing it was the border between their empire of prosperity and safety and the cold, dark wilderness to the south.

Chiloé isn't a large island—perhaps less than a hundred miles from north to south—but it's certainly the largest in the collection of small islands there off the coast of Chile. And to visit it is to go back in time. Green hills, mountains in the distance, the dark waves of the Pacific lapping on the shore where colorful houses are built on stilts to stay above the mud and rocks.

Darwin described it as beautiful in 1835. He wrote of the mixture of evergreen trees and tropical vegetation, of rolling hills and thick forests. And all of that green, Darwin postulated, was due to the enormous amount of rainfall. Gray skies and wet soil are a constant of life in Chiloé, then as now.

And while most people have never heard of the place, the unique churches there have an architectural style that has earned them classification as a UNESCO World Heritage Site. There are churches because Jesuit missionaries built them shortly after arriving at the beginning of the seventeenth century. But don't let these European artifacts fool you; the culture the Jesuits encountered when they arrived was far outside their realm of experience.

The Chiloé of old was home to a vast collection of myths and legends that informed almost every aspect of everyday life. And because much of the economy and culture of the island was built around the fishing industry, just as it is today, many of those stories have elements of the sea in them.

One example is the legend of the ghost ship known as the *Caleuche*. According to the stories, the *Caleuche* patrols the waters off the coast of the island, moving both above the water and below. The ship itself is a sentient being, and has the ability to sense when someone from the island has drowned.

After they die, these people are brought onto the ship by two sisters and a brother, where their new life can begin. That life consists of both an eternal party aboard the ship and working as sailors in the transport and unloading of illegal cargo for the island's merchants. Even today, there are many in Chiloé who claim to have seen the ship, still patrolling the cold waters offshore.

There are other legends that haunt the island. Stories speak of the Trauco, a sort of forest troll or little person who lives in hollow trees deep in the forest. This creature's task is to protect the trees, but it has also become a convenient scapegoat for unwed mothers. The Trauco, they say, is irresistible to virgins who wander into the forest, and those women frequently return home pregnant.

La Pincoya is said to be a woman who appears to fishermen along the coast. She is described as young and beautiful, but her hair is covered in wet kelp. And the locals consider her to be an omen, although the outcome depends on the circumstances. If she appears facing the sea, your fishing nets will overflow. If she's facing you, though, those nets will be empty. And in the rare instances when she appears right in front of a person, the legend says it is best to close your eyes and run as fast as you can, lest she seduce you and lead you down into the sea.

One more legend is that of the basilisk, a creature that appears elsewhere around the globe. In Chiloé, though, the basilisk is more than just an enormous snake. Here it also has the head of a rooster and hatches from an egg. Some stories tell of how the basilisk will nest beneath a person's house. During the night it will slither out and suck the air from the lungs of the people sleeping inside.

As frightening as some of these creatures and stories might be, though, none of them compares to the legends of the Brujos de Chiloé, the warlocks of the island. Those stories have struck fear into the hearts of the locals for centuries, shaping many aspects of the culture. The warlocks have been blamed for tragedy, for loss, and even for illness and death.

Most frightening of all is the simple fact that, unlike all the other legends found on the island, the Brujos were *real*.

The Dark Mafia

We know the Brujos were real because they were brought to trial in 1880. Almost overnight, what was once little more than a whispered legend—a sort of Chilean bogeyman, if you will—took on flesh and bone. And what the investigation uncovered was truly shocking.

Let's step back, though. It's important to understand where the warlocks came from. And the short answer is that we don't really know. But there are ideas, and many of them hold promise and truth. The most common theory is that something powerful was formed as a result of the collision between the indigenous culture and the Catholic faith of the Spanish when they first arrived.

The ingredients for this new breed of legend had been there for a very, very long time, though. On one side, we have the Machi. These were the traditional shamans of the Chilean culture, the healers and wise people. Their realm was that of revelations, interpretation of dreams, and serving as the oracle of the community.

On the other side, there was the Kalku. These were the practitioners of black magic, considered to be witches and warlocks by most people. Unlike the Machi, who sat at the center of their society and were documented religious figures, the Kalku were more mythical, spoken of in stories and whispered about at night.

The Kalku are described as Machi gone bad, those who become more interested in selfish gain than serving the community. I know this will be a gross oversimplification, but think of the Machi as the Jedi and the Kalku as the Sith. The light side and the dark. And as Han Solo recently said, "It's true. All of it."

Enter the Spanish conquistadors. They arrived in 1567 and brought countless stories with them of European witches. But the culture in Chiloé has always been very male-driven, and so the idea of the female witch was converted to the male warlock in the public narrative. This melding of religions has actually happened in many countries across the centuries, where the Catholic faith would meet ancient beliefs and, rather than wipe out those ancient beliefs, would blend with them, unintentionally becoming something new.

And that's how the Brujos were born. Maybe. Some scholars make reference to a story from the seventeenth century, of a Spaniard named José de Moraleda who met the Machi and wanted desperately to impress them. He challenged them to a magical duel, and after they brought in one of their best Machi, Moraleda was defeated. As a prize, the Spaniard handed over to them a book of spells that he claimed had been gathered from around the world.

It was with that book of spells, the legend goes, that the Brujos built their cult. Some still refer to it by the original name, the Recta Provincia—the Righteous Province—and according to them, this secret group manipulated the culture on the island for two centuries.

Initiation into the group was complex and drenched with the occult. The first step was to wash away any remnant of Christian baptism, and they did this by bathing in one of the local rivers for fifteen nights in a row. Some were instructed to murder a relative or a close friend. And then when all of that was completed, they had to run around the island naked while invoking the Devil's name.

The Brujos maintained their power over the people of Chiloé through an odd mixture of supernatural rumor and mafia-like control. They would most commonly force local farmers to give them produce or money, but they were also known to bribe local authorities and even created a shadow government that ruled in the places where the Spanish didn't reach. And rather than use violence or traditional weapons to enforce their policies, they used the threat of a curse.

Ultimately, it was this game of blackmail and protection rackets that brought an end to their reign over the people of Chiloé. And so in 1880, over a hundred members of the cult were arrested and interrogated. Many were released when they turned out to be nothing more than Machi looking for a community to belong to, but some were held for trial on the charge of murder.

The darkest revelations from the trials, though, were never believed. The supernatural creatures. The book of spells. The secret, hidden cave where the cult maintained its seat of power. All of this was passed off as folklore and superstition.

However, eyewitness testimony says otherwise.

WARLOCKS GONE WILD

The trials revealed many new details about the Brujos and their beliefs, their practices, and the group's inner workings. Some almost sound like they were pulled right out of a children's book, they're so simple and benign, while others are downright chilling.

For example, one of the men on trial in 1880 revealed that each warlock carried a pet lizard with him. This lizard, according to the man, would be tied to the warlock's forehead, and because it was magical, it gifted him with powers.

These warlocks were even said to communicate and interact with the ghost sailors aboard the *Caleuche*, using seahorses as aquatic carrier pigeons to pass messages back and forth. Seahorses.

Other stories spoke of how the warlocks recruited new spies for their sect. According to the legend, these warlocks would kidnap young women, who would be given a special elixir to drink. Once it was ingested, these girls would vomit until their stomachs and intestines lay on the ground at their feet. Then they would transform into birds and do the bidding of their master.

None of this, though, compares to what the Brujos were said to have kept in their cave. One of the men on trial in 1880, an elderly man named Mateo, claimed that in the 1860s he had been asked to visit the cave to feed the creatures kept there. And although his testimony was rejected by the court as fantasy, some have been left wondering.

The cave, it is said, was difficult to locate, and rightly so. It contained multiple magical items, including the book of spells the group had received from the Spaniard Moraleda, as well as a bowl that was said to show the future to those who looked into it. And because these were objects of power for the warlocks, they needed to be carefully guarded.

The entrance was a door hidden beneath the grass and soil in a rocky canyon near the coast, and with it, a metal key. Mateo told the court that he opened the entrance to the cave, only to find two creatures inside that nearly defied description.

One was called a chivato, a humanoid creature that was briefly described as goatlike and walking on four legs. But Mateo had no trouble describing the other thing in the cave. Because at first glance, it seemed to be nothing more than a bearded man.

This man, though, was deformed. Not mildly or by birth, but intentionally and drastically twisted. It was called the Imbunche, and although the one that Mateo witnessed appeared old, he said that they typically begin as infants.

Now, this next part isn't for the faint of heart. But it's necessary to understand the level of cruelty and barbarism that this cult practiced. According to writer Bruce Chatwin, who visited the island in 1975, the locals still maintain a good amount of folklore around the creation of the Imbunche.

The warlocks would kidnap a male six-month-old child, Chatwin recorded, and then deliver it to the one known as the Deformer, who lived inside the cave. This man's job was to shape and disfigure the infant's body. The head would be twisted daily until, after many months, it faced backward.

Limbs and fingers were disjointed, and even its ears and mouth were distorted by the Deformer. The final characteristic, according to Chatwin, was the right arm. It would be bent backward, and the hand slipped into an incision made on the right shoulder blade. Then the wound would be sewn up, leaving the arm permanently affixed to the child's back.

Why this was done is something that history has forgotten over the years, but the impact is just as powerful today. Left to guard and inhabit the secret cave of the warlocks, the forming of the Imbunche was seen less as an act of torture and more as the creation of an essential part of the cult's society. When one Imbunche died, another was created to take its place.

This is the level of darkness these real-life warlocks were capable of. This is what powered the fear they used to enslave and control the people of the island. And this is what many of them confessed to on the stand that spring in 1880.

And as a result, many of the accused were sentenced to long prison terms. These were men who had killed, cursed their neighbors, and blackmailed businesses for protection money. And yet the courts couldn't make the ruling stick. Just one year later, nearly all of the warlocks were released.

The reason? It was impossible to prove they had belonged to a secret society of black magic, as horrible as the stories sounded. No one, they thought, could be that evil. Could they?

THE POWER OF FEAR

In a world where authority often falls to those with the most wealth, the most weapons, or the most connections, it's unusual to find cases where some other power allows people to rule. But if the story of Chiloé teaches us anything, it's that fear can be just as powerful as any government official. Fear of death. Fear of poverty. Fear of the unknown.

Those who called themselves part of the Brujos in 1880 were card-carrying members of a cult that wielded fear like a weapon. Thankfully, the trial helped put real faces to the shadows that had plagued the people of Chiloé for centuries. Whether or not they received punishment for their crimes was secondary; the warlocks had been exposed, shattering their illusion of fear.

But while many saw the trial as the end to that nightmare, there are some who aren't so sure.

In 2006, the local court in Chiloé issued a restraining order against Manuel Cárdenas and his brother-in-law. Due to a physical altercation they had with a sixty-six-year-old farmer named José Márquez, they were prohibited from coming within ten yards of the old man.

When asked why he attacked the farmer, Cárdenas said that it was because of an illness his father had been suffering through. Pain had become a constant part of the man's life, and it had gone on long enough.

Cárdenas claimed that his father's illness had begun after an encounter with the farmer all the way back in 1992. The pain hadn't stopped since, and after consulting with a local shaman, they were told why.

According to the shaman, the farmer had cursed their father with black magic. Which begs the question: did the trial of 1880 really put a stop to the cult of warlocks? Or did some of them carry on the old traditions, living on to spread and grow their sect into the twentieth century and beyond?

After all, neither the cave nor its occupants were ever found.

The King

SOME FEARS ARE obvious and visible. A dark, cobweb-covered basement. An old axe propped up in the corner of the garage, with something red along its edge—maybe rust, or maybe something else. Many fears, you see, can be documented, even photographed. But others can't.

Some fears are like the wind. The only proof the wind exists is in the way it affects other things—that cool feeling on your skin, the way the leaves on the trees sway back and forth. And just like the wind, there are fears that we can point out only thanks to their effects.

One of the best places to feel that breeze, so to speak, is Hollywood. The stories that entertain us the most seem to tap into the deep, unseen fears that we all struggle with. It's like touching the tip of your tongue to a nine-volt battery; you hate the sensation, but there's something disturbingly attractive about it.

One of the biggest themes to come out of Hollywood over the past few decades, by far, has been one of isolation, loss, and disaster. Films like *I Am Legend* and *Alien* dip into this pool, as do small-screen shows like *The Walking Dead* and *Battlestar Galactica*. We're obsessed with the idea. We fear it, but we also love it, because the questions feel important.

What would happen if humanity were reduced to a tiny population, left on the brink of extinction, and fighting for survival? In what ways would our civilization hold strong, and where would it crack? Could we rediscover order, or would chaos consume us all?

You would think this would be an impossible concept to understand firsthand, that human dignity and ethics would prevent us from testing it out to find the true answers. Then again, real life is rarely ethical, and thanks to the events that took place on a small island in the Pacific just a century ago, we have answers.

Odds are, though, that you won't like them.

ALL FOR GUANO

Roughly one thousand miles due south of Cabo San Lucas, in the Pacific waters off the coast of Mexico and Central America, is an island. When I say "island," your mind probably conjures an image of a large green mountain protruding from the water, with sandy beaches and luxury resorts along the coastline, but that would be wrong.

This island is small. Really small, in fact. It's perhaps two miles long, but from the air it's almost nonexistent. It's more of a coral ring than anything else, with very little vegetation. If you can picture a coffee stain, like a dark ring on a white napkin, that's what I'm talking about. Outside the ring, the waves of the Pacific crash against the shore. Inside, though, is a freshwater lagoon. It's not deep, but the water is drinkable.

The first European to stumble upon it, as far as historians can tell, was a man named John Clipperton. In the first two decades of the 1700s, he operated as a privateer, a pirate for hire, serving the British crown in its efforts to hinder Spanish expansion in Central America and Mexico. Due to the tiny island's proximity to the western coast of Guatemala and Mexico, Clipperton set up base there.

For as tiny as the island is, it offered a surprising amount of space for Clipperton. The highest point is a mere ninety-five feet above the ocean waves, but he found a number of serviceable caves, which he had his men expand for storage and defense. But his time there was short-lived.

Clipperton Island, as it became known, had another feature that attracted attention: guano. The island was actually one of many that were mined to supply a growing need for the chemical elements found in the manure of birds, bats, and seals. This guano would primarily be used to manufacture gunpowder and fertilizer, two products that growing nations lusted after.

Because of this, the island exchanged hands a number of times through the middle of the nineteenth century. For a while Mexico claimed ownership, but in 1856 the American government passed the Guano Islands Act, making it legal for U.S. citizens to claim guano-rich islands no matter where they were located, so long as they were uninhabited and unclaimed by another country.

In the late 1800s, Napoleon sent French troops to annex the island. They found a small group of American guano miners there and forced them out. Mexico wasn't too happy about the French claim, though, and they argued about it for years. While they did, in 1899, a group of industrious British men landed and got to work.

Not only did they start mining, but they built houses and created garden areas. They even planted more palms. These guys were serious about colonizing the island and wanted to do it right. But the island was harsher than they realized, and by 1909 they had given up. All but one of the Englishmen abandoned the island and headed home.

And that's when Mexico got serious. In 1910, President Porfirio Díaz put thirteen soldiers on a ship and transported them to Clipperton, where they would do their part in maintaining Mexican rule over the valuable resources there.

When they arrived, they found the homes and buildings that the British had constructed, empty and waiting for them. There was even a recently built lighthouse, complete with its own keeper. But it wasn't just thirteen men with guns who made the trip.

Most of these men brought wives with them, you see. And there were children, and servants, and all the supplies they would need to settle in and build a life there. Sure, no one had been able to make a go of it so far. Sure, the island was nearly inhospitable. And sure, it was expensive and difficult to transport supplies there. But they were determined. By 1910, nearly a hundred people had begun to call the island their home, and even more would be born there in the years to come.

What none of them could foresee, though, was just how many would die there as well.

GOING NOWHERE

One of those thirteen soldiers was a man named Ramón Arnaud. He was a thirty-three-year-old military officer with a checkered past. Within months of his enlistment years before, he deserted his post. It resulted in him spending over five months in a military prison, and then a series of unappealing assignments. Clipperton Island was, to him, just one more piece of the punishment, whether or not it came with the title of governor.

Children were born in those first few years. Governor Arnaud and his wife, Alicia, welcomed their first child, Ramón junior, in 1910, and two more followed over the next three years. During that time, life was a dull rhythm of island life and the occasional resupply ship. But that was all about to change.

Sometime in 1914, the supply ships from Acapulco stopped coming. Because the regular frequency was every two months, it was probably hard to tell at first if the ship was just late or if plans had changed. I imagine everyone on the island watched the horizon daily for a sign of help. Without that ship, they were essentially stranded. And every day that ticked by was another attack against their dwindling supply of hope.

In late summer of 1914, a ship did show up, but this one was American. It brought supplies, but its real mission was to pick up the last remaining member of the British mining crew who had stayed behind five years earlier. While there, the ship's captain informed Governor Arnaud of the situation back home.

Not only had Mexico erupted into revolution, but the world

was now at war following the assassination of Archduke Franz Ferdinand of Austria. They'd seen nothing like this global conflict before, and the captain had no idea if or when it would stop. Perhaps, he suggested, Arnaud and his community would like to come home, just to be safe?

Arnaud declined, and the community soon watched the Americans vanish over the horizon. By 1915, though, that decision was beginning to feel flawed. The vegetable garden that the British had installed had started to fall apart. The only naturally occurring food on the island was a small supply of coconuts and whatever fish and birds they could hunt. But what those foods lacked was vitamin C, and so by late 1915 many on the island had scurvy.

We tend to treat scurvy lightly, making pirate jokes about it when we're out with friends, but the reality of the disease is more horrible. The symptoms begin with bleeding gums and sore spots and eventually grow into depression, immobility, and open wounds. In the end, someone suffering from scurvy simply bleeds to death, and without vitamin C, those around them can only helplessly watch it all end.

The people died off one or two at a time. The disease seemed to hit adult men especially hard, and as the population dropped, the survivors struggled to bury their dead deep enough to keep them out of the reach of the island's crabs.

By 1916, nearly all of the men were dead, and many of the women and children as well. All told, there were perhaps two dozen survivors. By this point, Arnaud was motivated. His wife, Alicia, was pregnant with their fourth child, and if his family was going to survive, they needed to find help.

It was probably while they were all studying the dark storm clouds on the horizon that they spotted the ship. They tried jumping and waving their arms, but there was no sign that the vessel saw them. It was just too far away, and the approaching storm probably made it too dark for anyone on the ship to see them, anyway. Hope was slipping right past them.

Out of desperation, Arnaud made the decision to gather the last of the men into the only boat on the island and row after the passing ship, hoping to catch its attention. Their lives depended on it.

It was probably their last chance, after all. And so they rowed hard and fast into the rough waters.

Historians aren't sure what happened next. There might have been a struggle in the boat, according to some witnesses. Or the small boat might have started to take on water. What we do know is that the men stood up and seemed to grapple with each other, only to capsize the boat, tossing them all into the sea. And there, within sight of their families, all of the men drowned.

But Alicia Arnaud didn't have time for heartache. The storm that had been on the horizon was upon them within just two hours of the tragedy. The three remaining woman, along with perhaps half a dozen children, all gathered in the basement of the Arnauds' home to take shelter.

And that's when Alicia went into labor.

ALL HAIL THE KING

She named her new son Angel, and he was the last good news they would experience for years.

When the women stepped out of the basement the following morning, the rest of the house was gone. The storm had destroyed everything, it seems. All of the homes, the remnants of the garden, even some of the palm trees were gone.

But something new was there as well. Some*one*, actually. The reclusive lighthouse keeper, Victoriano Álvarez. They knew he'd been there, of course, but he was seen so infrequently that most had forgotten about him. He's described by historians as mentally unstable, and a lack of social skills drove him to hide in the lighthouse, away from the others, for years. How he got supplies, though, I have no clue.

Álvarez was a giant. Tall, powerful, and menacing, he must have been a shocking sight to the surviving women as they pushed their way free from the wreckage of their home. But there he was, and he had a mission.

He wandered the ruined settlement and gathered all of the weapons together. Some reports say that he tossed most of them into the deeper part of the lagoon, while others say he took them all back to the lighthouse. Whatever he did with them, the message was the same: *I am the law now,* he was telling them. *I am your only hope.*

Álvarez set himself up as king over the island, with no other men to challenge him, and only three young women who were doing their best to keep the children alive. But it wasn't a glorious reign; no, Álvarez quickly became a nightmare for everyone there.

The three women were helpless to stop him. For the next three years, Álvarez would rape, abuse, threaten, and beat the women like some sort of primitive clan elder. He would often choose one of them to return to the lighthouse with him, and only send her back to the others when he grew tired of her company.

None of the women angered Álvarez more than twenty-year-old Tirza Randon. Maybe it was her youthful rebelliousness, or her sheer will to live, but Randon constantly made life difficult for the lighthouse keeper. When she was with him, she was quick to voice her hatred of him, and when she was back in the settlement, she was a loud voice of dissent.

They needed to find a way to escape, but without a visiting ship, that seemed hopeless. Álvarez, though, was a monster, and something needed to be done. And he had made a mistake. You see, he thought of his captives as "just women." Yes, he was stronger. Yes, he was armed. And yes, he seemed to be in control. But Alicia and the others weren't "just women."

No, they were survivors. They were human beings fighting for dignity and safety. And they were powerful in their own ways. So when Álvarez walked into their collection of primitive shelters in July 1917 and demanded that Alicia Arnaud be the next to report to his lighthouse, they saw their chance.

Arnaud and Randon walked up to the lighthouse the next morning, with Ramón junior—now seven—following close behind. When they arrived, Álvarez was outside cooking a bird he had managed to capture. It must have been a rare catch, as the women later described how he was smiling. But that smile melted away as he saw Randon approaching.

There was an argument. Álvarez wanted to know why Alicia

had brought the other woman. And while the giant of a man was busy shouting at Arnaud, the other woman slipped silently into the lighthouse. When Randon stepped back out through the doorway, Alicia gave her a tiny nod. Álvarez saw this, and turned to see what was behind him, but it was too late.

Later, all three women were standing in their settlement on top of a small hill that was crisscrossed by the overgrown paths used by the mining companies years before. And it was at that moment that they saw the rowboat. It was a whaler, launched from an American gunship called the *Yorktown*, anchored farther out at sea.

An officer named Lieutenant Kerr landed on the beach, and after speaking with the women, he brought all of the survivors back to the ship with him. There, they were presented to the commander of the gunship, a man named H. P. Perrill, who listened to their story with deep interest. They told him of their ordeal during the past three years, and of the maniacal lighthouse keeper who had held them captive through force and violence.

"Where is he now?" Commander Perrill asked them.

"Dead," Alicia told him, and then added, as if it helped clarify the matter, "from scurvy."

SLAYER OF MONSTERS

Some people view humanity as just one more member of the animal kingdom. And much like a dog left alone in the house for hours, it's in our nature to create chaos and destruction when we're left to our own devices. We need rules and boundaries, these people would say, if we want to have any hope of maintaining order and civilization.

Others, though, disagree. They would say that our tendency toward society and structure is innate, that it's written in our DNA right alongside things like the blueprints for our circulatory system and eye color. We're hardwired to build community, and it's merely the trials of life that push us off course from time to time.

But both can be equally true, I suppose. What if humanity is really more of a creature in the balance? The events that played out on Clipperton a century ago certainly show us both sides of that coin. Some leaned toward order and peace, while others became animals.

Lieutenant Kerr witnessed this firsthand. After delivering the survivors to the *Yorktown*, he and Commander Perrill returned to the island later that day. They wanted to see for themselves who this monster was that had terrorized the women for so long, dead or alive. Both of them had seen scurvy kill men before, so they weren't afraid of what they'd find.

After walking the path from the beach and up the hill to the lighthouse, the men found the door wide open, so they stepped inside. It was eerily quiet inside the dimly lit room, but it didn't take them long to figure out why.

Stretched out on the floor was the largest man either of them had ever seen. Blood had pooled around the body, filling in low spots in the stone floor, but their eyes were drawn away, toward an area of the floor beyond the man's shoulders.

Two objects had been tossed there, a knife and a hammer. Both were small, easy weapons for a malnourished woman to hold and swing. And both were covered in blood.

The two Americans looked at each other across the body of the king of Clipperton Island, but neither of them said a word. They knew what had happened, what had really brought an end to the man on the floor. But neither wanted to remark on it.

With a nod, they turned and left the building. The survivors were safe, and that was all that mattered to them. The island could keep its king.

Alicia Arnaud would tell us that some people truly are monsters deep in their core—Álvarez certainly was one. But she also advocated a very risky balance, a wagering of her soul in the pursuit of freedom.

Because sometimes—even if only in the rarest of rare circumstances—we have to *become* the monster in order to *defeat* it. And then hope that we change back.

The Mountain

IN FEBRUARY 2010, restoration specialists were trying to preserve the hut used by Ernest Shackleton and his team during their Nimrod Expedition a century ago when they found something beneath the floorboards.

Keep in mind, Shackleton is something of a legend. Born in Ireland in 1874, raised in London, and exploring Arctic regions by his twenty-fifth birthday, this man was about as tough as they come. He was a naval officer, a real-life explorer, and a bestselling author, and he even had the honor of being knighted by a king. I can't think of *anyone* more interesting to invite to a party.

So when restoration began on the Nimrod base camp hut in 2010, there was a sense of awe. It was the structure that had once played host to impossible dreams and a spirit that few today are willing to embrace. That little hut was a refuge against a hostile environment. And it was also, apparently, the hiding place for a treasure, buried by Shackleton himself.

It wasn't gold or silver, though. It wasn't a relic or some piece of history. No, beneath those bare floorboards, restorationists found something else: three cases of Scottish whiskey. And this whiskey, trapped in the permafrost for a century, was insanely valuable.

Not just because of its age. And not just because of the opportunity it offered to explore a rare, lost blend of Scotch. This whiskey was valuable, you see, because it offered the chance to taste the liquid that fueled a legend.

We're obsessed with those who venture out into the wild. We resonate with those who risk their lives. And while the successful ones often live on as legends in their own right, it's the ones who fail who often stick with us the longest.

For some people, nothing is more frightening than when the natural world reaches out and crushes our best-laid plans.

Far from Found

When Sir John Franklin set sail from England in 1845, it was his fourth expedition into the Arctic Circle. For years, nations had been looking for the mythical Northwest Passage, a route from the Atlantic to the Pacific that didn't require sailing south to the tip of South America before heading back north.

Franklin and his team were never seen again. In some ways, it shouldn't have surprised anyone. After all, the expedition set sail in two ships, one named the *Terror* and the other named after the Greek god of darkness and chaos, *Erebus*. They were practically begging for tragedy.

It wasn't until a decade later when another explorer, John Rae, learned of the expedition's fate. Trapped in the ice, the crew had made their escape on foot. The cold and lack of food were their undoing, and some believe the party succumbed to cannibalism before the last of them perished. Nevertheless, Franklin and his crew have gone down in history as heroes.

History has long had a love affair with tragedy. Maybe it's the haunting nature of these lost expeditions and journeys gone wrong that seems to elevate them in popular culture. Maybe it's our obsession with anything that has a passing resemblance to an Indiana Jones movie. Or maybe it's just the simple fact that there are so many of them to talk about.

Norwegian explorer Roald Amundsen was the expedition leader for the team that beat Robert Scott to the South Pole in 1911. He and his team returned from their journey as heroes, and while he participated in more adventures, it was the South Pole that earned him his reputation.

Nearly two decades later, in 1928, an expedition to the North Pole crashed on the ice and vanished. Amundsen, fifty-five years old at the time, climbed into a rescue plane and headed north to find them. Apparently you can take the explorer out of the wild, but you can't take the wild out of the explorer. Amundsen was never seen again.

Percy Fawcett was an explorer and archaeologist from England who spent much of his professional life in the jungles of Brazil. He'd performed tasks for the Royal Geographical Society, and served as a member of the British Secret Service for a time. Fawcett even formed a close friendship with popular author H. Rider Haggard, who wrote the equivalent of Indiana Jones novels for late nineteenth-century readers. If you've ever seen or read *The League of Extraordinary Gentlemen*, the character of Allan Quatermain was a Haggard creation.

Maybe it was that friendship that filled Fawcett's head with visions of cities of gold and adventure. In 1925, he managed to raise enough funds to set off for South America with his oldest son, Jack, and one of Jack's close friends. Together, they planned to locate a lost city that Fawcett had named "Z." It was supposed to be the real-life location of the legendary city of El Dorado.

There are a lot of theories about what happened. Some say the explorer and his partners were all killed by natives of the region. Others say that they set up a commune in the jungle and lived out the rest of their lives there. There are even stories that say the end was much less exciting; that Fawcett and the others just walked into the jungle and vanished. Even today, there are those that are still looking for the truth.

In 1804, Alexander Hamilton engaged in a duel with United States vice president Aaron Burr. Hamilton's aim was off, but Burr's wasn't. As a result, Hamilton died from his wounds the following day. Burr lived a long life after the duel but suffered through the mysterious disappearance of his daughter, Theodosia.

In 1812, she boarded a ship that was meant to carry her away from South Carolina—where her husband was governor—to see her father in New York. An incredibly fast schooner known as the *Patriot* left Georgetown harbor in December of that year, and was never seen again.

One of the risks that travelers take upon themselves is that they might never reach their destination. Whether the journey is one of exploration, personal travel, or recreation, there is always the chance for failure. And the farther from civilization, the worse those chances become.

Which is why, when a group of hikers marched off into the Ural Mountains in 1959, the odds were decidedly—and tragically—stacked against them.

INTO THE WILD

If there was ever a textbook example of whiteout conditions, the night of February 2, 1959, would have been it. The team of ten was huddled together inside their tents against the wind and snow and freezing rain. I realize it would be odd to refer to a blizzard as "hell," but just because it lacked flames and heat didn't mean it wasn't a place of suffering.

The trip hadn't started out like that, though. They had intended it to be a pleasant expedition into the mountains. No glorious mission or treasure to seek. This was meant to be a recreational trip. That's not how it ended, though. Then again, life rarely turns out the way we imagined it would, does it?

The team consisted of nine college students from Ural Polytechnical Institute, all of whom were led by their instructor, Igor Dyatlov. Their journey had actually begun on January 27—a week prior—in the northern Russian village of Vizhay, east of the Ural Mountains. They had been transported there by truck, along with their camping equipment and supplies, because the small village was the most northern settlement in the region. Beyond those borders, they would enter into the wild. A literal no-man's-land. This was a region of Russia that had once been called home by the indigenous people known as the Mansi, sometimes called the

Voguls. Centuries ago they ruled the northern lands, even fighting against the Russians until they were finally assimilated in the thirteenth century. Today, most Mansi live in Moscow or other large cities, and there are very few who remain in their northern homelands.

The college students and their instructor were well prepared. Aside from the expected camping supplies that you might expect, they also set up a communication plan. The trip was a there-and-back journey, with the goal of reaching Mt. Otorten within a week, and then returning to Vizhay by February 12. If they failed to check in, Igor had told friends, start to worry.

It was going to be a dangerous expedition, without a doubt. The terrain was hostile, and there was no support network north of the village. Still, the trip began smoothly enough, and the team made good progress. They headed east, and when they reached the foot of the mountains they stopped and set aside a supply of food for their return trip. That was January 31. The next day they started their climb.

The weather in the mountains wasn't helping them out. It was clear early on that the trip was going to take longer than they expected, but that didn't stop them. Instead, they hiked slow and steady into the wind and snow, aiming north for Mt. Otorten. By the end of the day on February 2, though, Igor and the others realized they were more than a mile off course. Somehow, thanks in part to the disorienting blizzard, they had drifted west, and found themselves on the northern slope of the mountain known as Kholat Syakhl.

The smart decision would have been to hike north less than a mile and set up camp in the line of trees below. But they had worked hard to reach such a high altitude, and it would be exhausting to have to climb back up the next day, so the team decided to ride out the storm where they were. Exposed to the wind on the bare mountain, with temperatures as low as -25° Fahrenheit, it was going to be a long, cruel night.

It must have been frustrating for them. On a clear day, they would have been able to see Mt. Otorten from where they were. They knew it, too. They were so close to their goal, and yet it must have felt like they were miles away. Instead of feeling like they had accomplished something, they were left to make the best of their mistake.

They set up their single tent, unpacked, ate a meal, and then settled in for the night. We know all of this because it's documented in their journals. We have the notes about their travel decisions, the weather reports, and the challenges they faced. We even have photos of the team setting up camp right there on the snow-covered side of the mountain.

After that, though, the records of the team led by Igor Dyatlov are silent. We have no more words from the team members. No more reports. And no way to speak to them now about what happened to them all.

All we have left now are their corpses.

BREAKING CAMP

Let me be upfront here: we don't know what happened to the hikers. Well, that's not entirely true. We know they died, but we don't know how their deaths were brought about.

What we *do* know is that the details that were uncovered by a later investigation seem to point toward something odd. Something that doesn't seem to fit with preconceived notions of hiking accidents. In the end, though, all we're left with are assumptions, unprovable theories, and a feeling of dread. Dread, because the obvious explanation isn't something that leaves people with warm, fuzzy feelings.

The night of February 2 had been cold and snowy. But when the search party finally located the hikers' camp on February 26, they found the scene of a disaster, not a storm. The tent was covered in snow—something one might expect—but it was also empty. There was also evidence that it had been torn in half from the outside.

Scattered in the snow around the remains of the tent were items that had belonged to the hikers, including clothing and warm shoes. Which went a long way toward explaining why so many of the footprints that could be seen exiting the area of the tent had been made by bare—or at least shoeless—feet.

The prints all led down the slope of the mountain toward the line of trees that *should* have been the team's campsite for the night, had they made the right decision. The investigators followed along in that direction with hopes of finding the missing hikers. When they reached the trees, though, what they discovered only added to the mystery.

The first two bodies they uncovered were located at the outer edge of the forest. Both were clothed in nothing more than their underwear. They discovered signs of a campfire there, hinting that they had perhaps walked down the mountainside in search of better shelter from the storm, but other clues didn't support this.

Branches in nearby trees had been broken and snapped off as high as sixteen feet above the snow. Either someone had tried to climb them or something else broke them. Some have suggested that something very tall had chased the hikers into the trees, breaking off limbs as it entered—or exited—the woods.

Three more bodies were found buried in the snow on the slope between the torn tent and the broken trees. The five hikers were all said to have died of hypothermia, according to later medical examinations. But what had happened to the rest of the party?

In the end, it would take another two months of searching the pass to find the remaining four. On May 4, 1959—a full three months after the blizzard that ended their journey—they were located in a ravine just 250 feet from the camp. But their discovery introduced far more questions than answers.

These four were better clothed than their friends, but they hadn't died of hypothermia. Although what killed them remains a mystery to this day, the evidence points to something unusual. One of the hikers was said to have been missing her tongue. Some historians have suggested that she had simply bitten it off in a moment of panic, but that wouldn't explain why her eyes were missing as well.

Many others had suffered major skull trauma, and their chests had been crushed. The medical examiner who studied the bodies said that the level of force required to create such injuries was on the same level as that found in a high-speed automobile accident. Some experts have suggested an avalanche, or perhaps a deadly fall, but there was no evidence of either at the site of the bodies.

That same medical examiner also ruled out the theory of an attack from nearby Mansi people. According to him, the injuries could not have been caused by other humans, because the force of the blows had simply been too strong. In other words, the injuries that these hikers suffered were unexplainable, nonhuman, and mysterious.

These are, of course, all the ingredients a story needs to truly become legendary. Today the region is referred to as Dyatlov Pass. And it's the *unknown* element of the tragedy there that has pushed the events deep into the mind of popular culture. This story has a way of leaving many of us feeling haunted. Haunted, because it could very well happen to us.

We can plan for things we understand. We can find safety in them. The unknown, though, can leave us as vulnerable as hikers in a blizzard, exposed and unprepared.

PLACES AND NAMES

Our obsession with lost parties and expeditions, with people who wander off and disappear, is as strong today as it's ever been. Movies, novels, television shows, and comics have all spent time and effort to recapture the mystery and thrill of the dangerous unknown. Our world seems to be full of it.

Loose ends have a way of making people uneasy. We want answers because answers make us feel safe, but we also want the thrill of a good mystery. We hate not knowing, and yet we also love the idea of the unknown. Ironic, I know, but true.

Decades later, we still have far more questions than answers. We don't know what frightened the hikers enough to cause some of them to flee undressed from their tent in a subzero blizzard. We don't know what caused the severe trauma to their heads and chests. What we don't know about their demise vastly outstrips what we do know, and most people don't like that.

Maybe something deeper was going on, though. There are those who believe the Russian government knows the truth. You see, after the investigation was completed in May 1959, all of the related documents were packaged up and shipped to a classified archive. When they were finally released four decades later, many of those reports were incomplete, with pages or paragraphs missing.

One last thought: as I mentioned before, the hikers were deep in Mansi territory when the tragedy happened. The lazy explanation early on was to blame the indigenous people of the area for the deaths of the hikers. It's been a common crutch for many lost expeditions: civilized people wander too far into unexplored, untamed wilderness, and they are killed by native people who feel threatened by the newcomers.

There was, of course, no evidence of an attack. No clues pointed toward a group of outsiders. No footprints were found that didn't belong to the hikers. And none of the injuries could be explained away with a theory like that.

But in the end, the answers might very well be found among the Mansi after all. Interestingly, the Mansi name for Mt. Otorten—the mountain they had been hiking toward but never reached—is translated as "don't go there."

Were the Mansi hiding a warning in plain sight all along? Did they know of some reason why travel to that mountain might not be the safest idea? It's hard to say for sure.

And what about Kholat Syakhl, where the hikers camped, and died, that final night? That's a Mansi name as well, given to the mountain many centuries—perhaps even millennia—ago.

It literally means "mountain of the dead."

Within the Walls

WHEN DUKE WILLIAM II of Normandy crossed the English Channel in late September 1066, he brought something with him. It was a tool that he planned to use in his quest to take the throne from Harold Godwinson, a man William saw as a thief, a liar, and the pretender to a throne that was meant for him alone.

This thing that William brought to England was something that we all take for granted today: the castle. Yes, it's an invention that was already ancient by the time William landed on the shores of Sussex, but he brought a new style and approach to an old art. Before he did anything in England—before the battles and long marches across the countryside—he ordered his soldiers to build a castle.

He built it right there in Pevensey, near Hastings, where he would later defeat Harold in battle. His builders simply found a tall hill, built a wooden tower on top of it, and then surrounded the tower with a tall fence. No, it wouldn't stand the test of time, but that wasn't the goal. He simply needed a central point from which to make raids, to be a symbol of the Norman presence, and to put a figurative stake in the ground.

After the conquest, William's nobility replaced those wooden towers with stone. And stone, as you know, can last a very long time. In fact, some of those original castles, now a thousand years old, are still standing today. But those structures, and the ones that followed them, were built to serve a greater purpose.

Each was a physical representation of the king's power. They were majestic and grand and impenetrable. Yes, they were tools of horrible oppression, but they were also the armor plating that protected the new and fragile Norman rule of England.

But every tool can be misused. And within those stone walls, all of that power and oppression was brought to bear on the innocent and guilty alike. Blood was spilled, lives were ended, and mysteries were born. And in some castles, the echoes of those horrible deeds are still with us today.

LASTING IMPRESSION

The English word *castle* comes to us from the Latin word *castrum*. It simply means "a fortified place." The first European castles were built in the ninth and tenth centuries, but these were fairly unsophisticated compared to what William brought with him when he invaded England. His castles did more than just provide enormous walls to hide behind.

When the first London fortress was constructed in 1066, it was made of wood, like all his other early constructions, and it followed that new design. Roughly a decade later, the timber was replaced with a more permanent stone structure. When it was completed, the central building that we now call the White Tower became the center of the English universe.

Back then, it was the royal residence, a symbol of the king's power, and a military stronghold. Since then, it's been home to the Royal Mint and a zoo for exotic animals; it was even a prison until 1952. That's a whole lot of purpose to cram into just twelve square acres. Today, the castle is home to the Crown Jewels, a fantastic museum, and extensive tours that attract millions of people each year.

If the Tower is known for one thing over all the others, it's the imprisonment of those who became caught up in the sharp gears of the political machine. Sir Walter Raleigh, Lady Jane Grey, Guy

Fawkes, Anne Boleyn, and even Queen Elizabeth I were all held there for a time. Some walked out with their lives intact; others, though, didn't fare so well.

When Edward IV died in 1483, his brother Richard became regent until Edward's boys, nine and twelve at the time, were old enough to take over. Instead, Richard had both of them declared illegitimate, and a short time later they vanished from palace life. It wasn't until 1674—almost two centuries later—that a wooden chest was found buried in the ground outside the White Tower. Inside, workmen found a collection of bones that made up two small human skeletons, one slightly larger than the other.

The most common residents of the Tower of London, by far, are the yeoman warders, the ceremonial guardians of the castle. Today they function primarily as tour guides, and each warder lives with their family in an apartment within the walls. It was in one of those apartments, during World War II, that a warder and his wife were pulled from sleep by the sounds of their daughter screaming for help.

The young girl was crying and trembling when they found her. When they asked her what was wrong, she told her parents that she had seen something in her bedroom that had frightened her. It was so frightening that she refused to go back. When they pressed her, she told them that she'd woken up to discover that there were strange children in her room. Two boys, in fact. They were just sitting quietly on the edge of her bed. Each was dressed in old clothing.

Far to the north, Scotland has its own fair share of troubled fortresses. And sitting at the center of them all is Edinburgh Castle. But where the Tower of London was constructed almost exclusively within a small two-century window, Edinburgh Castle is more of a living, breathing creature. While St. Margaret's Chapel is the only remaining part of the original twelfth-century structure, other parts have been added throughout the centuries, giving it all sort of a sprawling, organic quality. But of course, where there's life, there's also death.

Like most castles, Edinburgh served as a prison for criminals and political enemies of the crown. In one tale, a prisoner managed to escape his cell and stow away inside a wheelbarrow full of manure, with the hope of being carted out through the gate. Instead, the entire load was dumped off the West Port side, where he plummeted to his death below. Visitors to the ledge have often described the overwhelming scent of dung and the odd sensation of being pushed by unseen hands.

The tunnels and dungeons of the castle's lower level have played host to countless stories of unexplainable experiences. Heavy breathing, sounds of knocking or hammering, and pained-sounding moans have all been heard in the dark, subterranean portions of the building. And these events, some say, are connected to the tale of Lady Janet Douglas.

In 1528, Lady Douglas was accused of witchcraft and conspiracy by King James V. First her servants and family were captured and imprisoned. Then they were tortured in order to produce forced confessions against her. She herself was rumored to be kept isolated in the dark for so long that she actually went blind. And all the while, carpenters in leather aprons wandered the lanes above as they built the wooden platform upon which she would soon be burned alive.

In 2001, a British psychologist named Dr. Richard Wiseman wanted to get to the bottom of stories like these. He managed to find and screen over two hundred participants for an unorthodox experiment. The screenings were designed to weed out anyone who might have knowledge of the stories told about Edinburgh Castle and its haunted past. Once Dr. Wiseman and his team had verified all of the volunteers, they set to work.

Wiseman and his assistants proceeded to take small groups of volunteers on tours through various parts of the castle. Admittedly, there were elements of these experiments that weren't the most ethical. In fact, some volunteers were actually shut up alone inside certain rooms. Dr. Wiseman said it was their chance to make personal observations without anyone around. But no matter how safe it might have been, I can't see how locking a person in a castle dungeon could be anything other than traumatic.

One woman reported that her time alone inside one of the castle vaults was filled with odd experiences. She reported heavy breathing that seemed to move closer and closer to her the longer she was in the room. She also said she saw flashes of light in the darkness. It goes without saying that she exited the vault completely and utterly terrified.

Others heard voices and caught glimpses of shadowy figures. One entire group of volunteers unanimously claimed to see the ghostly figure of a man slowly move across the end of a tunnel. They said he was dressed in old-fashioned clothing and wore something unusual over his torso.

It was a leather carpenter's apron.

PRYING EYES

There's a common idea about castles: that all those thick stone walls and floors make great hiding places for horrible secrets. After all, few castles were as orderly and perfectly structured as most modern homes. Whether it's a hidden dungeon or the bricked-up body of a victim, the strong walls of a castle can act like a prison, holding in centuries of suffering, tragedy, and death.

If the stories are to be believed, there's one castle in particular that holds a secret that's darker than most. Darker, because rather than playing host to some ghostly vision or spiritual inhabitant, this one is said to have been the home of a flesh-and-blood monster. It has been the subject of speculation for nearly two centuries and has intrigued the minds of locals and luminaries alike. And the name of the castle? Glamis.

Glamis Castle was built in the village of the same name on the supposed site of the murder of King Malcolm II in the eleventh century. By the late 1300s, the castle had been granted to the Lyon family. Sir John Lyon, you see, was married to the king's daughter, which apparently came with perks. And if Monty Python has taught us anything, those perks probably also involved huge . . . tracts of land.

Today, the castle is featured on the back of the Scottish ten-pound note, and it's famous for being the setting of Shakespeare's *Macbeth*, although the historical Macbeth predates the castle by centuries. But it is also the setting of a legendary tale about a fifteenth-century earl who loved to play cards.

According to the story, when the earl's houseguests refused to join him for an illicit game on the Sabbath, he erupted in anger. He made a threat about being willing to play with the Devil himself, as long as he got to play cards. And that's when a stranger showed up at the castle door. This stranger—who turned out to be the Devil, of course—proceeded to play cards with the earl, beat him, and then take his soul. Historians are unsure which fifteenth-century earl was the focus of this story. And of course, there's no documentable evidence of anyone having their soul taken away in a card game, so take it all with a grain of salt.

But I mentioned dark secrets, didn't I? Sorry . . . let's get back to that. You see, beginning sometime in the 1840s, rumors began to spread about a family secret. The Lyon family, they said, was hiding something horrible. So horrible that only the earl himself knew what it was. But there were whispers. Details that hinted at what the secret might be.

We can probably thank Sir Walter Scott—the famous novelist, poet, and playwright—for making the secret public. In 1830, he published an account of a visit he made to Glamis back in 1790, and in it he made note of a secret room. He knew little else, of course, but he couldn't help mentioning the words "secret room." And the public ate it up.

Whatever and wherever this room is, the access to it either was hidden very carefully or had just been removed entirely. Think *Harry Potter and the Chamber of Secrets*, I suppose, just without the giant snake. A room that only a select few ever get to see, or even know about, and the knowledge of which is passed down from one generation to the next.

Now, this isn't an impossibility. Some of the walls of the castle are up to sixteen feet thick, which makes it easy to see how a small room could be tucked away in there. There are even records of small chambers being built within the walls. One such room is recorded near the Charter Room, located at the base of the main castle tower. In a lot of ways, one of the main reasons for a castle's construction was privacy and safety, so hidden rooms—even if they weren't an early trend—were certainly a common occurrence.

As to what lay hidden inside the secret chamber of Glamis, though, no one except the earl himself knew any of the details. But of course, that didn't stop others from trying to find it, sometimes intentionally and sometimes by accident.

Back in 1850 the earl and his wife played host to a number of guests for a large celebration. One morning the men went off hunting and left their wives and daughters behind. Bored, the earl's wife suggested a game: let's find the secret room.

Hundreds of white rags were brought out, and everyone was tasked with the job of tying one rag in each window they could find. Up and down the castle, these women ran about finding windows and placing rags in them. And then, when they were sure they'd finished the job, they headed outside.

As a group, they walked around the perimeter of the castle, looking at every window, and noting the rags that hung in them. Finally, as the story goes, the women found it: a window on the tower could clearly be seen without a white rag hanging from it. The party all ran back inside to check their work. Surely someone had missed a window. But try as they might, after examining the tower a second time, they couldn't find the mistake.

The window was in a room they couldn't reach.

Unfit for the Title

Naturally, people wanted to know what was hidden away in the castle. Sir Walter Scott had made the rumor popular, and stories like that of the white rag mystery only fanned the flames. Plus it didn't help that the earls—from the eleventh earl all the way down to the fifteenth—were famously elusive about it all.

In 1903, Claude Bowes-Lyon, who was the thirteenth earl, said this about the secret: "If you could even guess the nature of this castle's secret, you would get down on your knees and thank God it was not yours."

Five years later, an article about the secret appeared in a historical journal called *Notes and Queries*. The author claimed to know more, revealed to him in the 1840s. According to him, the secret room held, and I quote, "a monster, who is the rightful heir to the title and property, but who is so unpresentable that it is necessary to keep him out of sight and out of possession."

Just what sort of monster are we talking about here? Well, that's the question, isn't it? A couple of rough descriptions of the monster of Glamis have survived through the years. One, from the nineteenth century, claimed the monster resembled a human toad. It was said to leave the secret room at night and wander the battlements, an area still referred to today as the "Mad Earl's Walk."

Another description gives us more detail. In the 1960s, British writer James Wentworth Day was staying at the castle as a guest of the sixteenth earl when he was told the story as it had been passed down to the earl. What he told Wentworth Day is the most detailed description we have on record.

The story confirmed earlier rumors. "A monster was born into the family," the earl told him. "He was the heir, and a creature to behold. It was impossible to allow this deformed caricature of humanity to be seen—even by their friends."

The earl went on to describe the deformity that this rumored heir suffered from. "His chest was an enormous barrel," he told the writer, "and hairy as a doormat. His head ran straight into his shoulders, and his arms and legs were toylike. However warped and twisted his body, though, the child had to be reared to manhood."

A physically deformed heir to the title, hidden away to save face—if this was really true, it at least made sense as to why each successive earl was entrusted with keeping it all a secret. Their eligibility for the title and castle were at stake, as was—in their minds at least—the honor of their family name. It also makes you question who the *real* monster of Glamis was: the deformed child, or the father who was so ashamed of him that he locked him away from the world.

So, as you can imagine, anyone who got too close to this secret ended up in some form of trouble. When the twelfth earl found out his wife and her friends had searched the castle for signs of the

hidden room, it's said that he divorced her and sent her away. She never spoke of her experience again, and died many years later in Italy. And she wasn't the last.

Fifteen years later, in 1865, a workman was searching for something in the castle when he stumbled upon a door he'd never seen before. Maybe he was new to the castle, or maybe he'd just never fully explored it. Whatever the reason, here he was, staring at a mysterious door. So he did what any of us would have done in his place: he pushed it open.

Behind it stretched a long, dark passageway. He summoned up some courage and stepped through, taking a few steps down the corridor. There was a shape at the end of the hall that he wanted to get a closer look at. Before he could figure out what it was, though, the shape moved, and the workman—frightened for his life—bolted back down the passageway and out into the open. And then he reported everything to his boss.

The very next day, the workman was told in very strong language that he should move to Australia, of all places. He was handed paperwork with the details of his emigration, all paid for and arranged by the earl himself. He was never seen again in the castle.

Another story is told of a young doctor who visited the castle for professional reasons. His visit required spending multiple nights, so at the end of the first day he was led to the Blue Room and left to himself. He settled in, unpacked, and was getting ready to turn in for the night when he spotted a portion of the carpet that looked . . . well . . . *odd*. So he lifted it up off the floor and peeked beneath it.

What he found, according to the story, was the wooden square of a trapdoor set into the stone floor. Curious—and clearly a lot braver than I could ever claim to be—the doctor forced the trapdoor open and then lowered himself down through the opening. Below, he found a passageway. After following it for a few paces, it came to an end at a blank cement wall.

The doctor claimed that this wall looked solid, but was in fact still wet, as if the cement hadn't dried fully before he discovered it. He even claimed to have pressed his finger into the surface and watched it give way. If the cement was there to cover an opening, then he couldn't help but wonder: what was behind it?

He climbed back up into his room and went to bed with a good many questions on his mind. When he awoke in the morning, though, he found an envelope on the floor near the entrance. Someone had slipped it under his door during the night. So he picked it up and tore it open.

Inside he found two things: payment for his services, and a note announcing that a carriage was ready to take him to the train station. He was required to leave *immediately*.

A Dark Burden

There's irony in the idea of a haunted castle. These buildings, by nature and design, are meant to be places of safety and refuge. A literal fortified home, if even on a grand scale. They were built to last centuries, and to keep the people inside them safe from any outside threat imaginable.

But instead, many of these stone fortresses have become home to more than just nobility. They've collected tragedy, intrigue, oppression, even murder. And as a result, the undeniable echoes of dark history walk their halls to this very day. Now, rather than worrying about outsiders breaking in, there's a new, more frightening threat.

A threat within the walls.

Surely, though, these stories can't be true. Yes, it's widely accepted that Edward IV's sons were imprisoned and killed, and quite possibly by their very own uncle. The discovery of those skeletons seems to support that legend. But without similar proof, most other stories will never be anything more than speculation and whispers. Evidence is always required to give truth a voice.

All that said, some historians think they have the answer to the Glamis mystery, and they trace it back to the eleventh earl, Thomas Lyon-Bowes. You see, in 1821, his son and daughter-in-law recorded the birth of their first son, also named Thomas. But the records show that little Thomas died the same day as his birth.

The young couple went on to have another son the following year. They named him, like his older brother, Thomas. Now, maybe it was a desire to carry on that family name. Maybe it was a way of honoring their loss. I don't think we'll ever know. But from that day on, according to some, there were *two* boys named Thomas in the castle, not one. One lived in the light, and the other was a captive, hidden away in the shadows.

Sixty years later, on April 1, 1882, a number of British newspapers ran a sensational story. The claim was that the Glamis secret had finally been solved, that a person kept in a secret room had passed away. This person, according to the article, had been old, and the body had been carried out for burial. Sadly, nothing more was added to the description.

It's interesting to note that all of the stories—the 1850 exploration with white rags, the workman, the doctor, all of it—all took place between 1821 and 1882. Outside those dates, there are simply no stories of the monster of Glamis. That, in itself, is more than compelling.

One last tale. I don't have a precise date on it, but it was published in the 1880 edition of *All the Year Round*, so at the very least, we know it took place prior to that. The story goes that a woman known throughout London society as a celebrated artist had once visited the castle for the very first time. She was given a luxurious room to stay in overnight, and found it to be very modern and comfortable for such an ancient place.

The morning after her first night of sleep, she came down for breakfast and joined her hosts at the table. The earl's wife politely asked how she'd slept.

"Very well, thanks," she answered. "Up until four o'clock in the morning, that is. Your Scottish carpenters seem to come to work very early. I suppose they put up their scaffolding quickly, though, for they are quiet now."

The hosts fell completely silent. After a moment, the earl reminded her of the bonds of friendship, and asked her to never speak of that event again. According to him, there were no carpenters working in the castle.

And there hadn't been for *months*.

The Tainted Well

WHEN YOU SEE the body, the first thing that strikes you is just how much detail you can see. The hair standing up on an arm. The dirty fingernails. The pull of the skin over the knuckles. It has a way of making the body seem permanent and real.

And it *is* real, don't get me wrong. It's just that most bodies don't look this good after death, even when they're relatively fresh. Which is what makes this particular body all the more amazing. Yes, he was a man from County Laois in Ireland, and yes, there's no doubt he was dead. It's just . . . well, he looks really good for his age.

The Cashel Man, as they call him, is roughly four thousand years old. He's older than the Egyptian pharaoh Tutankhamen by six centuries, and yet here he is, making eye contact and showing off the pores of his skin. All thanks to the preserving power of an Irish peat bog.

These "bog bodies," as they're called, tend to be easy books to read, telling a clear story to archaeologists. Age, social status, even their occupation. But the most important detail is how they died, and nearly all Irish bog bodies share one common cause of death: human sacrifice.

Some were run through with a sword. Others were clubbed over the head. Some were even strangled with a length of rope. All of it, though, was to send a message to the gods. Life was precious, so to willingly give up one of their own was a powerful way of making a point. It was a primitive email to their deities, typed in all caps, bold, and underlined.

Ireland is a beautiful country with a dark past. Long before the Troubles of the last century—before the country was divided, even before British rule itself—Ireland was already a land full of dark tales and frightening lore.

And like the Cashel Man, many of those stories have refused to stay buried.

HILLS AND HALLS

Ireland is a country that lives up to its reputation. The Emerald Isle is just as overwhelmingly green and lush as you might expect. In the countryside, rolling hills seem to go on for as far as the eye can see. In places like Dublin, ancient buildings play host to laughter and song.

But there's a deep history that swirls around those green hills and dark halls, like a cold wind. And while many of them have drifted beyond the boundaries of Ireland to influence global folklore, those are just a few samples from a much deeper—and much darker—well.

Of course, we all know of the *banshee*, the female spirit that is said to enter our world through one of the many ancient stone mounds, or *sîdhe*, that dot the Irish landscape. They come to announce impending death, and the legends say that if you can hear her cries and wailing, you or someone you love is not long for this world.

We've covered pooka and leprechauns before, but Irish folklore has a plethora of other little creatures skittering about. The *grogoch* is described as a small old man, covered in thick hair that's matted and tangled with sticks and leaves. Most legends say that the *grogoch* is half fairy and half human, but unlike the tales of the pooka, these are friendly creatures that help humans with daily life.

Then, of course, there's the human-stealing fairy known as the changeling, yet another of Ireland's popular folklore exports. But they aren't the only fairy creature to be afraid of. Irish legends speak of the *dearg-dur*, the "red bloodsucker," which may have had a bit of influence on Bram Stoker, who was born and raised in Ireland.

The *dearg-dur* is described as a pale young woman who lures men into a graveyard, where she then drains them of their blood. To stop her, folklore says that all you really need to do is find her grave and pile stones on top of it. That's an episode of *Supernatural* right there, just waiting to be written. Throw in some pie and it's perfect.

But Ireland is more than just spooky mythology, however entertaining it might be. For every wailing woman and tiny old man cobbling shoes in the night, there seem to be two or three local spots with their own unique stories.

One such tale comes to us from the coastline north of Belfast, in the small village of Ballygally. It was there in 1625 that a castle was constructed by a man named James Shaw. They say the castle was immaculate, that it was beautiful and well-designed, and that Shaw obsessed over every detail of it.

Naturally, he wanted to pass his beloved home down to his heir someday. But when his wife, Isobel, finally gave birth to their first child, Shaw was enraged to discover it was a daughter, not a son. Of course, this is the sort of frustration you're guaranteed to experience when you base your entire system of inheritance and power on the biological roll of the dice, but I doubt anyone could have convinced Shaw of the folly of it all.

His response, though, was brutal. He locked Isobel away in one of the towers and had the infant girl removed from the castle entirely. Shortly after, his wife fell to her death from the window of the tower. Some say it was suicide, driven by her grief over the loss of her daughter. Others say it was an accident, that her desire to see her baby again drove her to climb out and try to escape.

Ever since, people outside the castle claim to have seen a pale woman in the window of the tower. Today the castle is a hotel, but the tower prison cell, now known as the Ghost Room, is off-limits to guests. Still, those who've managed to spend time in it claim to have felt a dark presence. Laughter has been heard in the castle hallways, and some have even seen the ghostly figure of a woman disappearing around corners.

For another legend full of mystery and death, we need to travel to County Clare, home to the ancient McMahon Castle. It's nothing more than an abandoned shell today, absent of life and the comforts of home. But according to the legend, there *is* something there, hidden inside the castle's walls: a secret chamber.

No one is sure what the chamber was used for, but the story tells of how a great evil was locked inside and hidden away from the rest of the world. Locked away, that is, until the 1920s, when a local priest was brought in to cleanse the space. They say that the exorcist opened the room and stepped inside, but never walked back out again.

The following morning, someone found the priest's dead body lying just outside the chamber door. Most assumed the man had died of a heart attack, which wouldn't be entirely unusual. What *was* unusual, though, was the expression on the dead man's face: complete and utter horror, as if he had been frightened to death.

The list could go on and on, of buildings and bridges and public spaces that are filled with ominous echoes of another time. But there's one place in Ireland that seems to hold more darkness, more bloodshed, and more treachery than all the others combined. From its ancient roots in bloody conflict to Victorian tales of spiritualism, there isn't much that hasn't taken place within its walls.

If you're looking for frightening tales, dark history, and unsolved mysteries, there's no better place in Ireland than Leap Castle.

AN INSIDE JOB

The earliest mention we have on record in Ireland of the O'Carroll clan is a soldier named Cearbhall who fought alongside King Brian Boru at the Battle of Clontarf in 1014. And I want to point out right away that the word *cearbh* literally means "to hack." It's both appropriate, given the man's occupation, and more than a little bit of foreshadowing.

The O'Carrolls claimed descent from an ancient Irish clan that dated back at least a thousand years. By the sixteenth century, though, the O'Carrolls of County Offaly represented the last powerful fragment of that older clan. But it was sometime before then that the O'Carrolls took control of a castle in their territory, once held by a secondary clan, the O'Bannons. This castle was called Leap.

Dating the original structure has proven a bit challenging to historians, but there are a couple of things that are known for certain. First, there are signs of significant settlement on the site of the castle dating back at least twenty-five hundred years. Second, most scholars agree that the main keep was built around the year 1250. Which means that it was already well known and very old by the time the O'Carrolls moved in near the end of the 1400s.

Leap Castle certainly had a reputation, too. Originally built as a simple tower house—essentially a tall, solid rectangle of stone and mortar—its purpose was to protect anyone inside. Over the centuries, more wings and extensions were added on, but that protective nature never really went away. For a very long time, Leap was considered impenetrable.

From outside, at least. You see, the O'Carroll clan wasn't known for getting along with others—with neighboring clans, or even among themselves. Family discord like that has a way of creeping inside the walls, like a cold December wind. And if their story hasn't piqued your interest yet, don't worry—winter is coming.

The first O'Carroll to rule in Leap Castle was John O'Carroll, but he died of the plague around 1490, passing the leadership on to his son, Mulrooney. And this new clan leader filled his father's shoes beyond anyone's expectations. Through the years, he became known for his bravery in battle and his honor as a leader. He even earned the nickname the Great Mulrooney . . . at least among his clan.

When he passed away in 1532 after over four decades in control, he left Leap Castle in the hands of at least three sons. Teige was known as a hothead, always quick to move toward violence. Fearganainm seems to have been a bit calmer. Thaddeus had trained as a priest and served the family in the chapel at the top of the castle.

Following the death of their father, the three brothers fell into months of arguing over who should lead the clan and control the castle. The tensions were high, and with Teige that was never a good thing. And it was a stewing pot of frustration and entitlement that was about to boil over.

The legend says that Thaddeus—the family priest and one of the contenders for the leadership of the clan—had waited to start Mass until his brother Teige could arrive, but eventually gave up and began without him. Sometime later Teige walked through the door and, despite being late, was shocked to see that the service had already begun.

In a fit of rage, it's said, Teige drew his sword and rushed at Thaddeus, screaming about how insulting it was to be left out. Of course, Thaddeus was in the right, and would have explained that to his brother . . . if Teige hadn't run the sword straight through him instead.

The priest screamed as Teige pulled the blade free and blood began to spill out on the floor of the chapel. Mortally wounded, Thaddeus staggered backward, swaying in front of the others who had come for Mass. And then he toppled over the altar, facedown, and stopped breathing.

Because people are very good at giving incredibly obvious names to places, you might not be surprised to hear that, ever since, the site of this gruesome murder has been known as the Bloody Chapel. Creative, I know. But humor aside, there are those who believe that something dark took place that day.

Brother killing brother, putting ambition and petty disagreement ahead of loyalty and family . . . those things have a way of standing out as powerful. They're atypical in the grand scheme of things. On top of that, though, a priest was killed right inside his chapel, and in the middle of a religious service, no less.

It wasn't long after the murder of Thaddeus that Teige himself was killed by a nephew. In the end, the only remaining brother,

Fearganainm, took over leadership of the clan and castle, but even he wasn't immune to the bloodshed.

Legend says that during his reign, the O'Carrolls hired another clan, the MacMahons, to help them defeat a common enemy. The plan worked, and the O'Carrolls achieved victory in the battle. To celebrate, the MacMahons were invited to Leap Castle for a grand meal . . . with a hidden purpose. Some say they were given poisoned wine, while others say they were murdered in their sleep. Either way, the MacMahons never left Leap Castle alive.

Now, I'll admit, this is a lot of death for one family over the course of just a single century. Some would say it's so atypical that, given enough time, this sort of history could leave a mark. It's this, then—this dark cocktail of violence, betrayal, and blasphemy—that many think was enough to taint the well, so to speak. It tore a hole in the very fabric of reality.

Something the rest of the story only seems to confirm.

A TAINTED WELL

The bloodshed inside Leap Castle went on for generations, until 1659, when the fortress passed into the hands of a new family through marriage between Finola, the daughter of the ruling O'Carroll, and an Englishman named Captain Darby.

Over the years, Leap Castle was improved and extended. Gothic architectural elements were added, and the gardens were expanded. With every change it became less an Irish tower house and more an English manor house. It was being tamed, at least from the outside.

In 1881, the castle passed to Jonathan Darby, and after his marriage to Mildred Dill in 1889, the couple settled into their new life there. Perhaps inspired by the dark atmosphere of the castle, Mildred soon began to write novels in the popular gothic genre, that beautiful blend of horror and romance, terror and literature that attracted the likes of Mary Shelley, Ann Radcliffe, and Edgar Allan Poe.

She published under the pen name Andrew Merry, and her

novel *Paddy-risky* was well received. But it was more than the architecture of Leap Castle that inspired her fiction. The halls there, at least according to her, were full of something darker and more evil.

At first there were noises, as if furniture were being moved in distant parts of the house. But noises quickly evolved into something more sinister. One October night, Mildred was awakened after midnight by the sensation that someone was in the room with her. After looking toward the foot of the bed, she was horrified to see the shape of a person in the darkness. This figure was dressed all in red and had raised a hand toward her.

"What is it?" she said aloud, thinking a servant had come in to wake her, and then she reached for the bedside table to find a match. She struck it, lit a candle, and then lifted it to illuminate the darkness. When she turned toward the foot of the bed, though, she caught her breath. The room was empty.

Now, this was the sort of experience that would probably convince most of us to back off and avoid the castle's dark history, but not Mildred. She was obsessed. Instead of turning away, she rushed headlong into the world of the occult and paranormal. She held séances and occult gatherings, maybe just to deepen her reputation as a gothic novelist, or perhaps to quench a personal thirst.

The consequences, though, were darker than she could have imagined. Something was there in the castle with them, and her experiments only seemed to attract its attention. Then, one night, it made itself known.

According to Mildred, she'd been up late writing in her room when she heard something in the hallway bump against the door. She opened it to find the hallway filled with a putrid, rotting odor, but otherwise empty. So she closed it again.

Moments later, the bumping and scratching sounds returned, only this time she could also hear sniffing at the foot of the door. Expecting a burglar, Mildred picked up a loaded pistol and quickly pulled the door open once again, and then froze, the hair on the back of her neck standing on end. There was something squatting in the doorway. Something unnatural and gruesome.

"The Thing," she later wrote, "was about the size of a sheep, thin, gaunt, and shadowy in parts. Its face was human, or to be more accurate, *in*human, in its vileness, with large holes of blackness for eyes, loose slobbery lips, and a thick saliva-dripping jaw."

According to Mildred, the Thing stood silently in the doorway, locking eyes with her for what seemed like an eternity. And then, with a jump, it moved inside her room. She raised the pistol and fired, nearly point-blank, but still somehow managed to miss. She fired again, this time even closer to the Thing, and still the bullet exploded against a piece of furniture behind it.

Whatever the creature was, whether immaterial spirit or some demonic animal, the shots didn't seem to have any effect on it. Frightened out of her mind, she brought the pistol up for a third shot and, she claims, pressed the gun right against the Thing's chest, just as it brought its arms up to reach for her.

She fired, and then quickly pulled back from its grasp, tripping over something on the floor behind her. And then, she claims, everything went black.

Later, Mildred reported all of this in the most unusual manner. She wrote it up and had it published in a journal called *The Occult Review* in December 1908. But like her novels, she signed the name Andrew Merry to this new tale. The following month, the journal published letters from others that seemed to verify and support her stories, but whenever a novelist is involved, it's impossible to be 100 percent certain everything is being reported with undecorated accuracy.

Still, it's not difficult to believe, is it? This castle, designed for warfare and built around generations of bloodshed, was home to more than the people inside. Evil events have a way of filling a building like explosions; while the initial shock might eventually fade away, the echoes can still be heard ringing through the halls long after it's over.

Whether those echoes took the form of red ghosts and rotting elemental creatures, or just an overwhelming atmosphere of dread, we can't deny the power—and the *darkness*—of the explosion itself.

In the end, it seems, the only thing more frightening than our deepest nightmares might just be our own violent humanity.

Ireland certainly has a lush and fertile landscape when it comes to folklore. The stories that are still told around fires and in crowded pubs cover the spectrum, from the deeply mythological to the downright terrifying. And I wouldn't expect anything less from such a textured, poetic culture.

But that line between fact and fiction has a way of getting blurry when you add in our violent human nature. The events we hear about, or the things we ourselves do to others . . . those things have a way of giving birth to tales far more frightening than anything we could invent.

Reality, though, often fails to have the tidy ending we've come to expect from books and film. Leap Castle isn't the same today as it once was. In fact, it's literally a shell of its former self.

In early 1922, sensing a growing political tension in the country, the Darbys left their home and moved to England. On July 30, 1922, just one month after the Irish Civil War began, eleven men knocked on the castle door and demanded that the caretaker, Richard Dawkins, provide them lodging for the night. When he opened the door for them, though, they forced their way inside and began to cover everything with gasoline, and then set it all on fire.

The following day, more men arrived and burned the parts of the castle that had been missed the night before. Dawkins tried to save as much of the furniture and belongings as he could, but the outbuilding he hid them in was later broken into and looted. By the time the Darbys returned, Leap Castle was nothing more than a smoldering ruin of charred stone.

One of the tragic losses that resulted from the burning of Leap was the vast collection of stories and novels that Mildred had yet to publish. According to one report, she lost an estimated 150 short stories, roughly forty longer manuscripts, and two finished novels.

Some things, though, still remain. For decades, while the castle sat empty, locals would look up at night to see lights in the old fortress windows. It was as if someone were walking the halls armed with a dim candle.

Others who ventured closer to the property reported that the ruins smelled of rotting flesh, and although they could never find the source, many reported hearing the sounds of some animal or creature. *Sniffing* sounds.

Today, Leap Castle is being restored by the current owner, with work being done to rebuild the two wings that extend out from the original tower house. But it's something else, something that was discovered decades earlier, that might be the most chilling revelation of the castle's last century.

Upstairs, just north of the Bloody Chapel, workmen stumbled upon a secret chamber. Think of it more as a pit, because it was only accessible from a trapdoor. The room below was small, barely larger than a closet.

These sort of rooms were called oubliettes, a French term that loosely means "place of forgetting." Unwelcome visitors or betrayed family members might be led over to the trapdoor and tossed inside. If the fall didn't kill them, the large spikes protruding from the floor certainly would.

And this oubliette, it turns out, was filled with skeletons.

So many skeletons, in fact, that when the workmen began to remove them, they quickly filled up their cart. Three cartfuls later, they had finally moved all the bones out. When they were finished, though, they found something else in the pit: a watch.

A pocket watch, to be precise. And after studying the maker's marks on the watch, researchers were able to estimate its age. According to them, it had been manufactured in the 1840s—mere decades before it was rediscovered.

Which raises a very interesting question. If the oubliette had stopped being used when the Darbys took over the castle in 1659, how did the watch get there two centuries later?

It seems the oubliette of Leap Castle had been used a lot more recently than we'd care to admit.

 DEEP AND DARK

Rope and Railing

THERE IS THE world we all know, with its streets and houses and the bustle of everyday life. And then there is the other world, filled with places that are set away from the center of our lives, places that most of us rarely interact with. Graveyards are a good example of this, and maybe even hospitals; we go there for specific reasons, but only rarely, if we're lucky.

But standing at the farthest edge of society, in a place it has held for thousands of years, is a structure we rarely give a second thought to. Not because it's unimportant, or because it's irrelevant, but because it's *literally* on the edge of our world.

The lighthouse. There are few buildings that harbor such powerful meaning and purpose in our world. Without fail, though, they have stood watch for millennia, right on the border between safety and danger, between darkness and light, between hope and despair. And yet by their very nature they are isolated and nearly forgotten.

Since the earliest known accounts, right up to modern times, the purpose of these buildings has changed very little: to cast a light into the darkness so that sailors might better understand where they are and what's ahead. They rarely waver, they frequently save lives, and they're universally understood. Which is why we have such a hard time believing that even there, in the narrow walls and seemingly never-ending stairs, stories have taken root that chill the mind.

There doesn't seem to be a lighthouse in the world without some whisper of unusual activity, some tale of tragedy or rumor of lost love. Oftentimes those stories speak of dangers from the world outside. Others, though, hint at something worse: a darkness that's right inside the walls.

Because every now and then, horror is born where the light is brightest.

A Bright History

For thousands of years, sailors around the world have used coastal lights to avoid risky waters and locate safe harbors. In an age before GPS, electrical lights, or anything more complex than celestial navigation, a lighthouse was often the only thing standing between a ship's crew and certain death.

One of the oldest lighthouses in the world is the Tower of Hercules in Spain. It dates back nearly two thousand years and is the oldest known functional Roman lighthouse. It illustrates the simplicity of a design that has changed very little over the centuries: a bright light, held as high as possible, with room in the building for a caretaker.

And it's that last bit—the caretaker—that sits at the center of nearly every whispered tale of lighthouse folklore. After all, without people, there would be no tragedy. That's our legacy as humans. We bring pain and fear with us wherever we go, even to the edge of the world. And the staff who live inside each lighthouse eventually come to call the place their home. It's the center of their life. Occasionally, though, it becomes their final resting place as well.

There are hundreds, perhaps thousands, of stories of unusual activity inside the walls of lighthouses all around the world. One such place, the Heceta Head Lighthouse in Oregon, has a reputation that goes back decades. There is a long-forgotten grave on the property that belonged to an infant. According to local legend, the baby was the daughter of the lighthouse keeper and his wife, and when the child died, the mother fell into a deep depression from which she never fully recovered.

Since the 1950s, nearly every keeper on duty has reported unusual activity inside the lighthouse. Screams have been heard in the middle of the night. Cupboards that were purposely left open were often found closed, and objects were seen to move in front of people.

In the 1970s, a groundskeeper was washing the windows of the house, inside and out, and while he was in the attic, he turned to see a silver-haired woman floating inches above the floor. The man, clearly frightened, bolted from the attic and refused to return, and so he was given permission to clean the outside of the attic window by way of a ladder.

In his effort to rush the job, though, the man broke the glass, but rather than go back into the attic to clean it up, he left it. Later that night, the lighthouse keeper was pulled from sleep by the sound of glass moving across the floor above. When he checked the next morning, he found that the glass had been swept into a neat little pile.

Another lighthouse, this one near Fairfield, Connecticut, holds an equally chilling history. Three days before Christmas in 1916, keeper Fred Jordan set off for the mainland in his rowboat, leaving his assistant, Rudy, in charge of the light. Rudy watched Fred row off into the distance, which turned out to be a good thing, because Fred's boat capsized about a mile from the island.

Hoping to rescue his friend and boss, Rudy climbed into a second boat and rowed to help. Unfortunately, though, strong winds had pushed Fred far from the location of the accident, and Rudy never found him.

Two weeks later, Rudy claimed to have seen Fred's ghost inside the lighthouse. According to his entry in the logbook, a light descended the stairs right in front of him and then began to act strangely. It moved toward the keeper's quarters, disappearing into the room. When Rudy caught up, the light was gone, but the logbook had been opened. Rudy checked the date on the page it lay open to, and it was the day of Fred's death.

In 1942, two boys were fishing near the lighthouse when their boat capsized in an eerie echo of Fred Jordan's accident. Thankfully, a strange man happened to be there, and he pulled them both to shore on the island, telling them to walk to the lighthouse for help.

Once there, the current keeper of the light welcomed them in, gave them both warm drinks, and allowed them to dry off. They told the keeper about the man who had helped them, but he knew of no one else on the island who could have done such a thing. And that's when the boys saw an old picture on the wall and recognized their rescuer in the photo.

"That," they were told by the keeper, "was Fred Jordan."

There are countless stories like these, scattered all around the world like the debris of a ship that broke upon the rocks. The ghosts of the past have a way of finding us, it seems. Sometimes, though, it is we who create the most frightful experiences, not some otherworldly force.

More often than not, it is people—not ghosts—who haunt lighthouses.

THE SMALLS

The Smalls are a collection of raw, lifeless basalt rocks that stretch out into the Atlantic, roughly twenty miles from the coast of Wales. The first lighthouse built there was small and rough, not much more than a house lifted high above the water on half a dozen or so oak and iron pylons, which allowed the waves and wind to pass right under.

It had been financed in 1776 by a man from Liverpool named John Phillips, and constructed by Henry Whiteside. To show just how much faith he placed in the structure, Whiteside himself lit the flame and tended the light for the first winter.

But this wasn't a room at the Hilton, believe me. It was a simple one-room shack affixed to the top of the platform, with the light room above it. A rope ladder and trapdoor allowed access from below, and a narrow gallery and railing circled the perimeter, which allowed the keepers to step outside and do repairs. It was required that the trapdoor remain closed at all times unless someone was entering or exiting the house, because the door itself constituted the majority of the walking space of the room.

It was, for all intents and purposes, a treehouse strapped to a small rock in the cold Atlantic. But it served its purpose, and Whiteside survived the winter without incident. He even devised a system for passing messages to the mainland, using the old cliché of a paper note in a glass bottle.

After his short time in the lighthouse, Whiteside passed the torch—literally—to a pair of men who would be the professional keepers of the light. And that's how the Smalls Lighthouse operated for over two decades, with a pair of men living in isolation, twenty miles from the mainland.

Weeks would go by without contact from others. During the winter, that silence could even be months long. Now, I'm an introvert, so I have to admit that the idea of weeks and weeks of silence, with piles of books and lots of writing to keep me busy, sounds like heaven. But during the winter of 1801, things were far from utopian.

Thomas Howell and Thomas Griffith were the lighthouse keepers at that time. According to what we know of the two men, Griffith was a young, tall, powerfully built laborer. Howell, on the other hand, was a small, middle-aged craftsman who had worked for years as a cooper, making barrels. Both men were from Pembrokeshire, were married, and had families who lived on the mainland. But the thing people remember the most about them is that they didn't get along. They hated each other, and everyone knew it.

It was said that during their infrequent visits to the mainland, the men could be seen in local pubs arguing constantly. The fights covered a wide range of topics, and witnesses claimed there was nothing the men could agree on. Sometimes their shouting would get so out of control that the pub would empty, just so the other patrons could get away from them. But not once were they ever seen to come to blows. People expected it, though.

During the winter of 1801, the weather contributed to their intense isolation. Relief keepers couldn't dock at the island. Supply ships tried to reach the rock but failed, and because of that, fresh water and food began to run low. They tried to use Whiteside's method of sending a message in a bottle, but no one ever answered—most likely the work of those same storm-tossed waves that kept away the supply ships.

One thing they didn't run out of, though, was fuel for the light, so Howell and Griffith stayed busy. After all, those same storms that kept supplies and human contact from reaching them were also threatening the ships that passed through the Smalls. Their duty took precedence.

It was most likely in the service of that duty that Thomas Griffith took ill. Some reports say that it was a sickness that laid the big man low. Others make mention of an accident, of how Griffith slipped and hit his head one day while working in the house. Regardless of the cause, every record of the event agrees on the conclusion: after weeks of failing health, Griffith—so young and fit and full of life until then—tragically passed away.

And just like that, Howell found himself completely alone, stranded on a rock in the Atlantic, with only a corpse to keep him company.

ROOMMATES

Howell had a problem on his hands. Well, two problems, actually. The biggest of those was that he and Griffith were known to quarrel constantly, so he didn't have the freedom to simply toss the man's body into the sea and trust that others would consider him blameless. No, he needed to make sure everyone knew that Griffith's death was not his fault, and so he kept the body.

Which led to the second problem. With no burial, the body would be left exposed to the elements, leading to decomposition. It probably didn't take long for Howell to look around the small room he shared with the corpse to understand how bad an experience that would be, so he began to plan.

Taking apart some of the storage cabinets in the room, Howell constructed a makeshift coffin. He knew his way around a hammer and saw, and managed to build something that worked, but Griffith was big, and Howell was alone, and . . . well . . . he was in a hurry.

When he finished, he took the large box, along with Griffith's corpse, outside onto the gallery that surrounded the house like a porch. It was cold outside, and that would help delay decomposition, but it was also harsh there. Waves crashed against the lighthouse constantly, and so, as a precaution, Howell tied the box to the rails.

The winter storms had other ideas, though, and one night soon after he had moved the coffin outside, a great wave washed up and smashed the box to pieces. All the wood and nails and rope that Howell had cobbled together to contain the body of his dead partner disintegrated and fell onto the rocks and into the water below. All of it, except Griffith's body.

According to the reports from those who rescued Howell months later, Griffith's corpse had managed to get tangled in the rope and railing at the edge of the gallery. Even though waves continued to wash over him and the occasional seagull approached for an inspection, nothing knocked the body free. Which means that rather than spend the coming weeks in peaceful retreat, Howell had a front-row view of his partner's decomposition.

I have to imagine that there were many moments when he regretted his decision, when he had to fight the overwhelming urge to rush outside, cut the ropes, and kick Griffith's body down to the waves below. It certainly would have ended the nightmare that he found himself living in. But it also would have stirred up the suspicion and judgment that he was hoping to avoid.

And so week after week, month after month, Howell lived in the small room of the lighthouse, tending the flame and maintaining the building, all while the rotting corpse of Griffith stood watch outside. He later spoke of how one of the body's arms hung loose, and would swing and wave toward him.

It sounds like the sort of tale Edgar Allan Poe would scratch onto the page at night, echoes of the telltale heart thumping monotonously in the background. But for Howell, this was reality. And it drove him mad.

When a rescue boat finally landed at the small rock almost four months after the death of Griffith, they discovered the rotted corpse on the gallery and an emaciated, shell-shocked Howell inside. He was alive, but the prolonged exposure to the sight of the corpse had wounded him deep in his mind and soul.

It was said that even when he was finally on the mainland and brought into the care of his family and friends, many of them failed to recognize him.

Howell was alive, but there was very little of him left inside. Like an abandoned lighthouse, his flame had gone out.

EVEN THE LONELY ARE NEVER ALONE

Everyone loves a good ghost story. There is mystery and horror and moments that put you on the edge of your seat. They're great around the campfire or the kitchen table, and they have a way of uniting people. Fear, after all, is a universal language.

But not every scary story has a ghost at the center of it, and while many frightening tales from the lighthouses of the world contain some element of the supernatural, perhaps it's the stories without them that frighten us the most.

Isolation, loss, guilt, and hopelessness can happen to any of us, no matter where we live or what we've been through. Maybe that's what makes the story of Thomas Howell so chilling: it could have happened to us if we had been in his shoes. And everything he experienced would be just as frightening and traumatic to you or me as it was to him.

Alone and isolated in tight quarters with dwindling supplies. The rotting corpse of the man he hated swinging in the wind and rain outside the window of his bedroom. And no sign of a rescue ship on the horizon, day by day, week by week, month by month. It's a horror that would drive any of us mad.

Ironically, though, help *had* tried to reach him. Ships sailed.

People watched. But every time they came close, they turned back, satisfied that everything was all right. It wasn't the light that convinced them, though. It was something else, something that multiple ships and witnesses confirmed together afterward.

Every time they got close, they could see, high up on the gallery surrounding the light, the shape of a man. But he wasn't calling for help, or beckoning them to come dock on the island. No, according to those who saw him, this man did nothing but lean against the rail and wave. Over and over again.

I Die

THE MESSAGE TAPPED through the wires with a frantic, urgent beat. A British listening post picked up the first transmission in June 1947. If the Morse code message had arrived with intensity and speed, the message it carried was more sobering, capable of stopping people in their tracks.

"We float," it declared. "All officers, including the captain, are dead, lying in the chartroom and bridge." And then, as if it were unknown and only a pessimistic guess, it added: "Possibly whole crew dead."

It was 1947. The war that had ended less than two years prior was still a painful, vivid memory in the minds of most people. For the men working in a number of listening stations in the Pacific, it must have sounded like a nightmare.

The ship was identified as the *Ourang Medan*. Using a number of stations, both British and Dutch, a location was calculated based on the ship's signals, and a rescue vessel was sent to the Strait of Malacca near Indonesia to lend assistance. Before they reached the troubled ship, one final message was received, this time in the form of a voice over the radio.

It simply said: "I die."

Nothing Left

The *Silver Star* was the first ship on the scene, and her crew attempted to signal the *Ourang Medan* with both whistle and lights. When no one aboard responded to their attempts, a small team was assembled, and they climbed into a boat and rowed over.

The rescue team first headed to the bridge, where the message had come from. Music echoed down the steel hallway as they approached, giving them hope. But when they stepped into the room, it was lifeless. The bodies of several members of the crew, along with that of the captain himself, were found still seated at their stations. The communications operator—most likely their source of the mysterious distress messages—was still at his console, hands on the dials and teeth bared in a savage grin.

Something did not seem right.

They moved their search to the cargo deck and discovered more dead. There, the corpses all seemed to be frozen in place, arms outstretched, faces pointed toward the sky. Each body was the same: mouth gaping wide, as if in horror at some invisible thing.

There were no survivors on board. But neither were the bodies injured in any visible way. No matter where they looked or whom they examined, there was no logical explanation for the death of so many men.

During an attempt to search the cargo bay below deck, one of the crew noticed a fire that seemed to have broken out minutes before. The rescue team was evacuated as quickly as possible and was soon back aboard the *Silver Star*. Within minutes, the fire triggered an explosion, and the ship, along with its mysteriously dead crew, sank into the ocean.

No one knows what killed the men aboard the *Ourang Medan*. No one knows what might have happened to leave each man with a face twisted by an unseen horror. No one is even sure what cargo or mission the ship was entrusted with. There have been conspiracy theories about government shipments, experimental weapons, and even an encounter with extraterrestrial life. But seeing as how the only witnesses to the real events aboard the ship now lie at the bottom of the Indian Ocean, all we can do is guess.

Safely back on the *Silver Star*, one of the men in the rescue party told the others of one final mystery he had seen while there. He had seen a dog. It had been standing among some of the bodies inside the ship. At first he had thought it was alive, but quickly discovered that it, too, was frozen in place on its four legs.

Its head had been turned upward, lips pulled back in a snarl, with eyes that seemed locked on nothing but thin air.

All Gone

ON DECEMBER 15, 1900, the SS *Archtor* was somewhere off the northwestern shore of Scotland. It was the middle of the night, and the fog was thicker than most of the crew had ever experienced before. But they knew where they were.

In fact, they were nearly certain that they were within a few hundred yards of Flannan Isle, a tall, mountainous island that stands sentry against the cold, dark northern Atlantic. What was unusual, though, was that the lighthouse there—barely a year old—was not lit. The night was completely, utterly dark.

The lighthouse was operated by three men at a time, adhering to a standard set in place a century before, following the tragedy at the Smalls Lighthouse off the coast of Wales. So it stood to reason that the lack of light was just a brief glitch, and there was no need to worry. Still, it was unusual.

The *Archtor* didn't investigate, though, and for more than one reason. First, it would have been nearly impossible to try and dock against the rocky base of the island at night. Flannan Isle resembles a footstool in some ways. Tall, vertical cliffs thrust out of the water and end hundreds of feet above. And while a staircase had been carved into the stone face, finding it at night, in the fog, with the waves pushing them around . . . well, it would have been suicide.

The second reason they didn't try to reach the lighthouse was more practical. A relief team was scheduled for just five days later, and they would be bringing in fresh supplies, new lightkeepers, and materials for repairs. Why stop now when everything they needed would arrive in a few days? So the *Archtor* sailed on.

EMPTY HALLWAYS

When the relief crew arrived on December 20, they expected to see a flag flying above the lighthouse. This was a sign that the keepers had spotted the ship as it approached and were headed down to the dock to greet them and help with supplies. But the flagpole was bare, and when they rowed over to the staircase, it was empty.

They blew the whistle on the ship, but no one answered. So two of the sailors were given the task of climbing into a rowboat and making their way over to the island to see what might be going on. The two men, Joseph Moore and Jim McCormack, rowed to the stairs and exited their boat, and Moore climbed to the top of the island.

He found the lighthouse door locked. Being part of the crew sent to relieve the current lighthouse keepers, he had a key, so Moore unlocked the door and stepped inside. What he found was equal parts confusing and disconcerting.

The living area was empty. No fire burned in the fireplace, and the beds were empty. The clock on the wall was even silent, frozen on some previous time.

Most eerie of all, though, was the kitchen table, where a meal had clearly been prepared and served but still sat cold on the plates. And one of the chairs lay on the floor, almost as if someone had stood up too fast and knocked it over.

I don't think Moore knew what he was getting into. How could anyone expect to find a lighthouse, built out on the edge of civilization in the North Atlantic, to be missing all three men? James Ducat, Donald Macarthur, and Robert Muirhead—all three veteran keepers—were just . . . gone. So Moore ran.

THE INSPECTION

An inspection was mounted, and more clues were found, but they didn't help paint a picture that the sailors could understand. Inside, they noticed that a pair of oilskins, the waterproof outerwear that the keepers would wear outside in bad weather, had been left inside. If anyone had gone outside, they had done so without the proper gear.

Lamps were freshly filled, the house was clean, and a proper logbook had been maintained. And so the crew went outside to look around. They found that a storage building near the lighthouse had been broken open, almost as if something had exploded or collided with it, and the contents were strewn all around the grounds.

Metal railings near the pathway up from the dock, as well as in other places, were bent, twisted, and—in some cases—ripped from the concrete. There was even a portion of the island, nearly thirty feet of rock and soil, that seemed to have been torn right off and into the sea.

The men couldn't come up with a rational theory for what they had found. Someone suggested a powerful wave, one that might have crashed up the high cliffs, pounded the island, and swept away all three keepers. There'd even been a recent storm that had been strong enough to do that, in theory. It was plausible, but hard to believe, especially when you consider two important details. First, why would all three men be outside in a storm like that, without their raingear?

And second, if the waves that destroyed the outbuilding and railings had also pushed the three keepers off the cliffs into the sea, then there'd be no record of the damage in the logbook. Yet there, in the last entry of the keeper's log, was a complete description of everything that had been destroyed. If the keepers had indeed been swept away, it was after the damage was done. Who or what took them, though, remains a mystery to this day.

Rearranged

THE CITY OF Norwalk, Connecticut, was originally settled in 1649. It sits on the coast overlooking Long Island Sound and is split right down the middle by the Norwalk River, which empties into Norwalk Harbor. I know, creative names, right?

Guarding the harbor, like a team of stone sentinels, are three islands. There are others, of course, but these three are the largest along the coastline, and they form a sort of wall between the sound and the city. If you look at them on a map, Chimon Island is on the right, Shea Island is in the middle, and Sheffield Island is on the left.

Each of the three islands is roughly fifty acres in size, give or take. And they're beautiful, no doubt about it. As beautiful, I guess, as any North Atlantic island can be. And Sheffield has the added benefit of having a quaint, antique lighthouse on the southwestern end. It's very picturesque.

Sheffield was originally called Winnipauk Island. Like a lot of places in New England, it started out in the possession of a Native American tribe, and was sold off to a European. In 1804, a Revolutionary War veteran by the name of Captain Robert Sheffield purchased the island and gave it the name it still carries today.

Sheffield only lived there for a while, from what I can tell, but we do know that he loved music. Folks who tell his story say that he was known to play an instrument similar to a violin, but with a more haunting sound. It could be heard by anyone who was traveling toward the Sheffield home, soft and otherworldly.

Whatever it was, the music stopped just three years after Sheffield bought the island, as he passed away in 1807. His son-in-law Gershom Smith inherited the island, and in 1826 he built the first lighthouse there, with the help of the U.S. Treasury Department.

It was Gershom's son, Nelson Smith, who encountered the most tragedy on the island, though. One of the things that the younger Smith did was build a number of additional structures around the lighthouse. He built a barn, a place to store corn, even a hotel of sorts that they called a "house of entertainment." And he built all of this out of the local stone found there on the island. In 1832 Smith was loading stones into his boat to move to another location when he slipped and fell. He drowned, most likely a result of hitting his head and passing out. He was just twenty-seven at the time.

Today, the island is part of the larger Stewart McKinney Wildlife Preserve, which spans a few of the islands there. Tourists occasionally travel to see the old light and experience being off the mainland. But in the autumn of 1991, something odd happened.

An archaeology student named Karen Orawsky was working on Sheffield Island, compiling a history of the area as part of her degree program. She was there on a daily basis. She would dock her boat, conduct the research for the day, and then take the boat home. Day after day, this went on without incident. And then something changed.

One day, while approaching the island by boat, she heard music. It was soft, almost otherworldly, but it was clearly coming from the direction of the island. After docking, though, she was unable to find the source.

She would frequently hear other noises as well. A faint, barely audible cry for help. The blast of a foghorn on a perfectly clear day. Wind that whistled through the trees without moving a single branch. She even felt cold spots while standing in the warm sunlight. All of these events were unexplainable, and all of them remain a mystery to this day.

Oddest of all, though, were the stones. According to her story, she would leave the island by boat at the end of each day, and return the following morning to discover that things had changed. Specifically, stones that had randomly littered the coast before would be found rearranged in clear patterns. Some were placed in the shape of a ring, while others were lined up straight. Once they even resembled the beginning of a stone wall.

Faulty short-term memory, or the ghost of Nelson Smith hard at work on another project? We'll never know for sure. What we can be certain of, though, is that Sheffield Island is a place where the past floats very close to the present. And if you lean into the wind, you just might hear it.

The Big Chill

SOME PLACES ARE more frightening than others. It's hard to nail down a specific reason, but even so, I can't think of a single person who might disagree. Some places just have a way of getting under your skin.

For some, it's the basement. For others, it's the local graveyard. I even know people who are afraid of certain colors. Fear, it seems, can be triggered by almost anything. And while history might be full of hauntingly tragic stories that span a variety of settings and climates, the most chilling ones—literally—are those that take place in the harsh environment of winter.

The incident at Dyatlov Pass. The tragedy of the Donner party. Even the sinking of the *Titanic* in 1912, which happened in the freezing waters of the North Atlantic. Winter, it seems, is well equipped to end lives and create fear. And when I think of dangerous winters, I think of Maine, that area of New England on the northern frontier.

If you love horror, you might equate Maine with Stephen King, but even though he's tried hard over the last few decades to make us believe in Derry and Castle Rock and Salem's Lot, the state has enough danger on its own. Maine is home to nearly thirty-five hundred miles of coastline, more than even California. And *that's* where the *real* action happens.

The Maine coastline is littered with thousands of small islands and jagged rocks, ancient lighthouses, and even older legends. And all in the cold north, where the sea is cruel and the weather can be deadly.

It's often there, in the places that are isolated and exposed, that odd things happen. Things that seem born of the circumstances and climate. Things that leave their mark on the people there. Things that would never happen on the mainland.

And if the stories are to be believed, that's a good thing.

ISLAND LIVING

The coastline of Maine isn't as neat and tidy as the coastlines of other states. Don't picture sandy beaches and warm waves that you can walk through. This is the cold north. The water is always chilly, and the land tends to emerge from the waves as large, jagged rocks. Go ahead and pull up a map of Maine on your phone. I'll wait. You'll see what I mean right away; this place is dangerous.

Because of that, ships have had a long history of difficulty when it comes to navigating the coast of Maine. Part of that is because of all the islands. They're everywhere. According to the most recent count, there are over forty-six hundred of them, scattered along the coastal waters like fragments of a broken bottle.

One such fragment is Seguin Island. It's only three miles from the mainland, but it's easy to understand how harsh winter weather could very quickly isolate anyone living there. And when you're the keeper of the lighthouse there, that isolation comes with the job.

The legend that's been passed down for decades there is the story of a keeper from the mid-1800s. According to the tale, this keeper was newly married, and after moving to the island with his bride, they both began to struggle with the gulf between their lives there and the people on the coast. So to give his wife something to do with her time, and maybe to get a bit of entertainment out of it for himself, the keeper ordered a piano for her.

They say it was delivered during the autumn, just as the winter chill was creeping in. In the story, it had to be hoisted up the rock face, but that's probably not true. Seguin is more like a green hill protruding from the water than anything else. But hey, it adds to the drama, right? And that's what these old stories provide: plenty of drama.

When the piano arrived, the keeper's wife was elated, but buyer's remorse quickly set in. You see, the piano only came with the sheet music for one song. With winter quickly rolling in from the north, shipping in more music was impossible, so she settled in and made the best of it.

The legend says that she played that song nonstop, over and over, all throughout the winter. Somehow, she was immune to the monotony of it all, but her husband—the man who had only been hoping for distraction and entertainment—took it hard. They say it drove him insane.

In the end, the keeper took an axe and destroyed the piano, hacking it into nothing more than a pile of wood and wire. And then, still deranged from the repetitive tune, he turned the axe on his wife, nearly chopping off her head in the process. The tragic story always ends with the keeper's suicide, but most know it all to be fiction.

At least, that's the general opinion. But even today, there are some who claim that if you happen to find yourself on a boat in the waters between the island and the mainland, you can still hear the sound of piano music drifting across the waves.

Boon Island is near the southern tip of Maine's long coastline. It's not a big island by any stretch of the imagination, perhaps four hundred square yards in total. But there's been a lighthouse there since 1811, due to the many shipwrecks that have plagued the island for as long as Europeans have sailed in those waters.

The most well-known shipwreck on Boon Island occurred there in the winter of 1710, when the *Nottingham Galley*, a ship captained by John Deane, wrecked there on the rocks. All fourteen crew members survived, but the ship was lost, stranding them without help or supplies. As the unfortunate sailors died one by one, the survivors were forced to eat the dead or face starvation. And they did this for days until fishermen finally discovered and rescued them.

But that's not the most memorable story from Boon Island. That honor falls to the tale of Katherine Bright, the wife of a former lighthouse keeper there from the nineteenth century. According to those who believe the story, the couple had only been on the small island for a few months when Katherine's husband slipped while trying to tie off their boat. He fell and hit his head on the rocks, then slid unconscious into the water, where he quickly drowned.

At first Katherine tried to take on the duties of keeping the light running, but after nearly a week, fishermen in York on the mainland watched the light flicker out and stay dark. When they traveled to the island to investigate, they found Katherine sitting on the tower's stairs. She was cradling her dead husband's corpse in her arms.

Legend has it that Katherine was brought back to York, along with her husband's body, but it was too late. Just like the lighthouse they had left behind, she was cold and dark.

Some flames, it seems, can't be relit.

FROZEN

There's been a lighthouse on the shore of Rockland, Maine, for nearly two hundred years. It's on an oddly shaped hill, with two large depressions in the face of the rock that were said to remind the locals of an owl. So when the light was built there in 1825, it was, of course, named Owl's Head.

Give any building long enough, mix in some tragedy and unexplainable phenomena, and you can almost guarantee a few legends will be born. Owl's Head is no exception. One of the oldest stories is a well-documented one from 1850. It tells of a horrible winter storm that ripped through the Penobscot Bay area on December 22 of that year. At least five ships were driven aground by the harsh waves and chill wind. It was destructive and fierce, and it would be an understatement to say that it wasn't a wise idea to be out that night, on land *or* at sea.

A small ship had been anchored at Jameson Point that night. The captain had done the smart thing and gone ashore to weather the storm, but he left some people behind on the ship. Three, actually: first mate Richard Ingraham, a sailor named Roger Eliot, and Lydia Dyer, a passenger.

While those three poor souls tried to sleep that night on the schooner, the storm pushed the ship so hard that the cables snapped, setting the ship adrift across the bay. Now, it's not exactly a straight shot southeast to get to Owl's Head—it's a path shaped more like a backward C to get around the rocky coast—but the ship somehow managed to do it anyway. It passed the breakwater, drifted east, then south, and finally rounded the rocky peninsula where the Owl's Head light is perched, all before smashing against the rocks south of the light.

The three passengers survived the impact, and as the ship began to take on water, they scrambled up to the top deck. Better the biting wind than the freezing water, they assumed. They huddled there under a pile of blankets against the storm, waiting for help.

When the ship began to actually break apart in the waves, though, Eliot—the sailor—was the only one to make an escape from the wreckage. I can't imagine how cold he must have been, with the freezing wind and ocean spray lashing him from the darkness. But standing on the rocks with his feet still ankle-deep in the waves, he happened to look up and see the lighthouse on the hill. If he was going to find help, that was his best option. So he began the climb.

He was practically dead by the time he reached the lighthouse, but when he knocked, no one answered. A moment later, the keeper of the light rode up the path on a sleigh, having been out for supplies, and realized at once that Eliot needed help. He took him in, gave him hot rum, and put him into a warm bed.

But not before Eliot managed to whisper something about the others.

The keeper immediately called for help and gathered a group of about a dozen men. Together, they all traveled back down to the shore, where they began to look for the wreck of the ship and the people who were still on board, perhaps alive.

When they found the remains of the schooner, the men began to carefully climb across the wreckage looking for signs of the other two people. It was treacherous work; the wood was encrusted with ice, and with each step the planks swayed dangerously with the waves. When they finally found Richard Ingraham and Lydia Dyer, they were still on the portion of the deck where Eliot had left them.

But they seemed to shimmer whenever the light of a lantern washed over them. Climbing closer, the men discovered why: Ingraham and Dyer were both encased in a thick layer of ice, completely covering their bodies. They were frozen, *Encino Man* style, in a block of ice.

Not taking any chances, the men somehow managed to pry the two free from the deck of the ship, and the entire block was transported back up the hill to the lighthouse. All that night they worked fast and carefully. They placed the block in a tub of water and then slowly chipped away at the ice. And as it melted, they moved the limbs of each person in an attempt to get their blood flowing again.

And somehow, against all logic and medical odds, it worked. It took them a very long time to recover, but Ingraham and Dyer soon opened their eyes. Ingraham was the first to speak, and it was said that he croaked the words, "What is all this? Where are we?"

Roger Eliot didn't survive in the aftermath of the shipwreck. Maybe it was the trauma of climbing up the hill to the lighthouse, soaked to the bone and exposed to the freezing winds of the storm. Perhaps it was an injury he had sustained in the shipwreck itself, or on the climb to the lighthouse. But his sacrifice did not go unrewarded.

Dyer and Ingraham fared better, though. They eventually recovered and even married each other. They settled down and raised a family together in the area. All thanks to the man who died to bring them help when all seemed lost.

GHOSTS

Later stories from inside the Owl's Head lighthouse have been equally chilling. Although there are no other tragic events on record there, it's clear from the firsthand accounts of those who have made Owl's Head their home that *something* otherworldly has taken up residence there.

The Andrews family was one of the first to report any sort of unusual activity on the property. I can't find a record of their first names, but the keeper and his wife lived there, along with her elderly father. According to their story, one night the couple was outside and looked up to see a light swirling in the window of her father's room. When they climbed the stairs, they found the older man shaking in his bed from fright.

Some think he might have seen the old sailor, a common figure witnessed by many over the years. When John Norton was keeper in 1980, he claimed to have seen the same apparition. He had been sleeping, but when a noise woke him up, he opened his eyes to see the figure of an old sea captain standing over the bed, just staring at him.

The old sailor has also been blamed for mysterious footprints that tended to appear in the snow, footprints that could be found on the walk toward the house. The prints never seem to have an origin point, and always end abruptly in the middle of the sidewalk.

Others have claimed to feel cold spots in the house, while some have gone on record to swear that brass fixtures inside the lighthouse—fixtures that were usually tarnished and dark—would be found mysteriously polished. None of the keepers have been able to figure out who was doing the cleaning for them.

There have been other stories as well. Tales of a pale woman who has been frequently seen in the kitchen, of doors slamming without anyone in the room, and of silverware that has been heard to rattle in the drawers. Despite this, though, most have said that they've felt at peace with her there. More at peace, at least, than they are with the old bearded sailor.

In the mid-1980s, Andy Germann and his wife, Denise, moved

in and settled into life on the harsh coast of Maine. Andy divided his time between tending the light and a series of renovations to the old lighthouse, which left the yard outside rather chaotic and full of construction materials.

One night after climbing into bed, the couple heard the sound of some of the building supplies outside falling over in the wind. Andy pulled on his pants and shoes and left the room to go take care of the mess before the wind made it worse. Denise watched him leave, and then rolled back over to sleep with the lamp still on.

A short while later, she felt him climb back into bed. The mattress moved, as did the covers, and so she asked out loud how it had gone, if there had been any trouble or anything unusual. But Andy didn't reply, so Denise rolled over.

When she did, she found that Andy's spot in bed was still empty. Well, almost. In the spot where he normally slept beside her, there was a deep depression in the sheets, as if an invisible body were lying right there beside her.

Of course, it was just the dent where Andy had been sleeping moments before. At least, that's what she told herself then. But thinking back on it later, Denise admits she has doubts. There were moments when she was lying there, staring at the impression in the sheets, and could have *sworn* the shape was moving.

Maybe she was too level-headed to get upset, or perhaps she was too tired to care. Whatever the reason, Denise simply told whoever it was to leave her alone, and then rolled back over and fell asleep.

At breakfast the next morning, she wanted to tell Andy about the experience, thinking he would laugh it off and help her to explain it away. But before she could, he told her his own story. It turned out Andy had had an unusual experience of his own the previous night.

He explained how, as he had exited the room and stepped out into the dimly lit hallway, he saw what he could only describe as a faint cloud hovering close to the floor. And this cloud had been moving. According to Andy, when he walked down the hall, it moved right up to his feet and then passed on through him.

That's when Denise asked Andy where the cloud had been going.

"Into the bedroom," he told her. "Why?"

Imaginary Friends

You don't have to travel to a lighthouse to bump into tales of the unexplained or otherworldly. You can hear them from just about anyone you meet, from the neighbor down the street to your real estate agent. But lighthouses seem to have a reputation for the tragic. And maybe that's understandable: these are, after all, structures built to help save lives in a dangerous setting. It might be safe to say that the well for these stories runs deeper than in many other places.

But are they true? Like a lot of stories, it seems it all depends on whom you talk to. Keepers across the decades have had a mixed bag of experiences. Some see odd things, and some don't. Maybe some people just connect with the stories more than others and see hints and signs where others might see none.

One recent family described their time at Owl's Head as normal. They never saw ghosts, never observed objects move, and felt right at home the whole time they were there. Another family, though, acknowledged that something unusual seemed to be going on in the lighthouse. They would find lightbulbs partially unscrewed, and their thermostat would constantly readjust itself. Perhaps whatever it is that's haunting the lighthouse is just very environmentally conscious.

It's easy to laugh off most of these stories. But we've never lived there. We've never heard or felt something that can't be explained away. And like most samples of data, there's always the outlier.

Another family who lived at the lighthouse in the late 1980s claimed to have experienced their fair share of unusual activity, though. One night, while Gerard and Debbie Graham were asleep, their three-year-old daughter, Claire, quietly opened her eyes and sat up in bed. She stared into the darkness for a moment, as if listening carefully to something, and then climbed out of her bed and left her room.

Her little bare feet pattered on the cold floor of the hallway as she made her way down toward her parents' room. Inside, she slowly approached the side of their bed, then tapped her father on the arm to wake him.

When he did wake up, he asked Claire what was the matter. The little girl replied that she was supposed to tell him something.

"Tell me what?" her father asked.

"There's a fog rolling in," Claire replied, somehow sounding like someone infinitely older. "Sound the horn."

When he asked her who had told her this, the little girl looked at him seriously. "My friend," she told him. "The old man with the beard."

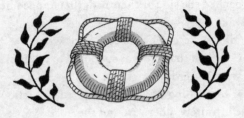

When the Bow Breaks

WE NEVER PLAN for the moments that frighten us the most. They tend to creep up on us, floating on chance and propelled by some twisted mixture of Murphy's Law and the worst side of humanity. Thankfully, those moments are rare.

In 2014, though, the people of Ireland came face-to-face with a real scare. A ship was slowly approaching the western coast of the green isle, and while countless ships do that every day, this one was different. This one, you see, was a ghost ship.

The *Lyubov Orlova* began life in 1976 as an ordinary Yugoslavian cruise liner. She was built to withstand sea ice, and spent a good portion of her career as a tourist vessel near Antarctica. But in 2010, the cruise ship entered troubled waters—figuratively speaking—and was taken out of service and docked in St. John's in Newfoundland. Turns out that the crew of over fifty people hadn't been paid in over five months, and so to cover the $250,000 in debts, the ship was impounded and sold for salvage.

In February 2012, the ship was pulled out of St. John's by a tugboat, headed to the Dominican Republic, but the tow line slipped free just a day into the journey. They tried to reconnect it, but somehow the effort failed. And thus began a journey that even a scriptwriter couldn't dream up, with the ship drifting back east, and then west, and north, until it was finally making its way toward County Kerry in Ireland.

Oh, one last detail. The abandoned cruise liner wasn't empty; it was full of cannibalistic rats. Left unchecked, they'd multiplied over the years, and after they had eaten every bit of food on the ship, they turned on themselves. So it was the thought of *that*—of thousands and thousands of starving, flesh-crazed rats reaching their shores—that left the people of Ireland in fear.

Ghost ships are a lot more common than you'd think. The good news is, most of them aren't overrun with cannibal rats. But that doesn't mean there's a shortage of stories. And just as with human settlements, it's the ships that have seen the most action that always seem to carry the biggest number of legends.

BRIGHT BEGINNINGS

In the century between the mid-1800s and the end of World War II, the primary method of transportation between Europe and North America was the ocean liner. Today we can easily hop on a plane and zip between locations, but in the era before powered flight, enormous ships did the job for us.

Ocean liners were different from the cruise ships of today, though. They were stronger, could hold more fuel, typically carried cargo and mail along with the paying passengers, and had thicker hulls. They could hold thousands of people at once, and made their round-trip journeys constantly, week after week, year after year.

America is a country of immigrants, and the vast majority of that immigration was aided by the ocean liner. My paternal ancestors boarded a steamship in Bremen in 1893 and rode it all the way to Ellis Island in New York. I have a copy of the ship manifest with their names listed right on it. My guess is that many of you could tell a similar tale. And at the core of all those stories is the ocean liner.

In the early 1930s, a new ocean liner was being built at a shipyard in Scotland. Legend tells of how the shipbuilders approached King George V and told him that they wanted to name the ship after England's greatest queen. They meant Queen Victoria, but before they could clarify, King George said, "My wife, Queen Mary, will be delighted to hear that." How do you say no to that, right?

The RMS *Queen Mary* set sail from Scotland on September 26, 1934. She was over a thousand feet long and weighed in at just shy of 82,000 tons. Throughout her twelve decks, she could carry over two thousand passengers and over a thousand crew members. And she was fast. Very, very fast. Between 1936 and 1952, there was only one year where a ship was faster than the *Queen Mary*.

And that speed caught the attention of the British military when World War II broke out. In 1940 she was converted into a troopship, bumping her passenger capacity up from two thousand to over fifteen thousand. For an empire with troops scattered all across the globe, the *Queen Mary* became invaluable in getting them all to Europe to aid in the conflict with the Axis powers.

In October 1942, as the *Queen Mary* was approaching Britain, an escort ship was sent to protect her during the final leg of the journey. The HMS *Curacoa* was tiny in comparison, but that wasn't unusual. The *Queen Mary* was enormous. What *was* unusual, though, was the navigational error that the *Curacoa* made. She mistakenly crossed directly in front of the larger vessel and was essentially run over, like an elephant running over a small wooden fence.

The *Curacoa* was sliced in two, and 331 of the ship's 432 crew members perished in the disaster. The *Queen Mary*, though, was essentially undamaged, and it never dropped speed out of a fear of possible German submarine attacks.

In December 1942, over sixteen thousand American soldiers boarded the *Queen Mary*, headed to England, and in doing so set a world record for the most passengers on a single vessel. The record still stands today. But along the way, a freak wave nearly a hundred feet tall crashed against the ship and pushed her over. She came within three degrees of capsizing, and the events of that night went on to inspire the classic 1972 film *The Poseidon Adventure*.

At the end of the war, the ship stayed on call to transport American troops home, as well as making more than a few trips with war brides. Over twenty thousand European women and their GI-fathered infants were transported to the United States on the *Queen Mary*, allowing them to reunite with their loved ones. The trips were called "Bride and Baby Voyages."

In 1947, she was refitted for luxury passenger travel, and operated in that capacity until 1967. Nine years earlier, the first transcontinental passenger jet crossed the Atlantic, sounding the death knell for the world of ocean liners.

After completing her thousandth passenger voyage, the *Queen Mary* left port one last time and arrived in Los Angeles, California, on December 9, 1967. There she was converted into a luxury hotel, museum, and tourist attraction. She's never left port since.

One last detail that should be mentioned: due to her dark colors and stealthy missions around the globe, the *Queen Mary* was nicknamed the "Grey Ghost." But oddly enough, it was her arrival in sunny California that seemed to trigger countless echoes of her dark past.

ECHOES OF THE PAST

In a lot of ways, turning the *Queen Mary* into a hotel made sense. Economically, it was much less expensive than building a new one. This was a ship designed for long-term accommodations, so converting it didn't require reinventing the wheel. And given that the ship had transported over two million passengers during her career, there were a lot of people interested in staying aboard a ship they'd probably thought they'd never see again.

Former passengers could see a lot of familiar elements on the retired *Queen Mary*. The indoor pools remained untouched, as did the first-class lounge. They could, in theory, tour parts of the ship that few passengers ever witnessed, including the engine room and the boiler room. It's a hotel today, but the ship truly is a piece of living history.

And with that history, apparently, come ghosts. That was a reality that an engineer named John Smith came face-to-face with in 1967, shortly after the ship arrived in California. He was contracted to come in and help with some repairs to the bow of the ship, structural damage left over from the war. And it was during one of his times inside the ship that he heard sounds.

> I could hear the sound of metal tearing, water rushing, and then, men screaming. It sounded like there'd been a rupture of the ship's hull. It was frightful. I went up to the extreme bow section of the ship. The sound was there, but there was no water and nothing to cause it. I don't believe in supernatural things, but in all my experiences as a marine engineer, I'd never seen anything like this.

John experienced these sounds a number of times during the two months he worked inside the bow of the ship, but try as he might, he was never able to connect those sounds with actual, physical activity. Nothing he could see with his own eyes, at least.

It was only later, about a year after he completed his work on the ship, that he stumbled across a description of the *Curacoa* tragedy. It was John's knowledge of the ship's structure, and how it would have behaved in the event of a collision, that ultimately convinced him of what he had really heard: it had been the sounds of that collision playing over and over again, like an echo from the past.

Another area of the ship with a history of unusual experiences is the pair of pool areas. In its ocean liner days, there was one in each of the first- and the second-class sections. And while much of the ship's living areas have been modernized, these pool areas have been left exactly as they were decades earlier.

Only available on private tours, these pool rooms seem to contain echoes of their own. Witnesses have reported seeing visions of women in old-fashioned bathing suits, while others have heard splashing and the laughter of children, and even felt water spray their skin.

More than a few people have even claimed to see wet footprints on the floor. All of which is a lot harder to believe when you discover that the pools have been empty for over three decades.

One visitor to the first-class pool area reported more than just sounds, though. According to her, while she was walking through the changing stalls, her children and the tour guide all continued down the hall, while she herself stopped to soak in the atmosphere. The place seemed to vibrate with activity, and she couldn't get over the feeling that, despite the private tour through a no-access area, she wasn't alone.

She was turning to leave and catch up with the others when she felt something. She described it as the sensation of two small hands on her waist, with distinct thumbs that pressed into her kidneys.

Then, just as she was about to chalk it up to some kind of muscular sensation and a bit of superstition, something pushed her backward. Not a little, either. According to her story, she stumbled backward as much as a foot, and the force of the shove was enough to throw her balance off. She pinwheeled her arms and ended up catching hold of the doorway between two rooms.

Reports like this and many others have trickled in over the years, from the pool areas to the ship's lounge, called the Queen's Salon, and even the old kitchen section. Visions of men and women in clothing from another era, reports of voices and sounds in the inaccessible areas of the ship—all of it combines to paint the picture of a ship carrying the cargo of a painful past.

When push comes to shove, though, nothing leaves its mark on a place quite like death. And the *Queen Mary* has been around long enough to have picked up more than its fair share of deathly tales.

DRINKS AND DOORS

In the years after the *Queen Mary*'s service in the war, she transitioned back over to a commercial ocean liner, and for a while it was back to life as normal. The crew worked hard, and when they weren't on duty, they enjoyed their downtime in much the same way the military crew before them had: card games, laughter, and a lot of drinking.

In the fall of 1949, officer William Stark ended his shift and returned to his quarters to change and relax. His captain had given him permission to enjoy a glass of gin, so he started to search for the bottle. After a few moments, though, he realized it was nowhere to be seen.

Considering that this potential glass of gin was practically an order from his captain, he decided to go ask the captain's steward, Mr. Stokes, who always knew where everything was. That was his job, after all—to provide for the needs of the passengers and crew. And so when Stark told the captain's steward about this dilemma, Mr. Stokes located a gin bottle and handed it to him.

According to the ship's records, Stark took the bottle and returned to his quarters. The steward went back to his own work as well, but several minutes later, there was another knock at his door. Officer Stark had returned, and he didn't look well.

It turns out, the bottle had indeed been a gin bottle, but it had already been emptied by someone else long before. The liquid inside wasn't gin at all, but an acid cleaning solution. Apparently Stark had taken a deep swig of the contents before his taste buds alerted him to the danger. And by then it was too late.

Officer Stark died slowly and painfully over the course of the following four days. More than a few visitors to the captain's cabin over the last three decades have claimed to have heard the sounds of someone choking. Stark's death, some think, is set on eternal repeat.

Far below the captain's quarters, in the belly of the ship, where darkness and grease once stood in for the brighter amenities of the passenger areas, there are tales of another tragedy. Today the engine room is empty, but when the *Queen Mary* was active, it was the heart of the ship. And that meant it needed to be protected.

Part of the safety system was a series of doors that shut automatically in the event of disaster. They're called fire doors, but they were designed to fight far more than flames. When these doors swung shut, the compartments would become watertight, something that can help a damaged ship stay afloat.

In 1966, the ship conducted a routine fire drill. The alert was sounded, and safety systems were engaged, including the fire doors. But the doors closed slowly. Slowly enough, at least, to allow crewmembers to slip in and out of them a few times. According to the legend, eighteen-year-old John Pedder wanted to see how many times he could slip through before it shut.

No one remembers his final count, but they remember how it ended. When door #13 slammed shut, Pedder was halfway through. And these doors don't stop. Pedder was crushed instantly.

During the months the ship was being converted into a stationary hotel, the ship was patrolled at night by guards with dogs. One guard spoke of an experience he had while on the job. According to him, while walking through the corridor near door #13, his dog whined and growled at the darkness ahead, and then came to a halt and refused to walk farther.

That's when the guard heard the sound of metal rolling across metal, as if one of the fire doors happened to be closing between compartments. The guard did what most of us would have done in a similar situation: he ran for his life.

In the late 1980s, one of the tour guides was closing up areas of the ship after the last evening tour. According to her story, she was near one of the hotel escalators when she looked up and saw a man standing high on the escalator. She described him as dressed in filthy work overalls, with a young, bearded face.

She glanced around the area to see if anyone else was nearby. She wondered if maybe it was nothing more than a prank, or if there was a new construction project she hadn't been made aware of yet. When she turned back to the escalator, the figure had vanished. She had no idea who the man was, where he'd come from, or where he'd gone. But the experience left her feeling very unsettled.

It wasn't until many years later that this woman had a chance to see some old photos of crewmembers from the ship's history. In one of those photos, she recognized the youthful face and beard of the man she had seen on the escalator. The photo identified him as John Pedder.

Places where large numbers of people have lived—and died—have a habit of becoming a hotbed of unusual activity. The places with the reputation for being the most haunted often turn out to be locations where a constant stream of pain and suffering has taken place. Hospitals, hotels, old battlefields, and the ruins of ancient structures. Buildings that have stood for centuries in harsh environments. Places where people have suffered tragedy and unrest over and over again. Yes, we can debate whether or not these locations *really* contain ghosts, but it's clear that they harbor *something*, be it dark memories and tragic tales or actual ghostly figures.

These memories, though, have a way of bringing the past back to life. It's almost as if these stories shine a light on something from long ago, casting shadows in the present. Or maybe it's something deeper. Maybe when events are painful enough, some piece of that pain and loss is left behind, like a scrap of paper or a breadcrumb, pointing the way backward in time.

The stories that circulate today among guests and tourists on the *Queen Mary* certainly point toward the past. So it's ironic that a tale from the birth of the ship should be so significant.

On September 26, 1934, as the ship was being prepared for her maiden voyage, newspapers scrambled to cover the events. They spoke with engineers and members of the crew who would staff the vessel. And they spoke to a guest at the launch ceremony, a woman named Lady Mabel Fortescue-Harrison.

Aside from being from a family of creative English entertainers, Lady Mabel had developed a reputation over the years as a popular astrologer, offering up predictions to those who would listen. So there, with the enormous *Queen Mary* looming behind her, she spoke words that, looking back, have an eerie weight to them:

"The *Queen Mary*," she said, "launched today, will know her greatest fame and popularity when she never sails another mile and never carries another paying passenger."

 OFF THE BEATEN PATH

In the Dark

THERE'S A CAVE near the Red River in Adams, Tennessee, that's a lot like any other cave you might find in the middle of the country. That is, except for its connection to a local legend that refuses to let go.

You see, the cave is on land that once belonged to a man named John Bell. He and his family had moved to the Red River area back in 1804, and in the years that followed, they endured one of the most mysterious, more horrifying experiences in American history. Specifically, they were assaulted by an unseen spirit that identified itself as Kate, although history and local legend have always given her a different name: the Bell Witch.

The cave was probably used by the family as a storage room, which was a common practice two centuries ago in the days before refrigeration. With a constant temperature of about 55° Fahrenheit, it's the perfect place to store perishable food through the hot Tennessee summer.

There's a local legend that tells of how young Betsy Bell, along with some of her friends, went to the cave one day in 1817. Maybe she'd been sent there by her mother to retrieve some supplies, or maybe they just wanted to explore. Either way, the group of children found themselves in the cave, in the dark.

While they were in there, one of the boys managed to get himself stuck in a hole. The others tugged on him and tried their best to pull him free, but he seemed completely and utterly stuck. And that's when a voice spoke up. A voice without a body.

"I'll get him out," the voice of a woman said. And then, as if by magic, the boy was yanked free from the hole while everyone was watching.

Some think that was Kate's entrance to our world, that this was the event that connected her to the Bell family, for better or for worse. In the months to come, she would be unusually focused on Betsy. That focus would become the core of the Bell Witch story, but the cave . . . well, it seems to have drifted into the background.

Until, of course, the Bell Witch events wrapped up. Because when Kate finally left the Bells, legend says that she retreated back to her cave. And as a result, many think this dark hole in the side of the rocky bluff is, in fact, haunted.

Today the land is owned by a man named Bill Eden. Sometimes people will travel to the area in hopes of getting a glimpse of the cave, and Bill is pretty accommodating. Sometimes he even gives tours. And it was what happened on one of those tours a few years back that leaves us with more questions than answers.

Bill was leading a group of more than a dozen tourists down the winding path to the entrance of the cave when one of the women abruptly sat down, right in the middle of the trail. And she couldn't stand back up, either. When she was asked why in the world she'd decided to take a seat, she told the others that she hadn't.

Something heavy, she claims, had pressed down on her. So heavy, in fact, that she couldn't overcome it and stand back up. In the end, a number of the others had to pick her up and carry her back to their car, where she could recover.

Most would think it's all nerves and exaggeration. And maybe it is. But Bill Eden thinks there's something going on, mostly because of what he once witnessed inside the cave. While he was there by himself one day, Bill claims to have heard footsteps. When he looked up, he said he could see the shape of a person standing a few yards away, back turned toward him.

Bill was about to call out and ask why that person was in his cave uninvited, but he stopped when he noticed two very unusual, very disturbing details. First, the person was all one color, a pale, snowy white. Bill said he couldn't see through the shape, but at the same time, it just didn't seem normal.

But it wasn't a trick of the light or a wisp of fog that was fooling his eyes. Bill said that the shape was, in every way, just like a person. He studied the back of the head, and then slowly lowered his gaze, examining the pale white details of the body.

And then stopped. That's when he noticed the second disturbing detail. The figure, he said, had no feet. Instead, where the feet should have been, there was nothing but open space.

The figure, if that's what it was, was floating.

An Angel Among Us

THE TOWN HAD gathered in the meetinghouse for a day of focus. They prayed. They fasted. They talked quietly and encouraged each other. They did the best they could.

It was June 1676, and they were living on the edge of the frontier. While others had called the coastline of Massachusetts home for decades, their little village of Hadley had only existed for seventeen years.

They'd broken off from a community settled in what is now Wethersfield, Connecticut. They struck out in 1659 and followed the Connecticut River north for about fifty miles. The river was a safe place to be. A boat could take you south. South to Old Lyme and Old Saybrook, although those communities wouldn't exist for another two centuries. And the river could take you to the Atlantic.

But in Hadley, they were about as far as you could get from safety. Their sea, if you want to think of it like that, was a nation of indigenous people who had lived in Massachusetts for thousands of years. It was their land, and the people of Hadley were stealing it from them. There's no other way to put it, so let's not be coy. The English were thieves.

So the Native Americans fought them. They fought the English all over Massachusetts that year, actually. The leader of the Native Americans was a man named Metacom, but he'd been on good terms with early Puritan colonists and had started to call himself King Philip in an effort to build trust and also earn respect. But relations soured, and so he led his people to war.

And now war had come to Hadley.

So the people of the village had gathered to pray and fast. They felt endangered. They felt threatened. The original inhabitants of the area wanted the English to go away, and they were delivering that message with the sharp tips of their arrows and with the vicious curve of each tomahawk blow.

They had been in the meetinghouse for some time when a stranger burst into the building. No one had ever seen him before. He was deathly pale. His white hair hung limp and unkempt around his neck. To the people in the room the stranger seemed immeasurably old.

And this stranger told the people of Hadley to prepare themselves. An attack was coming that very hour, an ambush led by the tribes outside their borders. But they could stop it, if they acted fast.

Some of the people panicked at the news. Some were in disbelief. But many of them heard his words and fell in line. This stranger—this visitor from some other place, dressed in white and bringing a word of hope—had a plan. Within moments he was leading them out, calling them to arms, and instructing some of the men of the village how to operate the old, disused cannon that sat in the square.

Those villagers repelled the ambush that day. Yes, the Native Americans were on the side of right, but the English survived and lived to talk about it for centuries to come. They spoke about the battle and their victory over their attackers with pride. But they also whispered tales of the angel who saved them all. The angel of Hadley.

REGICIDE AND REFUGE

Decades earlier, when the English Civil War broke out in 1642, England was divided by military and political conflict. In 1649, fifty-nine military leaders signed the death warrant for King Charles I. Among those men was a young officer named William Goffe. He and the others succeeded, King Charles was executed, and soon Oliver Cromwell took over as lord protector.

For a while, at least. The king's son, Charles II, returned to London in 1660 and regained the throne. He granted amnesty to nearly everyone involved in the war, but not the fifty-nine signers of his father's death warrant. Those people were labeled with the name "regicide," or king-killers, and their fate was to be more in line with the execution they had demanded for his father.

As a result, many of the regicides fled the country. William Goffe, along with a friend, headed across the Atlantic to disappear into the wilderness of Puritan Massachusetts. They spent some time in the colony at New Haven, and then headed north. But through all of it, the key for Goffe was to remain in hiding.

He was a fugitive from the crown, and even though the Massachusetts colony was thousands of miles away from King Charles, it was a land full of loyalists. There was always the risk that someone would recognize him or hear his story and then turn him over to the authorities. Goffe had to hide, and stay hidden, for the rest of his life. No more public life. No more political influence. Exposure meant death now.

William Goffe had been living secretly in the cellar of a home in Hadley for over a decade when the people of the village gathered that June day in 1676 for prayer and fasting. I like to imagine there was a moment that day when he realized—for the first time in forever—there was no one around to see him. Maybe he risked a trip outside to feel the sun and wind against his face. And maybe it was while doing *that*—smiling up at the sky and taking it all in— that he saw the enemy approaching.

However he discovered the ambush, we know what he did next. He burst into the meetinghouse and warned them all. He became the military leader of his youth and led them in defense of the village. He showed them how to fire the cannon. In his seventies, far from home, with a price on his head, William Goffe became a hero.

This is how folklore works. It delivers truth, filtered through the lens of time and edited by the political views and social climate of the times. The stories we inherit—tales that we pick up and share with each other over the years—aren't new and shiny. They're antiques, tarnished by the years and incomplete.

The stranger who saved Hadley in 1676 was just a man, not an angelic visitor. But William Goffe took on great risk to warn the people of the approaching danger. He risked exposure and execution. He risked his safety and secrecy. He risked his life. I wonder if any of us could be brave enough to do the same, given the chance.

Maybe there *was* an angel in Hadley that day after all.

A Bridge Too Far

A**T 2:00 A.M.** on February 5, 1887, the Montreal Express was working its way up the cold iron nervous system of the North American railroad network. It had pulled out of Boston hours before and was weaving its way beside the Connecticut River along the New Hampshire–Vermont borders.

That's a lot of geography, I know. Just know this: the Montreal Express was a daily passenger train that ran back and forth between Boston and, you guessed it, Montreal.

This time, though, the train was running behind schedule. Nearly an hour behind, and it hadn't even left Vermont yet. They had a long, cold journey ahead of them. But as planned, the train pulled into the White River Junction railway station and stopped for passengers to enter and exit the cars.

When it pulled away minutes later, it was nearly -20°. Each of the passenger cars had small wood-burning stoves, but they struggled to fight off the creeping chill in the air. Everyone on board—seventy-nine passengers and six crewmen—bundled up against the cold and did their best to keep their minds off it.

As the train pulled away from the station, a conductor by the name of Smith Sturtevant walked up and down the aisles collecting tickets. Minutes later, as the tracks crossed the White River on the longest wooden railroad bridge in America at the time, the train gave a shudder. One of the crew, sensing something was wrong, reached for a bell cable and gave it a yank, signaling to the engineer to stop the train.

But you don't stop a train that quickly. That's a lot of weight, and a lot of momentum, and while the speed dropped rapidly, the train kept moving across the bridge. As it did, one of the sleeper cars snagged on a piece of railway track that had broken due to the cold. And when it did, the car veered away from the rest of the train, and plummeted sixty feet into the river below.

That car was joined by the three other cars behind it, and as it fell, they followed it down. Not to the rushing waters of the White River, though. No, with temperatures as low as they were, the river itself was frozen solid. It was as if the train had dropped onto pavement, or solid stone.

The woodstoves and oil lamps exploded inside the train cars, and within moments everything was a raging firestorm. And those flames licked up the support legs of the bridge, and minutes later it too dropped into the gorge, landing right on top of the train.

Five of the six crewmen died that night. Of the seventy-nine passengers, thirty of them perished. Most were burned to death in the fire. Some were crushed by the train or the bridge. A few even drowned as the heat of the flames melted the ice. According to one local paper, only eight of the bodies they recovered were identifiable.

Those who were rescued were transported across the river to a farmhouse, where the injured and dying filled up the house so quickly that the rest were moved to the barn. Rescuers found Sturtevant, the conductor, and were able to pull him to safety. He died the next day. A woman named Maria Sadler, who'd been returning home to Quebec, was also found alive and pulled free, although her ankle was broken in the process. She, thankfully, survived.

When they found Edward Dillon, he was alive and uninjured but pinned beneath a pile of debris. Heavy objects lay across his chest—a wheel from the train car, a thick timber, seats—and try as they might, the rescuers weren't able to lift the weight of it all in order to free him.

Dillon, to his credit, stayed calm and chatted with the crew, but then he turned his head and his eyes went wide. The fire that was consuming the train was slowly creeping toward his location. He begged. He pleaded. And the rescuers doubled their efforts, trying to dig him free. But it was no use: the debris was simply too heavy to move.

When the first of the flames reached him, he cried out one final time. And then he closed his eyes. The twenty or so men who had been trying to free him could do nothing more than step back and watch in horror as Dillon burned to death, right before their eyes.

He wasn't the only one to burn to death, either. David Maigret, from Quebec, was also pinned beneath debris near the fire. When it approached, he pulled his pocket watch and wallet out and handed them to his young son Joseph, and then said his farewells before the wall of fire surrounded him as well.

TODAY

Today locals still whisper about the ghostly figure of a man in a conductor's uniform who's been seen walking along the tracks. He's only ever seen at night, and only near the river. Maybe Smith Sturtevant has returned to help with the rescue efforts, and he's just never left.

The farmhouse across the river has survived, but not without some baggage. It's said that so much blood soaked into the floor-boards of the second floor that the stains can still be found on the ceiling of the kitchen. Another rumor says that animals refuse to go inside the old barn. The farm, by the way, was known by the family name: Paine.

And although the old wooden bridge has been replaced by a more modern one, the original abutments are still there. But the locals will tell you that more than just stone has survived.

According to some, the area surrounding the bridge still has a smell. Many who have traveled across the bridge have caught the scent and have described it as a mixture of burnt wood and something else. Something less common than the cool New England air. Something less pleasant than the autumn leaves.

It's the smell, they say, of charred human remains.

A Leg Up

JONATHAN BUCK WAS born in 1719 and grew up in the town of Haverhill, in the northern part of Massachusetts. That meant that he grew into adulthood before America declared independence from British rule, but it also meant that he got to be part of the initial expansion into Maine.

Most people don't know it, but for a long while, Maine was nothing more than a district of Massachusetts. It wasn't until 1820 that the territory was granted statehood, though Jonathan was long dead by then. But in the 1760s, he sailed up the coast between Rockland and Bar Harbor as part of a survey team and helped establish six individual plantations, areas of settlement that would eventually become towns. In 1762, though, it was a difficult task to plant new communities so far north. There were Native Americans who felt threatened by the expansion of the colonials, and rightly so. Later on, the British would also put up a fight.

Fifteen years later, the American Revolution would pit the colonies against the crown, and while the majority of the war was fought in places we easily recognize, some of the conflict found its way north to Maine. Like most wars, this one managed to come home. And home, for Jonathan Buck at least, was the location affectionately called Plantation No. 1.

In July 1779, Buck joined a group of soldiers who were headed south toward the coast to lay siege to the British hidden away inside Fort George. A handful of frontiersmen was no match for the garrison of troops there, though, and the colonists were defeated. But they had succeeded at doing something else: they'd kicked a hornet's nest.

Buck knew it, too. The moment he got home, he packed his family up and they fled north, up the river to Brewer. Once he was sure they were safe, he walked south. Over two hundred miles, in fact, step by step toward his hometown of Haverhill. And he did this while he was sixty years old. Not too shabby, I'd say.

Five years later, he led his family back to the ruined remains of Plantation No. 1 and began rebuilding, and this time it appeared to stick. His adult sons began to take a role in the community, and things blossomed. By the time Buck passed away in 1795, Plantation No. 1 had a new name: Bucksport.

But not all was well in Bucksport. The legend says that a few years before his death, Jonathan Buck oversaw the execution of a woman in town. Some stories say that she had been accused of witchcraft, while others paint a darker tale. They say that the woman was his mistress and she was pregnant with his child. In either case, Buck had the woman burned at the stake to stop her.

Both stories agree on one thing, though: there was a curse. As the flames began to climb up the kindling and flicker around her, the woman was said to have cried out that Buck would soon die as well. She predicted that once a tombstone was placed over his grave, something odd would happen: she would place her mark on it.

Some stories say that once the fire had consumed her, one of her legs broke free and tumbled into the dirt in front of the onlookers. It's a vivid image, and one that I can easily see being recreated in a film, or in an episode of *Supernatural*. But sadly, it's all most likely a lie.

You see, Jonathan Buck had no authority to execute a prisoner. And the last witch executions in America took place in Salem in 1692, a century before the story was said to have taken place. There are no records of the event, no documents or historical proof. Just the story.

Well, that's not true. There's a bit more than just a story. There's also the tombstone. You see, Jonathan Buck's grandchildren finally erected a stone monument over his grave in 1852. It was in honor of the founder of Bucksport, and to pay respect to a beloved ancestor. But it also set the stage for something strange to happen.

A mark appeared on the stone. It was a patch that seemed ever so slightly darker than the rest. People have tried to remove it, but it won't come off. It's not a stain or a manmade mark. It's just an eerie shape embedded in the very color of the stone monument. And of course, it's probably the source of the legend.

Why? Because the mark on Jonathan Buck's tombstone looks an awful lot like a leg.

A Head of Steam

JUST TO THE north of Boston is a city nearly as old. Malden, Massachusetts, was settled just a decade after Boston was, all the way back in 1640. Thanks to the Mystic River, which separates it from Somerville and Boston to the south, locals referred to Malden for a very long time as simply "the Mistick Side."

The Sandy Bank Burial Ground there next to the Malden River welcomed its first long-term resident around 1648, and many followed after that. People were dying to get in, I guess you could say. But if you try to picture the graveyard in your mind, don't arrange it in neat and tidy rows, like the cemeteries of our modern world. It's a little bit crooked, a little bit ancient, and a little bit creepy.

And maybe that's to be expected for a graveyard situated on "the Mistick Side."

According to local legend, at least one of the burial ground's occupants had trouble staying put. In the 1700s, there was apparently a man in town who loved to experiment with chemicals in his home laboratory. Neighbors often complained of the noxious smells that drifted out of his windows, and more than a few passersby choked on the fumes.

As neighbors are so very good at doing, they complained about the chemist. Not that the man himself cared, mind you. In his view, he'd been doing true scientific work, and all of that effort had finally paid off. So when his last moments of life came a few years later, he made a chilling prediction to the few who had gathered around his deathbed.

"In my life," he told them, "I have differed from other men. And by the foul fiend I will continue different after I am dead. My flesh is not common flesh, like yours. It will never rot."

It was a cryptic thing to say because there are so many possible meanings. He could have been suggesting that he would never truly die. Or maybe that his corpse would refuse to rot and decay like the rest of humanity. Either way, it was a bold declaration from a man that everyone wished would just go away. In his own way, he was telling them all to not hold their breath.

But he did die, and was soon buried in his family tomb. It's the sort that you might imagine in an old horror film, where a stone chamber is built into the side of a hill, buried in soil, and accessible only by an iron door. His coffin was placed inside, and the neighborhood released a collective sigh of relief. It was nice to breathe easy again, after all.

The legend doesn't give a reason, but some years later a medical student crept into the cemetery and broke into the old man's tomb. He'd heard the stories from others in town, and that had made him wonder. Had the old man's prediction come true? And if so, how?

When he got inside, he found that the old man's corpse had indeed refused to decay. No rot, no peeling flesh, no putrefaction. It had, though, turned brown, and—according to this medical student—rather hard. Whatever chemicals the old man had exposed himself to, they'd done the trick. His body had refused to rot.

Wanting to know why, this medical student is said to have taken a bone saw from his bag and then slowly, methodically, removed the old man's head. With the pale light of the flickering lantern behind him, he gripped his trophy by the hair and began to lower it into a sack. And that's when he heard the voice.

It was as if someone else was in the cold chamber with him, whispering softly in the corner. He turned toward the sound, but nothing was there. Nothing, that is, except for the other coffins.

But rather than fade away, the sounds grew. Whispers became moans, then wails, and then horrific cries. Shadows began to swirl through the chamber, around and above him, some black as night and others a sickly green. All of it was enough to frighten the man out of his mind.

He tossed the head on the floor of the chamber and bolted through the open door into the night, heading home as fast as his legs could carry him. And with that, the episode ended.

Months passed. Sometimes neighborhood children would cautiously push the iron door open slightly, and then squeal at the vision of the severed head sitting on the chamber floor. Even by the light of the noonday sun, it was a frightful experience—one that was hard to forget, and even harder to keep private. As a result, word spread.

That's the power of folklore, after all. It spreads like a low-burning fire, consuming rational thought and filling a community with a feeling of wonder, or horror, or dread. It rarely lets go once it's taken hold of you. In fact, given enough time, folklore can build up quite a head of steam. And the story of the old chemist is one of those tales.

One last bit of the legend. According to the story, a local man was bathing in the Malden River in 1825, just west of the graveyard near the Medford Street bridge. And while he was there, buck naked in the cold water, he glanced up the eastern bank, where he could see the edge of the Sandy Bank Burial Ground and the door of the old chemist's tomb.

That's when the door moved. It opened, and then, as if stumbling slowly between one world and the next, a man walked out.

The bathing man was horrified, and he bolted out of the river with a cry. He didn't even bother to grab his clothes. He simply ran as fast as he could, straight into town and down the streets in full view of the public. I doubt it's the first historical record of a streaker, but I'm sure it made quite the impression nonetheless.

The figure who had stumbled out of the tomb, however, was just a man. No ghost, no undead corpse, no vengeful spirit looking for his head. Just a local drunk who had found his way inside the night before, and curled up in a corner to sleep it off.

Whether or not the tale of the chemist was true, it's hard to ignore a story with the power to send a man screaming naked down the street. Sometimes folklore is significant for the history it preserves, and other times for the mark it leaves behind.

And that, my friends, is the naked truth.

A Deadly Past

LET'S BE CLEAR before I tell you this story: I have very little evidence it's real. But sometimes we have to entertain the possibility that odd things can happen and that folklore can carry them forward, like a scrap of paper on the wind. This, I think, is one of those scraps.

Henry lived in Honey Grove, Texas, located northeast of Dallas, up near the Oklahoma border. Today Honey Grove is a small town, but it was even smaller in 1893—perhaps eight hundred citizens or so. And Henry was one of them.

One day Henry ran out on his girlfriend. We don't know the reason for the split—maybe he left her for another woman, or perhaps they had an argument and this was one of those heat-of-the-moment things. We just know that Henry left her, and it broke her heart.

Some versions of the tale say that this unnamed woman killed herself over the loss. Some assume she moved on and found happiness later. But it was the act of breaking up, of Henry leaving her, abandoned and alone, that drives the tale. Because this unnamed woman had a brother, and *he* wasn't very happy with what Henry had done.

And so it was that one day Henry was outside his house in Honey Grove when the brother arrived to give Henry a lesson. I would like to believe that he didn't come with the intent to kill.

The line between crimes of passion and crimes of premeditation is wide and tall, and it takes a lot of planning and resolve to cross it. It's hard to say if this man had that sort of dedication in him. But at the very least, he had a gun.

They argued. They shouted. The brother demanded Henry make amends and set things right, fix his sister's broken heart. And when Henry failed to cooperate, he pulled his gun out. He held it straight out, hand trembling with rage and fear, and pointed it at Henry's head.

And then he fired.

Blood sprayed from Henry's head and his body fell backward, landing in a lifeless heap on the lawn near the large tree. That's when panic washed over the brother, and he bolted. Later, when he had locked himself up at home, that panic was joined by regret and distress. Fearing for what he had done, and what it meant for his future, he took the same pistol and turned it on himself.

It's a tragic story, and not a fun one to listen to if it ends there. But it doesn't. You see, Henry got back up from that spot on the lawn near the tree. He pressed his hand to his head and felt pain. There *was* indeed blood, but not as much as he'd expected. So he went to the doctor, who patched him up and sent him home.

Twenty years went by. Two decades of life that Henry probably viewed as a gift. He had been shot in the head, after all, but the bullet somehow only grazed him and then disappeared. So here he was, healthy, older, and enjoying his life in Honey Grove, Texas.

One day in the summer of 1913, Henry walked outside to take care of an old problem. The large tree in his front yard had grown too close to the house, and the shade was causing problems. Today was the day to remedy that by getting rid of the old tree.

Now, we have to lean into the story here and trust in the details. We're told that Henry didn't have an axe or saw or anything that might help him take the tree down in the usual manner, and we have to believe that. I know, not having an axe would indeed be unusual, but then again, most folklore is born out of unusual moments, isn't it?

So Henry grabbed the next best thing: a stick of dynamite. He took a piece of rope and tied the explosive to the trunk of the tree, low to the ground opposite the house. Then he lit the fuse and ran for cover.

And it worked. The explosion went off, and the tree toppled to the ground away from the house. But as the tree was slowly falling, Henry was doing the same thing. And both of them hit the ground at the same time. Neither would move again.

I have to assume a neighbor found Henry's body. Someone did, at least, and they took him to the doctor to find out what the cause of death had been. The carnage in the yard seemed to suggest that a piece of the tree had perhaps pierced Henry's skull. There was certainly enough blood to validate that theory.

But they were wrong. When the doctor opened Henry's skull to find the source of the fatal wound, he found something unusual, something very much unlike a piece of wood.

A bullet.

In fact, it was a bullet from a pistol. *The* bullet, you see, that had been fired at Henry two decades earlier. After grazing his skull that fateful day in 1893, the bullet had embedded itself in the tree behind him. And there it had waited, motionless and benign, left to slowly vanish into an ever-expanding prison.

It would have stayed there, too, if it hadn't been for the dynamite.

Sometimes our past has a way of tapping us on the shoulder and reminding us that it's still there. We think we're clear, that we made it out or got away, and then—with a sudden flash—it all comes rushing back into our mind.

Or, in the case of poor Henry, back into his *head*.

For Want of Cider

THE ROOM WAS packed with visitors. That wasn't an unusual thing, though. The home of Gabriel Godefroy was known far and wide as a friendly space. Many of the older settlers gathered there on a regular basis, along with some of the men from the local Native American tribes.

Godefroy was one of the oldest men in town, actually. So old, in fact, that he could remember when Detroit had been under French rule, long before the Americans took over, and the British before that. In 1805, few could make that claim.

So they gathered there under his roof. They lounged and drank and laughed. But the centerpiece of their time in Godefroy's house was the storytelling. Man after man would recount dramatic stories of their dangerous pasts.

One moment a powerful chief such as Okemos or Tecumseh would thrill the crowd with accounts of amazing hunts, and the next it would be Antoine Beaubien or Whitmore Knaggs detailing some harrowing escape during their youth.

It wasn't a pretty place. They say the candlestick holders were nothing but empty bottles. And no servants waited on the men gathered there. Everyone helped themselves, like a big family more than a fancy dinner party. And that's the way they liked it.

In the winter, the fire was warm and bright; in the summer, the cider was cool and refreshing. But on this night, the cider had run out. So the men asked their host for something stronger.

"Go ask Jean," Godefroy told them. "He has the key to the cellar."

Jean was Jean Beaugrand, Godefroy's clerk, who lived in the barn out back. He was an older man with a sour disposition. The story says that children in the neighborhood avoided him because he had a habit of talking to himself, mumbling under his breath as he walked through the streets. He was creepy and rude and always kept to himself.

The oddest thing about Jean Beaugrand, though, was his horse. First, it was older than anyone could remember. Even Godefroy, who had been there longer than the rest, remembered the old horse from his childhood in French Detroit. But despite this, the animal still managed to make its way all over the town, eating from gardens and jumping over fences to escape.

The horse—known as Sans Souci to the locals—could apparently jump pretty high, too. Higher than they would expect from a young horse, let alone that ancient, emaciated thing that walked around their neighborhood. One legend claims she jumped a fence over twelve feet high.

But the weirdest thing of all, they say, is how the horse would stand in the street near a crowd of people, and when something humorous was said, Sans Souci would laugh along with everyone else. It was off-putting, to say the least.

So when Godefroy told the men to go find Jean Beaugrand, they didn't really know what to expect. One of the Native Americans volunteered to go look around the property for the man, but when he came back, there was a look of fear on his face.

"He's in the barn," the man told the others. "But he's with that horse. They're sitting at a table together. Laughing. And *talking*."

Everyone glanced around at their neighbors and then chuckled nervously. After a moment of awkward silence, Godefroy himself stood up and motioned to some of the others.

"We'll just see about this," he said coldly.

The group headed around back to the old barn, and then the

men climbed the ladder to the landing outside the loft area. When they reached the top, they peered through a gap in the door and saw something almost otherworldly. The man and the horse were seated together at a table, and they were sharing a cup of some golden liquid. And playing cards.

Godefroy had seen enough. He kicked the door open and barged into the room, along with two of his guests, and that's when all three of them saw something unexplainable: the horse, startled by their sudden entrance, leapt into the air and flew out an open window.

Someone in the crowd accused Jean Beaugrand of witchcraft, but he laughed and flatly denied the charge. "The horse has been in the stable below all evening," he told them. "Go look for yourselves."

The horse was right where he said it would be. So the men dismissed it all as a trick of the light or the result of an evening of drinking. After they had gathered back inside, the night went on as it always did. But still, they couldn't help but wonder if the horse had really flown.

So word spread. Rumors always follow unusual events like that. They are the leaves on the ground that tell us what the tree once looked like. They are the footprints in mud that help us track the animal. They hint that something else is going on.

And the rumor mill was running at full speed in the weeks following. Because the tale of Sans Souci flying out a window into the night seemed to confirm all of their fears. The horse wasn't a horse at all, but a monster of some kind. A shape-shifter, able to take the form of a horse when it wanted, but still able to talk and laugh and act like a person.

It was only weeks later when all of the pieces seemed to fall into place for those who believed the tales. It was later that spring, on the morning of June 11, 1805, that a fire broke out in the stables of a local baker named John Harvey. When it was done, the fire had burned all of Detroit to the ground, save for one lonely warehouse building and a forest of chimneys.

Some people saw more than flames that morning, though.

More than dark smoke and toppling walls. More than the bucket brigade running water from the river to the fires. According to the legend, they saw something else. A little red man, standing atop the Godefroy barn.

And this red man, they say, was laughing.

In the Woods

NOTHING CAN BE as isolating or confining as the woods. They seem to cut us off from the rest of the world, leaving us alone, balanced on the edge of being lost. Even in these thoroughly modern times, the woods seem to exist as a reminder that so much of the world is outside of our control.

Sure, we could stay on the path, but those narrow routes between the trees only give us the *illusion* of control, like a trail of breadcrumbs. They're fragile and fleeting, and somewhere in the back of our minds we understand that if we were to leave the trail, we would be stepping into the unknown.

The woods hide things from us. For centuries, criminals have used the dark cloak of the forest to conceal everything from bootlegging and poaching to drug use and murder. The woods hide wildlife from us, and instill just enough doubt and mystery that we end up believing that anything could be living out there.

Anything.

Some areas, though, are darker than others. In some places, the woods are more than just a gathering of trees and undergrowth. There are locations in our world that are consistently avoided, plagued by rumor and dense with fear. To step into one of these places is to abandon all safety, all reason, and all hope.

THE BRIDGEWATER TRIANGLE

Between the three Massachusetts towns of Abington, Rehoboth, and Freetown exists a triangular slice of land that has become home to hundreds of reports of unexplainable phenomena. It's known as the Bridgewater Triangle, though some call it the Black Triangle or the Devil's Triangle. It might not be swallowing up fighter jets and Colonial-era ships like the Bermuda Triangle far to the south, but its history is just as storied and mysterious.

One of the areas within the Triangle is the Hockomock Swamp. It's a 17,000-acre wetland near Bridgewater, Massachusetts. In the 1600s, it was inhabited by the Wampanoag tribe of Native Americans, and the fort they built inside it became a strategic location for them during King Philip's War in 1674.

One legend details how, during this time of upheaval and invasion by the colonists, a powerful artifact was lost in the swamp. Now, I can't find anything beyond a small Wikipedia entry to confirm this, but the story tells of how an object known as a wampum belt was lost during the war. And as a result, the swamp became a home to restless spirits.

Ever since, the swamp has been the source of a nearly endless supply of unexplainable sightings. One of the most dramatic and best-documented reports was made by a local police officer, Sergeant Thomas Downy.

On a summer night in 1971, Downy was driving toward the town of Easton, near a place known as Bird Hill, which sits at the edge of the swamp. As he approached the hill, he caught sight of an enormous winged creature. Downy claims it was over six feet tall and had a wingspan of almost twelve feet.

After reporting the sighting to the Easton police, he quickly earned the nickname "Birdman." I don't know about you, but it seems odd that a police officer would risk his reputation on such an unusual claim if it was just a joke. Officer Downy clearly saw something that night. Just what that thing was, of course, is open to debate.

Decades earlier, in 1939, a Civilian Conservation Corps crew was working on the edge of the swamp near King Philip's Street. While there, workers claimed to have seen a huge snake as large around and as black as a stovepipe. According to the report, the snake coiled for a moment, raised its head, and then vanished into the swamp.

And what wooded area would be complete without Bigfoot sightings? Although a tall, hairy creature has been sighted dozens of times over the years in various parts of the Bridgewater Triangle, the most common appearances have been near the swamp.

In 1983, John Baker, a local fur trapper, had a similar experience. He was on his canoe in the swamp when he heard a splash. He turned to see "a hairy beast slog into the river and pass within a few yards" of his boat.

In 1978, local man Joe DeAndrade was standing on the shore of a pond known as Clay Banks. He claims that he turned and saw what he described as "a creature that was all brown and hairy, like an apish man-thing." Oddly enough, I went to high school with a guy who fits that description.

But there's been more than just weird animal sightings in the swamp. As far back as the late nineteenth century, locals have reported seeing unusual lights. One report was made by two undertakers who were traveling past the swamp on Halloween night in 1908. They claimed to have seen a light that hovered in the sky for almost an hour.

Whether the reports of creatures and lights are true or not, it might be worth mentioning that the word *hockomock* literally means "the place where spirits dwell."

LIGHTS AND LITTLE PEOPLE

Another hot spot, in the southeastern corner of the triangle, is Freetown State Forest. If all the stories are to be believed, it's the quintessential haunted forest.

Deep inside the park is a cliff, known as Assonet Ledge, that overlooks an old quarry. There have been reports of hauntings near the Ledge, of visions and ghostly figures. Some stories tell of a woman in white who lingers near the precipice. Others claim to have heard voices while visiting there.

The most common report is of mysterious lights. Some researchers think they know exactly where those lights come from, too: they're the tools of a creature known as the pukwudgie.

In ancient Wampanoag folklore, the pukwudgie is a small forest-dwelling creature, something like a troll or a goblin, that lives in the wooded areas around the swamp. Aside from having one of the most entertaining names to say out loud, they are said to be small, hairy people, roughly three feet tall, who hide in the woods and cause trouble for people who discover them.

What kind of trouble? Well, Wampanoag folklore tells of how the pukwudgies used lights to lure travelers into the woods, where they would meet their death. These lights, according to legend, are known as the Tei-Pai-Wankas, a North American version of the English will-o'-the-wisp, sometimes referred to as "ghost lights." Rather than attacking hikers outright, though, apparently the pukwudgies prefer to let the land itself kill their victims.

Coincidentally, one of the most common experiences reported by visitors to the Ledge is an overwhelming urge to jump. Normal, healthy people have felt nearly suicidal standing atop the Ledge. Many of them claim that upon approaching the edge of the cliff, they felt an almost uncontrollable desire to jump off into the dark, rocky water over one hundred feet below.

BILL RUSSO

One story in particular bears retelling. Bill Russo was a welder from Raynham, Massachusetts. He worked long hours, and for the six years prior to his retirement, he worked a late shift from 3:00 p.m. until midnight.

By the time he got home from work each night, Bill's dog, Samantha, would be in desperate need of a walk. So before bed Bill would take her out and let her get some exercise. They kept this habit up, each and every night, no matter the season or weather.

On a night in 1995, Bill took Samantha out for their usual midnight walk. Their typical route was to stay on the sidewalks and head toward the center of town, but on this night Bill decided, on a whim, to cut through his own backyard and head along a trail through the woods alongside the swamp. Not a choice I would have made, mind you, even with a German shepherd–Rottweiler mix as my companion.

About half a mile into their walk, at a place where the path was crossed by a road, Samantha began acting odd. She was tugging at the leash and trembling, and kept glancing back at Bill with worried eyes. Bill tried to lead her home, but the dog wouldn't budge. She just whined and quivered where she stood.

After a moment, Bill began to hear the sound that had frightened his dog. It was a thin, high-pitched voice, faint at first but growing louder as it continued. And even though Bill couldn't understand what the voice was saying, it kept repeating the same sounds.

"Eee wah chu," it seemed to say. "Eee wah chu."

It was midnight in the woods, so of course Bill couldn't see anything. But he tried. He scanned the trees and bushes for whatever could be making the sounds. There was even a streetlight nearby, casting a circle of pale light on the pavement, but he saw nothing there.

Suddenly something stepped into the light. According to Bill, it was perhaps four feet tall, covered in hair, walked on two legs like a human, and looked to weigh no more than a hundred pounds. It was naked and potbellied and looked nothing like anything Bill had ever seen before in the swamp. And as it stepped out of the trees and into the light, it continued to speak to him.

"Eee wah chu," it said again. "Keahr. Keahr."

Bill and Samantha stood frozen to the ground, paralyzed with fear. And as the dog continued to whine and shiver, the creature lifted its arms and beckoned them to follow.

"Eee wah chu," it said again, motioning to them. "Keahr."

Bill claims that he tried asking the creature a few questions, but it only replied with the same nonsense it had already said. Not knowing what else to do, Bill managed to tug Samantha after him, and they both turned and headed home.

They didn't look back.

The Unknown

It's not the trees that make the woods a frightening place. It's what the trees conceal. There's no telling what creatures hide behind the green leaves and thick branches of the forest landscape.

Cryptozoologists, ghost hunters, and believers in the supernatural are often seen as abnormal, as believing in things that can't possibly be real. But when we step into the woods, when we surround ourselves with the dark embrace of the unknown, somehow the impossible begins to seem more likely.

Maybe we want to believe. Maybe that feeling we get in the pit of our stomachs when we step into a strange wooded area is a cry for answers. There has to be something more out there, right? Maybe that's what we all want to know, but we're simply too afraid of the answers.

Bill Russo experienced such a fear on that night in 1995. He and Samantha managed to find their way home safely, but he was beyond shaken up. Even though it was one o'clock in the morning, he went into the kitchen and brewed himself a large pot of coffee. There was no way he was going to let himself sleep that night.

Cup after cup, hour after hour, Bill relived the experience over and over again, playing back everything he had heard and seen. He experienced doubt and fear and regret. He wondered if maybe he should have tried harder to speak with the creature. Perhaps he should have approached it—if Samantha would have allowed him to, that is.

But the question that plagued him the most that night was more difficult: what had the creature been saying to him? Bill wrestled with his memory of those sounds all through the night.

"Eee wah chu," it had said. And then, "Keahr."

Before sunrise, Bill was almost positive that he had his answer. It wasn't another language the creature was speaking, after all; it had been trying its best to use English. And the words it kept repeating?

"We want you," it had been saying. "Come here."

Broken Fingernails

OR MANY CULTURES, the funeral is the last goodbye. It's the final chance to say what needs to be said, or do what needs to be done, in order to honor the ones we've lost. But while the methods and purpose behind these rituals can vary drastically from one culture to the next, one thing is common among the vast majority: the burial.

We bury our dead. We've done it for an incredibly long time, and we've gotten very good at it. Every year, archaeologists open new tombs that date back millennia, each one teaching us something new about the cultures that time has caused us to forget. And central to each of these discoveries is the burial itself. The techniques, the beliefs, the ritual.

But it's not just about the dead. The practice of honoring and burying our loved ones is just as much about our own feelings of loss and grief as it is about our responsibility to care for those who have passed away.

No place personifies the act of burial more than the local cemetery. With their green lawns and neat rows of pale stones, the graveyard is unique among urban constructions. Cemeteries are respectfully avoided by some, obsessed over by others. But whatever beliefs you might hold, whatever opinions you might have about them, graveyards are a special place.

Stephen King explores the allure and power of the graveyard in his novel *Pet Sematary*. In his story, the cemetery is a portal between our world and another. It's a place of transformation, of transition, of mystery. And while we might not be digging shallow graves for our pets in hopes that they'll return to us in the night, we've never lost our fascination with those places.

Cemeteries have always been seen as the end of the journey. Whether you believe in a heaven or not, the graveyard is where most of us will go when our time is up. For some, however, the story doesn't always end there. Some things, it seems, can't be buried.

FERTILE GROUND

For a very long time, burial in Europe was limited to churchyards. It made sense: with a vast majority of Europeans holding to the Christian faith, all of them wanted to be buried close to their place of worship.

Politics held sway even in these quiet, humble places of burial, though. Throughout Europe, it was common to find cemeteries that separated Protestant and Catholic graves. There's a touching example of this near the Dutch town of Roermond, where a couple was buried in the late 1800s. The husband had been Protestant, while the wife held to the Catholic faith. Despite strict rules regarding their burial, the couple managed to cheat the system by picking graves on opposite sides of the dividing wall. Their tall headstones included carved hands that reached out to touch each other.

Economic status played a part in burial as well. Those wealthy enough could purchase space inside the church itself, while the less well-off had to settle for graves outside the church walls. And even then, social status determined where in the yard a person might be buried. The higher the status, the closer to the chapel. But no one wanted to find themselves in the north corner. That was where people of uncertain birth, strangers from out of town, and stillborn infants were buried.

But churches filled up fast, as did the yards around them. As the population of Europe swelled, churchyard space began to disappear at an alarming rate. At first, graves were simply moved closer together, like the parking lot at your local mall. Smaller spaces meant more occupants, and that was good for business. But it only worked for a while.

Next, people opted for the vertical approach: coffins were stacked one atop the next. But as earth was filled in between the newly added graves, the churchyards were rising, sometimes as high as twenty feet.

Greyfriars Cemetery in Edinburgh, Scotland, is a horrific example of this problem. It used to be a depression in the ground, but over time it's become more of a hill. With more than half a million recorded burials, the cemetery has risen over fifteen feet in elevation, introducing problems that are unique to a graveyard so old and so full. According to reports, there's such a high concentration of human remains that on especially rainy days, remains that aren't sealed within a casket have a tendency to float to the surface, bursting through the mud like white teeth.

All of this left cities in need of some seriously creative thinking. In some places, the solution they chose was a drastic one. In France, for example, the government actually had to step in. Churchyards had gotten so full that they would often collapse outward, spilling soil and human remains onto the streets. Walls were built around them, but they rarely worked. The dead were getting out of hand, so to speak. In 1786, they removed all the bodies from Holy Innocents Cemetery in Paris and moved them to a series of disused stone quarries that became known as the Catacombs. It's estimated that the Catacombs hold close to six million bodies.

Sometimes it wasn't a lack of space that ruined a cemetery, but a lack of popularity. That's the fate that awaited the cemetery built on the former property of Sir William Ashhurst in the north end of London. Named for the small hilltop community that once existed there, Highgate Cemetery was established on the grounds of the old manor house, which had been demolished and replaced with a church in 1839.

At first the cemetery was popular. Karl Marx is buried there, as are many relatives of Charles Dickens and Dante Rossetti. But when the owners lost money and fell on hard times, the graveyard was left to the elements. Monuments and crypts became overgrown with vegetation, and sometimes trees would sprout up right through the graves themselves.

Highgate is a wonderful example of what we all imagine a haunted cemetery might look like. Filmmakers and authors have been drawn to it for decades, tapping into its arresting visual atmosphere to create works of gothic horror and fantasy. It was even the inspiration behind Neil Gaiman's beautiful novel *The Graveyard Book*.

But while there are plenty of stories about the history of graveyards throughout Europe and America, cemeteries have always been known for something darker, something less tangible than what we can see above ground. Perhaps it's all those neat rows of bone-white headstones, or the notion that hundreds of bodies lie waiting beneath our feet.

Whatever the reason, it's in the local graveyard, more than any other place, that we find rumors of the otherworldly and unexplainable. Inside those walls, between the pale stones and dark trees, almost everyone has heard tales of those who refuse to stay in the grave.

Buried or not, sometimes the past is too traumatic to leave us.

HERE AND THERE

Just south of Chicago, between the curving arms of I-80 and I-294, is a graveyard known for a level of activity unusual in a place of the dead. Bachelor's Grove Cemetery isn't big; there are only eighty-two plots there, and many of those have never even been used. But that hasn't stopped the stories.

It's said that the famous gangster Al Capone used to use the pond nearby as a dumping place for the bodies of those he had killed. Other rumors make reference to satanic rituals and meetings that have taken place in the graveyard over the years. But there are those who swear they have seen unusual things there.

The most famous sighting has been called the White Lady, the ghostly image of a woman that was said to appear only during a full moon. In 1991, the *Chicago Sun-Times* featured a photo of the White Lady on the front page, taken by a researcher on one of her visits. The woman appears to be semi-transparent, sitting on a tombstone near the trees, and dressed in white. Other visitors have seen glowing orbs, apparitions, and even vehicles and a farmhouse that seem to fade in and out of existence. The site is off-limits to visitors now, but it's remained a favorite haunt—no pun intended—of ghost hunters across the country.

In 1863, an outbreak of smallpox moved through a Civil War POW camp in Columbus, Ohio. The camp held close to ten thousand Confederate soldiers, and thousands of them died from the epidemic. As a result, the Camp Chase Confederate Cemetery was formed—unusual in that the site was so far north into Union territory.

Miles away, in New Madrid, Missouri, a Confederate sympathizer sent his young daughter north to avoid the destruction caused by the war. Louisiana Briggs settled in Ohio and eventually married a Union veteran, but she apparently never lost touch with her southern roots. It was said that later in life she would often visit the Camp Chase Cemetery, where she would place flowers on various graves there. She wore a white veil each time she went, in an effort to hide her face. Nevertheless, she acquired a reputation in town as the Gray Lady, and was known for her passion for the old burial ground.

She passed away in 1950, but flowers would still appear regularly on the graves there. Visitors to Camp Chase have heard the sounds of a woman quietly weeping, while others have seen the figure of a woman in a veil. Something drew Louisiana Briggs to that location; that much is clear. According to the stories, though, she never left.

Across the country in Connecticut, yet another graveyard plays host to a mysterious story. Mary Hart was born in New Haven in 1824 and lived a very modest life there. She was a corset maker and machine stitcher by trade, working hard to support her family.

On October 15, 1872, Mary fell into a deathlike state from an unknown cause. She was only forty-seven—young even for the late nineteenth century—and this tragedy rocked her family to the core. By midnight Mary had expired, and her grieving family set about to arrange for a quick and immediate burial. There was a lot of pain, and I can imagine they just wanted to get it over with.

It's said that Mary's spirit still wanders Evergreen Cemetery, close to the site of her home on Winthrop Avenue. More than one story has been told about drivers pulling over to pick up a hitch-hiking woman, only to have her disappear.

Others say Mary was a witch, although you didn't have to look far in the late 1800s to find a woman who had been accused of something like that. According to the stories, local college students have frequently visited Mary's grave, which is said to be cursed. Anyone who visits her grave at midnight, goes the legend, will meet a horrible fate. As a result, most people refer to her today as Midnight Mary.

There are no records of New Haven college students who've died after visiting Mary's gravesite. But whether or not the stories are rooted in fact, it hasn't stopped them from spreading. Mary still has one foot in our world, it seems. It's just not clear who's keeping her here.

RUTH'S STORY

South Cemetery in Portsmouth, New Hampshire, is really a collection of many smaller graveyards. It's the site of the oldest burial ground in town, dating back to the 1600s, and is a wonderful mixture of styles and centuries. Together, the old Auburn Cemetery, the Proprietor's Burial Ground, Sagamore Cemetery, and Harmony Grove all combine to showcase everything from an Egyptian-style sarcophagus to winged skulls and Victorian funerary imagery.

It's a peaceful place, and much of the grounds have been planted with flowering trees, creating a parklike atmosphere. But that wasn't always the case. In the 1700s, South Cemetery served double duty as both a graveyard and the site of several public executions. All of them were hangings, and more than a few of them were women. And the reasons were often tragic.

The early eighteenth century was a very different era from our own, and the law books were filled with rules that might seem barbaric or cruel by today's standards. Provincial laws of the time required capital punishment for a wide assortment of crimes—close to six hundred of them, in fact—including murder, rape, abortion, bestiality, burglary, treason, and counterfeiting. Another capital crime, though, was known as concealment.

If a woman found herself pregnant outside of marriage in the mid-1700s, her life was effectively over. Social stigma, loss of employment, fines, and even physical punishment were all expected to follow upon discovery of adultery and the possible resulting bastard birth. To avoid this fate, it had become common for women in that situation to hide their pregnancy, and then abandon the newborn baby to die of neglect and exposure.

This was concealment. And it was the situation that a woman from South Hampton, New Hampshire, found herself in during the spring of 1768. Ruth Blay was twenty-five and split her time between teaching in the nearby towns and working as a seamstress. She was single and poor, but she did her best to hide the pregnancy for as long as she could.

No one knows where she gave birth to the child. We don't know if she labored alone, with no hand to hold or companion to help her through it. All history remembers is the baby, but even then, there are still questions.

According to Ruth, the baby had been stillborn. It didn't erase her crime of adultery, of course, or the stigma that was sure to follow, but it did mean that she didn't kill the child. She had been afraid, and so she buried the tiny body beneath the floorboards of a local barn, most likely the site of one of her traveling classrooms. And that, she thought, was the end of it.

But what Ruth didn't know was that some of her local students had watched her bury the child's body. They didn't see the birth itself. They didn't feel her pain and loss and fear and hopelessness.

All they saw was a young woman placing a body in the space beneath a loose board. They saw a crime, and so they reported it.

Ruth was soon arrested by Isaac Brown, the local constable, and was quickly brought to trial. A jury was formed—all men, of course—and they soon ruled that the child had died by violence after birth. Ruth, they said, was a liar. And a murderer.

Ruth was held at the constable's home until she could be transported to the jail in Portsmouth. But she was still recovering from the birth, and so she remained there for over a month while her body healed. By July 19, she had been formally accused, and two weeks later she was brought before the provincial court. She pleaded innocent, of course, but no one listened. Her final trial date was set for nearly two months later, toward the end of September.

I can't imagine how lonely she must have felt, how hopeless. Ruth didn't have a chance; I think it's safe to assume she knew that. Society wasn't kind to women in her position, and when you added in the dead infant . . . well, Ruth was pretty sure how it was going to end.

Her trial began on the afternoon of September 21, 1768, and a little over twelve hours later, the jury handed down their verdict: guilty. She was, according to their instructions, "to hang by her neck until dead." But not just yet.

No, the royal governor of New Hampshire, a man named John Wentworth, issued three consecutive reprieves, postponing her execution. He said it was to give her time to prepare herself for death, but I can't help but wonder if it was really just one more punishment. Rather than walking to the gallows before the end of September, Ruth would have to wait three long months.

Just before noon on December 30, over a thousand people gathered at Gallows Hill in South Cemetery. It had snowed earlier that day, and now a cold, freezing rain was covering everything in a layer of ice. Sheriff Packard, the man presiding over the execution, had Ruth placed atop the back of a wagon, a rope draped around her neck. Parents stood with their arms around their children, who craned their necks to catch a glimpse of the woman about to die.

There are rumors that a pardon was on its way from the governor but that Sheriff Packard was in a hurry to eat his lunch, so he rushed the execution rather than waiting for the governor's letter to arrive. At noon, the horses pulling the wagon were driven away from the tree, and Ruth Blay fell off the back, where her body swung slowly at the end of the noose. She died soon after.

Those same rumors say the governor's stay of execution did arrive, just moments after Ruth's body stopped moving, but there's no record of a pardon. Instead of freedom, Ruth was given an unmarked grave about three hundred feet north of the small pond in the middle of the cemetery.

Today, visitors to the pond report anomalies in their photos: ghostly images, orbs, and indefinable shapes. Some say their cameras stopped working altogether. According to local legend, a pair of glowing lights has been seen there, and some think it's Ruth and her infant child.

STAYING BURIED

Between life and death, between the places most familiar to us and that vast expanse of the unknown, sits the graveyard. It has represented the beginning of a journey for countless cultures across the history of humankind. From the Egyptians to the khans, from ancient Europe to modern America, the cemetery is a constant thread, tying us all together.

Philosophy aside, these are places born out of loss and filled with deep emotion. And so it's no wonder that so many stories exist of the ones who refuse to stay buried. Maybe ghosts are real after all, or maybe we just wish they were. Perhaps it's both.

One final note: Midnight Mary, the New Haven corset maker who fell into a coma at the age of forty-seven, was buried on October 16, 1872. That night, after the funeral was over and her extended family had traveled back to their homes, Mary's aunt had a horrible nightmare.

In her dream, she saw Mary still alive in her coffin, scratching at the lining in an effort to get out. She was screaming and moan-

ing with desperation, and the image of that stayed with Mary's aunt long after she awoke. So much so that she managed to convince both her family and the authorities to exhume Mary's grave.

After the coffin was removed from the earth, the men opened it. What they found inside would haunt them for the rest of their lives: Mary's corpse had moved. Her hands were covered in blood and many of her fingernails were broken. The reason was clear after examining the coffin's lid.

The cloth lining had been shredded. Apparently Mary had finally awoken from her coma, and in her panic, she had tried to claw her way out.

Going Viral

ON AUGUST 31, 1944, a man in southern Illinois woke up in the middle of the night to the smell of something . . . *odd*. It wasn't a skunk, or the telltale odor of smoke from something burning. This was different. Partly because of the acrid, almost *venomous* nature of the smell. But mostly because of the effect it had on him.

The man said that the smell left him feeling weak and nauseous, and that it induced a violent fit of vomiting. His wife didn't fare any better. She wondered if maybe their gas stove was still on, so she tried to get out of bed and go check on it. But she couldn't. In fact, she seemed to be completely paralyzed.

The next day, another resident of the same town reported a similar experience: an odd smell followed by paralyzing effects. Day after day, more reports just like those trickled in. The result, as you might imagine, was group panic. And everyone wanted to find the person responsible. They called him the Mad Gasser of Mattoon, and even now—over seventy years later—no one's really sure what happened.

It's amazing how quickly hysteria can spread, isn't it? One minute there's nothing, and the next, an entire community is wrapped up in something dark and horrifying. It might be political panic, or religious fervor, or a simple, primal fear of the unexplained. Whatever its flavor, it always has the potential to be powerful. Sometimes even deadly.

Over two centuries ago, something took place that fit the definition of hysteria to the letter, but with a *twist*. This event had more depth and more power than usual. In fact, it had everything a good folktale needs: cryptids, and witchcraft, and ghosts, oh my. But it also had something else. Something that's helped it survive to this day.

You see, with hundreds of witnesses on record, this one just might be *true*.

Unknown Territory

The first British settlers along the Atlantic coast of North America stayed pretty close to the ocean, and for good reason. Those early colonies were deeply dependent on ships from England to bring them supplies and help, and to stray too far from the Atlantic meant putting yourself and your family at risk.

But as time went on, settlers felt more and more comfortable moving farther inland. They followed the rivers. They aimed for the mountains they could see on the western horizon. They chased the dream of wide-open territory, ripe for the taking. Which wasn't a pleasant idea for the tens of thousands of Native Americans who already called those lands home, and had done for millennia.

The British issued the Proclamation of 1763, which prohibited moving westward past the Appalachian Mountains. But when the British were forced out after the American Revolution, that political borderline evaporated. Thousands of newly independent Americans flooded westward, and by 1800, places like Kentucky and Tennessee had been transformed from wilderness into rustic civilization.

By the time John and Lucy Bell rolled into the newly formed state of Tennessee in 1804, there were already a good number of people there waiting for them. Not that they needed more company; John and Lucy were traveling with five of their children.

Their oldest wasn't with them, having gotten married before the family left North Carolina.

True to the social climate of the pre–Civil War South, the family also traveled with a number of slaves—nine, by most accounts. The entire group aimed for the flatlands around the Red River, where a number of other settlers had put down roots. And then they did what settlers are born to do: they built a new life in a strange place. A couple of years later, they welcomed another daughter. Then a son. Then another son. And as the family was growing, they also deepened their friendship with the neighboring family, the Gunns.

In 1817, something unusual happened to John. He was out in the cornfield one day when he looked up to see an odd animal a dozen or so yards away. It was odd because it seemed to be a mixture of two very different creatures. The body was very clearly that of a dog. The head, though . . . well, John was sure it was a rabbit.

John raised his gun—no settler on the edge of civilization went anywhere without a gun, after all—and fired at the unusual creature. The shot missed, so he fired again. And again. But whatever it was just turned and ran off toward the woods.

By the time he walked back into the farmhouse that evening for dinner, he'd almost forgotten about it. There was a lot on his mind: the crops, the livestock, the approaching winter. Being a practical man, he wasn't one to dwell on what had so clearly been a figment of his imagination. That, however, is when they heard the noises.

The sounds came from outside and sounded, for all they could tell, like someone was beating on the house. They ran out to see who it was, but found nothing. A few days later, John's son Andrew was outside when he saw what he described as a giant turkey. It was larger than any bird he'd ever seen before, but it flew away before he could shoot it.

Not long after that, John's daughter Elizabeth, known as Betsy, claimed to have seen a dead woman hanging from a tree on the property. She was just eleven, and the sight of it frightened her enough to send her running back to the house, but when she glanced back over her shoulder, there was nothing there.

One of the most unusual stories came from one of their slaves, a man named Dean. Years before, he had found true love with another slave at the nearby Gunn farm, and the couple had married shortly after that. And so each night, after Dean finished his work, he would walk over to the Gunns' to see his wife and spend time with her.

It was always late when he came back. Late, and dark. But even though the frontier wasn't the safest place to walk alone, Dean knew the road well enough. It's just that . . . well . . . lately he had been seeing things that didn't seem normal. One thing, specifically. A dog. Every night on his return trip home, a large black dog would step out of the darkness and cross his path. It wasn't random, according to Dean. It was regular, happening each night, and had for at least a week before he reported it.

Large and unusual animals on the property. Noises. Visions of dead people. Ominous black dogs. None of it was comforting, and all of it went on for months. But they could always run home, shut the door, and feel safe again. It was upsetting, sure, but at least it was containable.

And that's when the unexplainable moved *inside* the house.

Close Encounters

At first it was just knocking sounds. They seemed to creep in through the walls like a winter chill. Odd sounds in a distant part of the house, always without an explanation. But then it changed. Or maybe it *adapted* . . . it all depends on how you look at it, I suppose. Because not long after the noises moved indoors, the children began to complain about disturbances in the night.

It sounded to them like rats were chewing on their bedposts. Some of the children claimed they could hear chains being dragged around the house. Others said that their blankets were being pulled off them while they slept.

On at least one occasion, Betsy ran into her parents' room in the middle of the night, crying hysterically. They lit a lantern and discovered that she was covered in red welts and bruises, as if she'd been beaten. That night set off a string of attacks that all seemed focused on her . . . noises that followed her, physical assaults, visions.

This new focus wasn't contained to the house, either. One story tells of how Betsy even tried spending the night at the home of a school friend. She hoped the distance would help. She hoped it—whatever *it* was—would leave her alone. But it followed her. It always followed her.

One other odd symptom of these unexplainable attacks was that John began to have trouble eating. He said it was like his tongue had a mind of its own. He would put food into his mouth, but it would be pushed back out. It didn't happen all the time, but once was enough to put him on edge.

John Bell was apparently a patient man. For a long while, he assumed all the trouble would soon go away and eventually be forgotten. For over a year, he and his family bravely endured their mysterious torment. The beatings. The noises. The blankets and chains and all of it. But when Betsy's friends found out, word began to spread. And John didn't like that, because he had a reputation to maintain.

That might seem selfish, I know. On the surface, it looks like John was content to do nothing while his family suffered. And then, the moment his reputation seemed to be at risk, he gave in and started to worry. But before you judge him, you have to keep in mind the common beliefs of the time, especially in his part of the country.

This all took place long after the witchcraft panic of the seventeenth century had died out. The Salem trials were the last of their kind in America, and those had taken place over 125 years before the Bells began having odd experiences. But on the edges of the frontier, away from the civilized, modern cities of the coast, old superstition still ran deep.

So deep, in fact, that half a century later, in the very same town as the Bells, a man named James Smith would be murdered. The reason, according to his killers, was that Smith was a *witch*. So yes, John Bell's obsession with his reputation does seem a little petty, but it was also rooted in self-preservation.

To find help, John called on his local minister, James Johnston. Johnston arrived later that day with his wife, and the couple agreed to spend the night at the farmhouse and offer their own opinion on the activity. And they apparently had a plan to help with whatever might come their way.

After dinner, the Johnstons led the Bell family through a selection of Bible readings, and then followed that up with a few hymns and a prayer of blessing for the house and the people inside it. Then, with the evening at an end, everyone retired to their rooms for the night.

It was only when the lights went out and darkness took over that the invisible force became active. And that night, it seems, the focus would be on the newcomers. The Johnstons woke to the sound of loud noises, and then later their blankets were pulled off the bed.

Frustrated and more than a little frightened, the minister jumped out of bed and shouted into the darkness, "In the name of the Lord, who are you, and what do you want?"

His demand was met with silence. No more noises. No invisible forces tugging on the blankets. Just silence. But that silence wouldn't last long. In fact, it turned out to be the calm before the storm.

Within hours, the spirit did something that no one in the house expected. It *spoke*.

A Voice in the Wilderness

When the Bell family gathered for breakfast the following morning, the Johnstons joined them. There was conversation about the previous night. There were panicked looks. There were frustration and fear and a lot of hopelessness. If the minister couldn't help them, what chance did they have?

It was during that conversation that something unexpected happened. Something that defied all laws of nature. Because according to everyone at the table, that's the moment when the spirit in the house actually spoke to them.

What did it say? Well, it appears to have taken a liking to the words of the minister. The otherworldly, disembodied voice repeated back, word for word, the Bible passages the group had listened to the night before. It repeated the prayers, too. And then it vanished.

After that, word spread fast. John and Lucy received a letter from their oldest daughter back in North Carolina, who mentioned hearing of their troubles from someone else. This was more than just a bit of family drama now. It was a public spectacle. And the odd occurrences kept piling up.

Weeks later, the Bells hosted two local ministers for lunch on a Sunday afternoon. The two men were from churches separated by thirteen miles, and both had preached their sermons at the same time that day. Yet the spirit seemed to have heard both, reciting each of them back to the people gathered at the table.

Which didn't help solve the mystery. Because if we assume one of the older children was responsible for all of this, then how could that one person have listened to—and memorized—two sermons so far apart at the same time?

Of course, they tried to figure out who or what the spirit was. Some thought maybe it was the ghost of a local Native American, angry about the settlers' presence. Others thought it was the demonic spirit that inhabited a local witch. The voice even identified herself as Kate, apparently named in honor of the witch in question. But having a name didn't make the problem go away.

Things began to escalate. It got so bad that the family started to discuss moving away. Some of the older children suggested returning to North Carolina. Others didn't care where they went; they just wanted to leave the farmhouse forever. But could they really get away from it?

The spirit did, however, reveal a helpful side at least once during the spring of 1820. That's when Betsy's mother, Lucy, became horribly sick with a lung infection. It hurt to cough. It hurt to breathe. And she wasn't getting better.

That's when Kate, if that was her name, literally dropped a remedy in Lucy's hands. Grapes and hazelnuts, which at the time were thought to have powerful medicinal qualities, simply appeared out of thin air. Lucy apparently recovered a short while later.

The worst of it all, however, fell on John Bell. Maybe it was because he was the most prideful and resistant to believing the spirit actually existed. Perhaps it was because he was the one dragging the local church into the situation. All we know is that the spirit did not care one bit for John.

Sometimes it was verbal. Insults would often be heard shouted at him from thin air. He was called names and told that his life wasn't worth carrying on, that he should end it. Other times, though, the spirit became violent. And that odd thing with his tongue returned in force, leaving him unable to eat or even speak.

Whether it was the lack of food or some other influence from the spirit, John spent much of 1820 very ill. By autumn, he was forced to spend over a month resting in bed. When he did recover, it wasn't for long, but John tried to make the most of it.

His son Richard told the story of how John followed him outside one day when he needed to check on the pigs. I can imagine John was feeling a bit helpless and just wanted to contribute. Farms are a lot of work, after all. But while they were out of the house, Kate decided to attack.

First it was his shoes. Richard described how, no matter how tightly John tied the laces, his father's shoes would fly off his feet. When they turned around to return to the house, Kate slapped John across the face. The older man sat down to recover himself, and the spirit filled the air with laughter and song.

In early December 1820 he took a turn for the worse and took to his bed again. On the nineteenth, John slipped into a coma, and no matter what the family or neighbors did, they couldn't wake him up. They didn't know what had brought it on, but they had a theory.

John's wife, Lucy, found a small glass vial among their household medicines, but she had never seen it before. There was a dark liquid inside it . . . or at least there had been. There wasn't much of it left. So Lucy did what any desperate person would do in her situation: she shouted out to the spirit for answers. What was this mysterious medicine?

The spirit refused to tell Lucy what it was, but she admitted giving it to John the night before. Horrified, Lucy opened the vial and gave the last few drops to one of the cats, who died just moments later. The following day, John's breathing slowed and his heartbeat became harder and harder to find. Finally, hours later, it stopped for good.

The Infection

If fear were a virus, it would be declared highly infectious by the Centers for Disease Control. Fear has this way of spreading from person to person like the common cold in a grade-school classroom. Give fear enough time, and it'll infect everyone in the room, or the house, or the *town*.

Which is why we have folklore. Because folklore has this way of inoculating us against fear. It provides us with explanations and answers when there's just too much mystery. Folklore creates the illusion of logic, and that can stop the spread of fear.

Unless, of course, that folklore is more frightening than the mystery it explains. It's hard enough to not be afraid of odd noises in your own home. But when the only explanation involves evil spirits and witchcraft . . . well, you can see how that might fan the flames.

Of course, it could all have been a hoax. History is full of hoaxes that prey on the fears of the superstitious. It's possible that a few of the Bell children were in on that hoax, and that they somehow managed to work together to pull it all off. It's also possible that the whole family sat down, planned it out, and then performed the entire mystery. But for what reason?

It's been two centuries since those events, and we still don't know what really happened. What we do know, however, is that the stories have fascinated people—and still do. Even while they were taking place, word spread far enough that hundreds of people traveled to witness them firsthand. And most of them got what they wished for.

One story stands out above all the others. Five years before the events on the Bell farm, John's three oldest sons fought in the War of 1812. They were participants in the Battle of New Orleans, serving under General Andrew Jackson. So when the spirit's reputation reached Jackson's ear, he decided to come see it for himself.

He arrived one day in 1819, along with several other travel companions. Just outside the Bell farm, though, their wagon became stuck. The men worked hard to make sure none of the wheels was caught on a rock or in thick mud, but no matter what they did, they couldn't get the wagon to roll free.

That's when a voice spoke up and welcomed Jackson and his friends to the farm. A voice without a body. It called itself Kate, and told them it would see them all later that evening. After that, the wagon miraculously unstuck itself, and they were able to move on.

One of Jackson's friends didn't care for the suggestion that there was something supernatural going on at the farm. Later that night after dinner, the man waved his pistol around in the air, claiming there was a silver bullet in the chamber and threatening to shoot the spirit or witch or whatever it was.

Instead, the man was struck with a fit of seizures. He shouted out that someone was poking him with needles. That he was being beaten violently. But no one was touching him. Then the front door of the house opened on its own, and the man was kicked out into the night by an invisible force.

Jackson and his men left the following morning.

The Red Coats

I F YOU LIVED there, you just sort of accepted the fact that at some point, things were going to disappear. But of course, that was the price you had to pay if you wanted to live in one of the most beautiful parts of Maine.

It was a vast expanse of old-growth forest, just twenty miles north of Augusta, Maine's capital city. Those miles and miles of deep green treetops are broken only by the occasional lake—Great Pond, East Pond, The Narrows. And for as long as anyone could remember, if you had a cabin in that area, you'd be wise to lock it up, because things had a way of going missing.

Then, on April 4, 2013, a police officer responded to a silent alarm in a cabin at a summer camp called Pine Tree. Minutes later, he arrived and caught the thief. His name was Christopher Thomas Knight. He'd lived there in the forest for nearly thirty years, subsisting entirely off nature and stolen supplies—and he'd been perfectly happy doing so.

Until his arrest, though, he was just one of hundreds of people who step into America's forests each year and just . . . *vanish*. After he'd gone missing, everyone had just assumed Knight was dead. Because when you slip away like that—into the dark embrace of the wild and wooded backcountry—your chances are pretty slim.

We humans have tamed much of the world with our roads and maps, but there are still a lot of unknown places out there. And the unknown always has a way of inspiring fear. Add in the chance of disappearing and never coming back, and the woods can be downright terrifying.

Some locations, though, seem to attract a disproportionate amount of mystery. They act like magnets for tragedy, or a dark beacon designed to lure people to their doom. And one of the most mysterious places of all is right here in the wilds of New England.

So let's take a walk. Let's wander along the trail, and explore the shadows within the trees. But watch your step; you never know what's waiting for you just beyond the edges of the path.

BOUNDARIES

Benning Wentworth was a greedy, egotistical man, which made him a perfect fit for the age of British colonial expansion in the New World. In 1741, at the age of forty-five, he was appointed governor of the colony of New Hampshire. Eight years later the crown gave him the power to distribute land grants.

In 1761, he drew up charters for new territory that would one day become Vermont, arbitrarily drawing township squares all over the map. One of those random boundaries was drawn around a mountain in the southwestern corner of the state, just northeast of Bennington, a town named by Benning Wentworth after himself. And this mountain, and the township around it, borrowed a magical name from England: Glastenbury.

This mountain is an interesting piece of folklore jutting up from the landscape. Long before the British began to spread into the region, the land there belonged to the Algonquin nation of Native Americans, specifically the Abenaki tribe. And they have stories about the mountain there. Stories that are not tourist-friendly.

The Abenaki stayed away from the top of the mountain because they believed it was cursed. Hunters would frequently get lost there, thanks in part to the erratic wind that seemed to change direction every few minutes.

But the biggest reason for staying away was the legend of an enchanted stone. They say it looked like any other boulder on the mountain, but if you were unlucky enough to step on it, you would vanish into thin air. So quickly, in fact, that you wouldn't even have time to scream.

Because of all of that, when the first European settlers arrived in southern Vermont, the Abenaki strongly urged them to avoid settling on the mountain. Which, of course, they did anyway. In 1791, at the time of the first state census, Glastenbury township had a total of six families living there. But it wasn't until the Civil War was over that the population broke one hundred.

That's when people started to realize, "Hey, there are a lot of trees here!" So they built a sawmill. And then another. Soon they were building kilns, too—dozens of them, all running nonstop to create charcoal that was then exported to places like New York for use in iron production. And with all that economic growth came a lot more people.

In 1872 the Bennington-Glastenbury Railroad was constructed as a way to move the charcoal down the mountain faster, and to bring settlers back up. But wherever humans gather in large numbers, so does darkness. It's like a cloud that follows us around. Wherever we build communities, tragedy and loss and death just sort of come with the package.

In 1892, a sawmill worker named Henry McDowell attacked another man, John Crawley, by picking up a rock and beating him to death. Before the authorities could capture McDowell, he skipped town and headed south. He made it as far as South Norwalk, Connecticut, before he was taken into custody, but it only got weirder from there.

He confessed to the murder, but blamed it on the voices in his head. They wouldn't stop, he said, and they wanted him to kill again. So he was returned to Vermont and placed in the state asylum there. For a while, at least.

Local legend says that McDowell escaped the facility and made his way back to Glastenbury by hiding on one of the train cars that headed up the mountain. If the legends are true, he lived out the rest of his days right there in the forest.

Five years later, in 1897, John Harbour and his brother Harry were out hunting just south of Glastenbury Mountain. They had separated a bit, although in the forest all you really needed was a few dozen feet of distance before you felt isolated and alone. At one point, Harry heard a gun go off, and then a cry for help from somewhere nearby. "I've been shot!" the voice of John shouted.

Harry searched the area, but he couldn't find his brother. He gathered some friends to help, but still had no luck. It wasn't until the following morning that they finally stumbled upon his body. But there was something not quite right about the scene they discovered.

First, John's body was found lying under the wide branches of an old cedar tree with his rifle beside him. But the gun was loaded and seemed to be just out of reach, as if someone else had placed it there later. And there were also drag marks in the pine needles and dirt, indicating that John had been dragged to the tree.

No one ever figured out how John Harbour had been killed. No other hunter came forward to confess to having accidentally shot the man, and no other clues came to light. It was a murder, that much was clear, but it would forever remain a tragic cold case.

Which, in most other towns, might stand out on the pages of local history as a major story. But Glastenbury wasn't like most towns. The people there were no strangers to unusual occurrences. Yes, John Harbour's death was mysterious, but it wasn't the first time something unexplainable had happened.

And, tragically, it wouldn't be the last.

OFF THE TRAIL

There's a story about something that happened near Glastenbury way back in the middle of the nineteenth century, a few decades before the murders of John Crawley and John Harbour. If it's true, though, it paints a frightening backdrop for a lot of the events that followed through the years.

Before the train route was constructed between Bennington and Glastenbury, people who didn't want to hike all the way up the mountain were transported by stagecoach. On one particular day the trip departed Bennington late in the evening, and by the time they were halfway to their destination, the skies had opened up and a torrential downpour had begun to fall.

Glastenbury Mountain wasn't a great place to be in weather like that. The mountain is steep, rising an average of 250 feet every mile. The stagecoach would have been making that journey on a wide dirt path—dirt that would have quickly transformed into mud as the rain continued to fall.

First the driver slowed down, but then he was forced to pull over and stop. Despite the rain, he picked up his glass-enclosed lantern and climbed down from his seat. Then, careful not to slip, he began to inspect the wheels and the depth of the mud they were buried in. And that's when he noticed something odd.

There were footprints in the mud around the coach. Footprints that were much larger than his own, and if the impressions were any indication, the feet that made them weren't wearing shoes. So, like any expendable extra in a horror flick, he turned and followed them, only to discover that they vanished into the forest.

That's when something large and powerful slammed against the side of the carriage. Passengers began to exit the coach, spilling out into the mud and rain. A moment later, the stagecoach toppled onto its side. Then, slowly emerging from the darkness at the side of the road, a shape stepped into the weak lantern light.

They say it was tall, perhaps two heads taller than a grown man. The thing was covered entirely in wet, matted hair, and its eyes seemed to reflect a yellow light back from the lantern. For a long, tense moment, the creature stood there beside the wreckage of the overturned stagecoach before turning away, blending into the shadows once again.

Life in Glastenbury was certainly never boring. Between the nighttime encounter with what would become known as the Bennington Monster and the murders to follow a couple of decades later, people in the area never really felt completely safe in their isolated woodland community.

But there was more to worry about than mysterious creatures. Glastenbury, you see, was dying. It was inevitable, really. When your only business is cutting down trees, chopping them up, and then burning them, it has a way of transforming a place. By the late 1880s, all the local forest was gone, stripped away by the economic greed of the town.

They tried to fight it, though. Beginning in 1894, everything was reinvented with an eye toward bringing in summer tourists. The old coal-powered train was converted over to electric passenger trolleys. Buildings in town were gutted and remodeled to serve as hotels and a casino. It was expensive, sure, but it was also their only hope. If they could no longer sell the forest, they had to market something else to the public.

And for one season, it worked. During the summer of 1897, scores of people traveled from far and wide to experience life in a frontier resort town. The hotels were full, and the casino offered ample entertainment. But a mountain stripped of its forest is a mountain ill-prepared for spring, and when the calendar rolled around and the snow began to melt, something happened.

A *flood*. The technical term for it is *freshet*, when snow and rain overfill a river and cause flooding. And in the spring of 1898, a powerful flood rushed down the mountainside and washed away the trolley tracks. In one tragic moment, the town's new lifeline had been severed, and like a garden without water, everything began to dry up and die.

Over the years to come, Glastenbury all but vanished. The hotels and casino fell apart. Homes disintegrated until nothing but their foundation stones remained. By the 1930s, the entire population of Glastenbury consisted of just three people: Ira Mattison, his wife, and his mother. In 1937, Glastenbury became the first town in Vermont to be officially disorganized. And then, for the next two decades, it was empty.

Well, not entirely. You see, the trees eventually returned, and with them came that siren's call that lures people into the woods. Except these were probably not the best woods to wander around in—the Abenaki had been pretty clear about that, after all. Nevertheless, people returned to Glastenbury Mountain. But when they did, they discovered a very difficult truth.

It seemed that the darkness that inhabited the mountain had never really left.

LONG GONE

On November 11, 1943, two men went hunting just north of Glastenbury Mountain. There was a chill in the air that morning as Carl Herrick and his cousin Henry set up their camp, and then the men grabbed their rifles and headed out into the woods. It was deer season, and they wanted to make the most of their time.

During the hunt, the men split up. It was a common thing to do, even though it left each of them alone in a forest full of dangers. By afternoon, Henry had given up and wandered back to their camp, but Carl wasn't there yet. So he waited.

When daylight had faded into that hazy gray twilight between day and night, Henry finally decided something was wrong. So he hiked his way back out of the trees and ran to the police. Shortly thereafter a search party returned to the woods near the campsite to begin looking for Carl.

It took them three days. Three days of slowly walking through the trees. Three days in the snow and cold. Three days of worry. But in the end, they found him. Carl's body was lying flat on the ground, and his rifle was nearly a hundred feet away, just leaning against a tree.

Interestingly, the ground around his body was covered in enormous footprints. The hunters who found him weren't sure what sort of animal had made them, but they guessed it had been a bear. Which was odd, because Carl Herrick hadn't been mauled or injured in any way consistent with a bear attack.

He'd been *squeezed* to death.

Sadly, Carl wouldn't be the last to experience the dangerous nature of the woods around Glastenbury Mountain. Just two years later, in 1945, a seventy-four-year-old hunting guide named Middie Rivers was leading a group of visiting hunters through the trees when he slipped out of view ahead of them. One of the others hurried to catch up to Rivers, but he wasn't there. After searching for over a month, locals gave up hope. No one ever saw Middie Rivers again.

Paula Welden was the next to go missing. A year after Rivers vanished into the unknown, Paula left her college dorm in Bennington to go for a hike. At 3:00 p.m. on December 1, she pulled on her bright red jacket and hiking shoes, and set off on the well-known Long Trail, where many people remembered seeing her. But she never returned.

One elderly couple who noticed her that day claimed that she had been about a hundred yards ahead of them, but they lost sight of her when she rounded a bend where two trails intersected. When they reached the same crossing, they were surprised to no longer see her. She'd simply vanished.

There was a massive search effort. There was a large cash reward. They had helicopters and dogs and over a thousand people. Everything that *could* have been done to find her *was* done. And with that bright red jacket on, you'd think she'd be easy to spot. But after three long weeks of fruitless searching, they all went home empty-handed.

Four years later, on October 9, 1950, Paul Jepson was out with his mother in their truck. I've read that the Jepsons ran the town dump, or maybe were pig farmers, so I'm not exactly sure what Paul's mother was doing that day. But she pulled over near the tree line and got out for a moment, leaving eight-year-old Paul inside.

When she returned, he was gone. She shouted for him, but no one answered. Overcome with panic, she called the authorities for help, and soon a whole team of rescue workers began to scour the woods there. It also might be worth pointing out that, like Welden, little Paul was wearing a red jacket.

But it wasn't meant to be. Paul's scent was followed by bloodhounds all the way to an intersection, where it vanished. The same intersection, according to some locals, where Paula Welden had disappeared a few minutes before the elderly couple arrived there. The Glastenbury woods, it seems, had claimed another life.

Later that same month, Frieda Langer and her family were camped on the east side of the mountain. Frieda was fifty-three, incredibly knowledgeable about the area around the mountain, and a skilled hiker. So when she and her cousin Herbert Elsner headed out for a hike on October 28th, they expected a good workout through some beautiful scenery, nothing more.

About ten minutes into the hike, Frieda slipped while crossing a small stream. She wasn't hurt, but the fall had soaked her shoes and clothing, which she knew was not going to make for a comfortable walk. So she told her cousin to hold tight, and she ran back toward camp to quickly change.

After waiting for almost an hour, Herbert started walking back to camp. He wasn't sure what was taking Frieda so long, but he assumed he would bump into her on the trail at some point. But he didn't. And when he stepped out of the trees into camp, no one else had seen her either.

Over the decades since all of the disappearances occurred, there have been a lot of theories tossed around. Perhaps that creature witnessed in the rain that night near the Long Trail was still alive and active. Or maybe other humans are to blame, even a local serial killer. Some have suggested that after Henry McDowell escaped from the state asylum, he took up residence in the forest there, and was somehow still alive and healthy enough in the 1940s and 1950s to kidnap and kill people.

It's all guesswork, though. What is clear is the historical record. Real people have stepped into those woods and vanished. People with lives and families and futures that all came to an abrupt end in the shadows between those trees. And all of that loss comes with its own fair share of real pain.

It's a sobering thought: the one thing we *wish* would vanish into the woods—all of that loss and pain and grief—seems determined to stick around.

CONNECTING THE DOTS

The woods have always been a dangerous place. We can hurt ourselves there. We can get hurt by other things. It's wilderness, after all, so it's about as far from safety as we can get. But when you take all of the stories into account, it feels like there's something more than dangerous about Glastenbury Mountain.

Some people believe that wearing the color red is a surefire way to guarantee your disappearance, as noted in some of the cases.

But I can't find any evidence that Frieda Langer had been wearing a red coat the day she disappeared. Same for Middie Rivers. Sometimes coincidence is nothing more than just that, random details that *appear* to line up in a neat row, when maybe they really don't.

Our brains like to connect the dots, though. We look for patterns, like red coats or geographic epicenters. Patterns are like ruts in a dirt road, easy to slip into and hard to avoid. They feel significant, even though they often aren't.

Rationally, all of these disappearances could be viewed as nothing more than pure coincidence. These are dense woods, after all, and hikers go missing all over the world every single day for a variety of simple reasons. They lose their way, they get hurt, or they encounter a wild animal. Whenever something like that happens, their chance of survival drops below 100 percent. The truth is a bitter pill: sometimes people just don't come home.

Still, we whisper stories. Local Vermont folklorist Joseph Citro was the first to call the area the Bennington Triangle, drawing comparisons to the more famous triangle off the coast of Bermuda. But rather than ships and fighter jets, the Bennington Triangle just seems to be interested in people. And the name has stuck, probably because it feels like such a good fit.

Some people think it's all because the mountain is cursed. Those enchanted stones, the ones the Abenaki claimed would swallow people whole, are like supernatural flytraps, and the hunters and hikers who encounter them can never return.

Interestingly, a number of small cairns—stone mounds or towers used to mark special locations—have been found on the mountain. The local Native Americans won't take credit for them, and they're too high up to have been built by the loggers and farmers who once inhabited the town below. No one knows where they came from. It's *just* mysterious enough to make you wonder, isn't it?

That wonder has a way of inspiring us. The legendary horror writer Shirley Jackson connected so deeply with the story of Paula Welden that she included elements of the disappearance in her 1951 novel *Hansaman*, and then again in a 1957 short story called

"The Missing Girl." To Jackson, there was a disturbing beauty in a life that was thriving one moment and completely gone the next.

Others, though, are drawn to the story of Frieda Langer. The thing that makes her disappearance so different from the others isn't some small detail in what happened or how or where. It's the conclusion of it all.

You see, long after the search-and-rescue teams had given up and gone home—after autumn and winter and well into spring—someone finally found Frieda Langer. Her body was discovered in a wide-open area that had been thoroughly searched by hundreds of volunteers seven months before, just lying in the grass in plain sight.

No cause of death could be determined.

ACKNOWLEDGMENTS

Lore would not be alive today without the electrical surge that each and every fan imparts to it. So, whether you've been with Lore since the first podcast episode landed on your phone more than three years ago, stuck around after the television show caught your attention, or even just discovered it all for the first time today, please know that you are part of my team, and I'm so proud to have your support.

There are others, though. Chad, Carl, and Marcet are essential parts of my daily team. Susan keeps my publishing career on a smooth path. My wife and kids provide a constant source of laughter and support when things get stressful. And friends like Nora, Chuck, Myke, Pete, Helen, and Charles contribute equal parts encouragement and wisdom on a daily basis.

BIBLIOGRAPHY

DARK IMPORTS

"Savannah Like Beautiful Woman with Dirty Face, Lady Astor Says," *Savannah Morning News*, February 20, 1946, page 12.

"Savannah's Great Fire of 1796," Go South! Savannah, date unknown, http://gosouthsavannah.com/history/fire-of-1796.html.

Preston Russell and Barbara Hines, *Savannah: A History of Her People Since 1733* (Frederic C. Beil, 1992).

"The Weeping Time," *The Atlantic*, July 10, 2014, https://www.theatlantic.com/business/archive/2014/07/the-weeping-time/374159.

"Beneath the Surface," *Savannah Magazine*, March 15, 2017, http://www.savannahmagazine.com/beneath-the-surface.

Alan Brown, *Haunted Georgia: Ghosts and Strange Phenomena of the Peach State* (Stackpole Books, 2008).

Michael Harris and Linda Sickler, *Historic Haunts of Savannah* (Arcadia, 2014).

Walter J. Fraser, *Savannah in the Old South* (University of Georgia Press, 2005), 16–17.

"First African Baptist Church, Savannah, Georgia," BlackPast.org, date unknown, http://www.blackpast.org/aah/first-african-baptist-church-savannah-georgia-1777.

"The Haunted Hamilton-Turner Inn," Ghost City Tours, date

unknown, https://ghostcitytours.com/savannah/haunted
-places/haunted-hotels/hamilton-turner-inn.

A Dead End

"Richmond's Belle Isle and the Mixed Blessing of Water,"
Abandoned Country, January 2013, http://www
.abandonedcountry.com/2013/01/14/richmonds-belle-isle-the
-mixed-blessing-of-water.

"Belle Isle Prison," Civil War Academy, date unknown, http://
www.civilwaracademy.com/belle-isle-prison.html.

"Where Raw Dog Was a Luxury," Civil War Richmond, date
unknown, http://www.mdgorman.com/Written_Accounts
/National_Tribune/national_tribune_991882.htm.

"Hollywood Cemetery," Colonial Ghosts, August 2015, https://
colonialghosts.com/hollywood-cemetery.

"Richmond's Urban Legends," Richmond.com, October 2003,
http://www.richmond.com/entertainment/article_85098414
-d1f6-5aad-8945-cd08a0789cca.html.

"Richmond Vampire," OddThingsIveSeen.com, April 2012, http://
www.oddthingsiveseen.com/2012/04/richmond-vampire
.html.

Everything Floats

"Voodoo, Ghosts, and Werewolves at Louisiana's Cursed Swamp,"
Mysterious Universe, January 2016, http://mysteriousuniverse
.org/2016/01/voodoo-ghosts-and-werewolves-at-louisianas
-cursed-swamp.

"The Difference Between Voodoo and Hoodoo," Knowledge Nuts,
December 2013, http://knowledgenuts.com/2013/12/26/the
-difference-between-hoodoo-and-voodoo.

"Saint Louis Cemetery," Haunted Houses, date unknown, http://
www.hauntedhouses.com/states/la/saint_louis_cemetery.
htm.

Carolyn Morrow Long, *A New Orleans Voudou Priestess: The Legend
and Reality of Marie Laveau* (University Press of Florida,
2007), 60.

"The Sultan's Palace," About Travel, December 2014, http://

goneworleans.about.com/od/ghostsandhauntings/a/The
-Sultans-Palace.htm.

Troy Taylor, *Haunted New Orleans* (History Press, 2010), 101–106.

DOWNRIVER

"Welcome to Europe's 'Most Cursed Town,'" *Daily Mail*, May 2015,
http://www.dailymail.co.uk/news/article-3076473/Witches
-evil-eye-unexplained-calamities-Welcome-Europe-s-cursed
-town-feared-Italians-dare-not-speak-name.html.

"Lafayette Fires, Setting the Record Straight," New Lafayette, date
unknown, http://www.newlafayette.org/lafayette-history
/lafayette-fires-setting-record-straight.

"An Ax Murder, a Hanging, and a Curse," New Lafayette, date
unknown, http://www.newlafayette.org/lafayette-history/an
-ax-murder-a-hanging-and-a-curse-in-lafayette.

Troy Taylor, Mark Moran, and Mark Sceurman, *Weird Illinois: Your
Travel Guide to Illinois' Local Legends and Best Kept Secrets*
(Sterling, 2005), 49–50.

"Students, Residents Battle Flood Threat to Historic Kaskaskia
Island," *Chicago Tribune*, April 5, 1973, 6.

"Curse of Kaskaskia," Prairie Ghosts, 2000, http://www
.prairieghosts.com/kaskaskia.html.

"Curse of Kaskaskia," *Jonesboro Gazette*, March 2, 1901, transcription
here: genealogytrails.com/ill/kaskaskia/news_curse.html.

A WAY INSIDE

S. G. Drake, *The New England Historical and Genealogical Register* 2
(1848): 290.

"Haunted Guide to Granary Burying Ground," Ghosts and
Gravestones, date unknown, https://www.ghostsandgravestones
.com/boston/granary-burying-ground.php.

Renee Mallett, *Haunted Colleges and Universities of Massachusetts*
(Arcadia, 2013).

"Bizarre Boston: Ghosts of the Parker House Hotel," Spare Change
News, December 2015, sparechangenews.net/2015/12/bizarre
-boston-ghosts-of-the-parker-house-hotel.

"Haunted Guide to the Omni Parker House Hotel," Ghosts and

Gravestones, date unknown, https://www.ghostsandgravestones
.com/boston/omni-parker-house.php.

"Charlotte Cushman, Cross-Dressing Tragedienne of the 19th
Century," New England Historical Society, date unknown, www
.newenglandhistoricalsociety.com/charlotte-cushman-cross
-dressing-tragedienne-of-the-19th-century.

"The Women Who Fought in the Civil War," *Smithsonian*, April 2011,
www.smithsonianmag.com/history/the-women-who-fought
-in-the-civil-war-1402680.

"Lady in Black Ghost George's Island Folklore," Celebrate Boston,
date unknown, www.celebrateboston.com/ghost/georges-island
-lady-in-black-ghost.htm.

"Fort Warren's 'Lady in Black' . . . Debunked?," Historical
Digression, October 2012, https://historicaldigression.com
/2012/10/17/fort-warrens-lady-in-black-debunked.

BEHIND CLOSED DOORS

"Triangle Fire's Haunted Brown Building," Seeks Ghosts, 2014,
https://seeksghosts.blogspot.com/2014/03/triangle-fires
-haunted-brown-building.html.

"Remembering the Triangle Shirtwaist Fire," Untapped Cities, 2011,
http://untappedcities.com/2011/03/12/remembering-the
-triangle-shirtwaist-fire.

"Second Old Burial Vault Found Beneath Washington Square Park,"
ABC7NY.com, November 2015, http://abc7ny.com/news/photos
-second-old-burial-vault-found-beneath-washington-square
-park/1068922.

"Beware of Zombies: The Grim Origins of Washington Square
Park," New York Public Library, March 2011, https://www.nypl
.org/blog/2011/03/10/grim-origins-washington-square-park.

"Terror on 10th Street," *New York Post*, October 28, 2012, https://
nypost.com/2012/10/28/terror-on-10th-street.

"The Manhattan Well Mystery," Murder by Gaslight, December
2010, http://www.murderbygaslight.com/2010/12/manhattan
-well-mystery.html.

"William Axtell," Metropolitan Museum of Art, date unknown,
http://metmuseum.org/exhibitions/view?exhibitionId
=%7Bba1dd6f3-fcbc-4918-81ec-27f8b5fd3e3c%7D&oid=13338.

"A Flatbush Legend," *Brooklyn Daily Eagle*, June 22, 1884, 9.

F. L. Perine, "A Long Island Homestead—Melrose Hall," *American Magazine* 7, no. 3 (1888): 323.

"Walkabout: The History and Legend of Melrose Park," Brownstoner, June 2013, http://www.brownstoner.com/history /walkabout-the-history-and-legend-of-melrose-park-part-1.

ECHOES

"Ice Pick Lobotomy Anyone? Take a Ride on the 'Loboto-mobile,'" CCHR International, March 2013, https://www.cchrint.org/2013 /03/18/ice-pick-lobotomy-anyone-take-a-ride-on-the-loboto -mobile.

Katherine Anderson and Robert Duffy, *Danvers State Hospital* (Arcadia, 2018).

Carla Yanni, *The Architecture of Madness: Insane Asylums in the United States* (University of Minnesota Press, 2007).

SOUTHERN DRAMA

"The Myrtles Plantation: Legend, Lore, and Lies," American Hauntings Ink, date unknown, https://www .americanhauntingsink.com/myrtles.

"The Slave Girl of Myrtles Plantation: Louisiana Ghost Story," The Moonlit Road, date unknown, http://themoonlitroad.com/slave -girl-myrtles-plantation-louisiana-ghost-story.

BEHIND THE DOOR

"The Mistress of Death," Prairie Ghosts, date unknown, https:// www.prairieghosts.com/lalaurie.html.

Victoria Cosner Love and Lorelei Shannon, *Mad Madame Lalaurie* (History Press, 2011).

"A Portrait of Cruelty," *Vice*, March 2015, http://www.vice.com /read/a-portrait-of-cruelty-madame-marie-delphine -lalaurie-982.

A Bad Spirit

Michael Norman and Beth Scott, *Historic Haunted America*
    (Macmillan, 2007), 111–113.
"Haunted Libraries: Peoria Public Library," The Witching Hour,
    June 2013, https://4girlsandaghost.wordpress.com/2014/01/03
    /haunted-libraries-peoria-public-library.
Mark Leslie, *Tomes of Terror: Haunted Bookstores and Libraries*
    (Dundurn, 2014).

Steam and Gas

Rebecca F. Pittman, *History and Haunting of the Stanley Hotel* (23
    House, 2011), 60–61.
"Freelan O. Stanley, Motor Car Inventor," *New York Times*, October
    3, 1940, 25.
"The Stanley Hotel," Haunted Places in America, date unknown,
    https://www.hauntedplacesinamerica.com/the-stanley-hotel.
"Stanley Hotel Ghost Story Supported by Evidence of Room 217
    Event," Estes Park News, March 2014, http://www.eptrail.com
    /estes-park-news/ci_25288538/stanley-hotel-ghost-story
    -supported-by-evidence-room.

In the Bag

"Solitary Confinement," Prairie Ghosts, 2003, http://www
    .prairieghosts.com/eastern.html.
Paul Kahan, *Eastern State Penitentiary: A History* (History Press,
    2008).
"Eastern State Penitentiary: A Prison with a Past," *Smithsonian*,
    September 2008, https://www.smithsonianmag.com/arts
    -culture/the-daring-escape-from-the-eastern-state
    -penitentiary-180947688.
"Timeline," EasternState.org, date unknown, https://www
    .easternstate.org/research/history-eastern-state/timeline.
"Is Eastern State Penitentiary Really Haunted?" NPR, October 2013,
    http://www.npr.org/2013/10/24/232234570/is-eastern-state
    -penitentiary-really-haunted.

"A Real Knockout," Doctor's Review, August 2012, www
.doctorsreview.com/history/real-knockout.

"Dorothea Lynde Dix," History.com, date unknown, www.history
.com/topics/womens-history/dorothea-lynde-dix.

Kim Jacks, "Westin State Hospital," master's thesis, West Virginia
University, 2008, UMI: 1458739.

Rosemary Ellen Guiley, *The Big Book of West Virginia Ghost Stories*
(Stackpole Books, 2014), 178–180.

"Trans-Allegheny Lunatic Asylum and the Haunting Enigma of
Lily," America's Most Haunted, July 2016, www.americas-most
-haunted.com/2016/07/01/trans-allegheny-lunatic-asylum
-and-the-haunting-enigma-of-lily.

Eric Olsen and Theresa Argie, *America's Most Haunted: The Secrets of
Famous Paranormal Places* (Penguin, 2014).

WITHERING HEIGHTS

"Lessons in Iceman's Prehistoric Medicine Kit," *New York Times*,
December 8, 1998, http://www.nytimes.com/1998/12/08
/science/lessons-in-iceman-s-prehistoric-medicine-kit.html.

"Ballsy," *Discover*, April 2015, http://blogs.discovermagazine.com
/bodyhorrors/2015/04/30/tuberculosis-plombage.

"Collapse Therapies," Museum of Healthcare, date unknown,
http://www.museumofhealthcare.ca/explore/exhibits/breath
/collapse-therapies.html.

"An Echo in Time: The Waverly Hills Sanatorium," Liberty Voice,
July 2012, http://guardianlv.com/2012/07/an-echo-in-time-the
-waverly-hills-sanatorium.

Randy Russell, *The Ghost Will See You Now: Haunted Hospitals of the
South* (John F. Blair, 2014), 76–79.

"Waverly Hills Orderly Held for Killing Another," *Courier-Journal*,
March 2, 1954, 15.

"The Ghosts of Waverly Hills," Mysterious Universe, October 2013,
http://mysteriousuniverse.org/2013/10/the-ghosts-of-waverly
-hills.

"Curses! Fungus Dispels the Myth of King Tut's Tomb," *Los Angeles Times*, July 30, 1985, 11.

"Nine Victims of King Tut's Curse (and One Who Should Have Been)," *Mental Floss*, November 2009, http://mentalfloss.com /article/23321/quick-10-nine-victims-king-tuts-curse-and-one -who-should-have-been.

Mary Jo Ignoffo, *Captive of the Labyrinth: Sarah L. Winchester, Heiress to the Rifle Fortune* (University of Missouri Press, 2010).

Colin Dickey, *Ghostland: An American History in Haunted Places* (Penguin, 2016), 49–69.

Pamela Haag, *The Gunning of America: Business and the Making of American Gun Culture* (Basic Books, 2016).

Laura Trevelyan, *The Winchester: Legend of the West* (I. B. Tauris, 2016).

"New Room found at San Jose's Winchester Mystery House," ABC 7 News San Francisco, October 2016, http://abc7news.com /society/new-room-found-at-san-joses-winchester-mystery -house/1548352.

"Three Ghost Stories of the Winchester Mystery House," *Mercury News*, October 10, 2016, https://www.mercurynews.com/2016 /10/06/three-ghost-stories-of-the-winchester-mystery-house.

BITE MARKS

Jan-Andrew Henderson, *The Ghost That Haunted Itself: The Story of the Mackenzie Poltergeist—The Infamous Ghoul of Greyfriars Graveyard* (Random House, 2012).

"The MacKenzie Poltergeist," Unexplained Mysteries, January 2012, https://www.unexplained-mysteries.com/column. php?id=220743.

Paul Roland, *Hauntings: True Stories of Unquiet Spirits* (Arcturus, 2008).

THE CAVE

Charles Darwin, *Works of Charles Darwin* (D. Appleton, 1915), 268–270.

Shafik Meghji, Anna Kaminski, and Rosalba O'Brien, *The Rough Guide to Chile* (Penguin, 2015).

Bruce Chatwin, *In Patagonia* (Penguin Classics, 2003), 109.

"Into the Cave of Chile's Witches," *Smithsonian*, February 19, 2013, http://www.smithsonianmag.com/history/into-the-cave-of-chiles-witches-20138093.

"Myth and Magic Infuse Chilean Island," last modified November 5, 2014, NPR, http://www.npr.org/2008/06/26/91931716/myth-and-magic-infuse-chilean-island.

"The Trolls, Witches and Sorcerers of Chile's Huilliche," last modified February 15, 2015, IndianCountry, https://newsmaven.io/indiancountrytoday/archive/the-trolls-witches-sorcerers-of-chile-s-huilliche-uRYUXRadkUmHbZzkkCoTkw.

The King

"The Tyrant of Clipperton Island," DamnInteresting.com, updated March 2016, http://www.damninteresting.com/the-tyrant-clipperton-island.

"Guide to Islands You Never Want to Visit," Atlas Obscura, May 2011, http://www.atlasobscura.com/articles/atlas-obscura-s-guide-to-islands-you-never-want-to-visit.

"The Explorer," TheSmartSet.com, June 2010, http://thesmartset.com/article06021001.

"An Island the World Forgot," *The Age*, February 22, 1960, 13.

The Mountain

"Spirits of the South Pole," *New York Times*, July 2011, http://www.nytimes.com/2011/07/24/magazine/drinking-ernest-shackletons-whisky.html?_r=0.

"Dyatlov Pass," *Daily Mail*, August 2013, http://www.dailymail.co.uk/news/article-2401175/Dyatlov-Pass-Indicent-slaughtered-hikers-Siberias-Death-Mountain-1959.html.

Keith McCloskey, *Mountain of the Dead: The Dyatlov Pass Incident* (History Press, 2013).

"William the Conqueror's Castles," BritainExpress, date unknown, http://www.britainexpress.com/articles/Castles/william.htm.

Geoff Abbott, *Ghosts of the Tower of London* (David & Charles, 2012).

"The Princes of the Tower," Historical Royal Palaces, date unknown, http://www.hrp.org.uk/tower-of-london/history-and-stories/palace-people/edward-v/#gs.tZXifbM.

"The Ghosts of Edinburgh Castle," About.com, February 2016, http://paranormal.about.com/od/hauntedplaces/fl/The-Ghosts-of-Edinburgh-Castle.htm.

"The Monster of Glamis," Smithsonian.com, February 2012, http://www.smithsonianmag.com/history/the-monster-of-glamis-92015626.

Y. K. Wha, "The Glamis Mystery," *Notes & Queries* 10, no. 251 (1908): 311–312.

Thomas Firming and Thiselton Dyer, *Strange Pages from Family Papers* (Sampson Low, Marston, 1895), 102.

THE TAINTED WELL

Lionel Fanthorpe and Patricia Fanthorpe, *The World's Most Mysterious Castles* (Dundurn, 2005), 212.

Jeff Belanger, *The World's Most Haunted Places* (Career Press, 2004), 15–20.

Allison Vale, *Hell House: And Other True Hauntings from Around the World* (Sterling, 2008), 112–115.

"The House of Horror," *Occult Review* VIII, no. 6 (December 1908), 308–347.

"Correspondence," *Occult Review* IX, no. 1 (January 1909), 44–47.

ROPE AND RAILING

Christopher Nicholson, *Rock Lighthouses of Britain: The End of an Era* (Whittles, 1995), 58–59.

I DIE

Roy Bainton, *The Mammoth Book of Unexplained Phenomena: From Bizarre Biology to Inexplicable Astronomy* (Little, Brown, 2013).

ALL GONE

Christopher Nicholson, *Rock Lighthouses of Britain: The End of an Era* (Whittles, 1995), 168–179.

REARRANGED

"History of Sheffield Island Lighthouse, Norwalk, Connecticut," New England Lighthouses, date unknown, http://www .newenglandlighthouses.net/sheffield-island-light-history.html.

Joseph Citro, *Passing Strange* (Houghton Mifflin, 1996), 276.

"Sheffield Island, CT," LighthouseFriends.com, date unknown, http://www.lighthousefriends.com/light.asp?ID=786.

THE BIG CHILL

"History of Owl's Head Lighthouse, Maine," New England Lighthouses, 2012, http://www.newenglandlighthouses.net /owls-head-light-history.html.

"Owl's Head Lighthouse," Alan's Mysterious World, March 2012, https://alansmysteriousworld.wordpress.com/2012/03/05/owls -head-lighthouse.

"Haunted Memories," *Bangor Daily News*, October 31, 2006, http:// archive.bangordailynews.com/2006/10/31/haunted-memories -keepers-of-owls-head-light-tell-tales-of-ghosts-in-their-bed -plastic-pumpkins-that-move-by-themselves.

"Haunted Owl's Head Lighthouse," Angels and Ghosts, http:// www.angelsghosts.com/haunted_light_houses_owls_head_ lighthouse.

"Horrific Boon Island Wreck Has Portsmouth Link," SeacoastNH .com, 2012, http://www.seacoastnh.com/History/History -Matters/horrific-boon-island-wreck-has-portsmouth -link/?showall=1.

WHEN THE BOW BREAKS

"Lyubov Orlova," *Independent*, January 23, 2014, http://www .independent.co.uk/news/uk/home-news/mystery-of-the -lyubov-orlova-ghost-ship-full-of-cannibal-rats-could-be -heading-for-british-coast-9080103.html.

"A Brief Overview of the Queen's Wartime Service," SkyLighters
    .org, date unknown, http://www.skylighters.org/special
    /queenmary/qmww2.html.
"Ghosts of the Queen Mary in Long Beach," Legends of America,
    March 2013, http://www.legendsofamerica.com/ca-queenmary
    .html.
"The Queen Mary," Unsolved.com, September 2015, https://
    unsolved.com/gallery/the-queen-mary.
"The Ghost Ship Queen Mary," Weird U.S., date unknown, http://
    www.weirdus.com/states/california/ghosts/queen_mary.
"The Queen Mary, Part 2," Seeking Ghosts, February 2015, http://
    seeksghosts.blogspot.com/search/label/John%20Pedder.

IN THE DARK

"The Bell Witch Cave," Prairie Ghosts, 2013, www.prairieghosts
    .com/b-cave.html.

AN ANGEL AMONG US

Diana Ross McCain, *Mysteries and Legends of New England* (Morris,
    2009), 29–40.
Sylvester Judd and Lucius Manlius Boltwood, *History of Hadley:
    Including the Early History of Hatfield, South Hadley, Amherst and
    Granby, Massachusetts* (Metcalf, 1863), 145–147, 214–219.

A BRIDGE TOO FAR

Frank Leslie's Illustrated Newspaper, February 12, 1887.
An Appalling Disaster (Cranbury Press, 1887).
J. A. Ferguson, "The Wrong Rail in the Wrong Place at the Wrong
    Time," *Vermont History Journal* 81 (2013), 52.
Joseph Citro, *Weird New England* (Sterling, 2005), 192–193.

A LEG UP

"The Legend of Jonathan Buck," *Bangor Daily News*, October 28,
    2015, http://bangordailynews.com/2015/10/28/living/a-close
    -look-at-the-legend-of-jonathan-buck.

"Colonel Buck's Cursed Tomb," Roadside America, date unknown,
    http://www.roadsideamerica.com/story/6159.

A HEAD OF STEAM

Charles M. Skinner, *American Myths and Legends* (J. B. Lippincott,
    1903), 100–103.

A DEADLY PAST

Howard Zimmerman and Robert Le Roy Ripley, *Ripley's Believe It
    or Not! Strange Coincidences* (Tor Books, 1992), 11.

FOR WANT OF CIDER

Marie Caroline Watson Hamlin, *Legends of le Détroit* (Thorndike
    Nourse, 1883), 180–188.

IN THE WOODS

Jeff Belanger, *Weird Massachusetts: Your Travel Guide to
    Massachusetts's Local Legends and Best Kept Secrets* (Sterling,
    2008), 78–82.
Loren Coleman, *Mysterious Creatures* (Paraview Pocket Books,
    2001), 33–39.
Cheri Revai, *Haunted Massachusetts: Ghosts and Strange Phenomena of
    the Bay State* (Stackpole Books, 2005), 84–87.
"Bill Russo Survived a Puckwudgie from the Bridgewater
    Triangle," HubPages, September 8, 2015, https://hubpages.com
    /religion-philosophy/I-Survived-the-Bridgewater-Triangle.

BROKEN FINGERNAILS

Cheri Revai and Heather Adel Wiggins, *Haunted Connecticut: Ghosts
    and Strange Phenomena of the Constitution State* (Stackpole Books,
    2006), 68–69.
Roxie J. Zwicke, *Haunted Portsmouth: Spirits and Shadows of the Past*
    (History Press, 2007), 45, 47.

David Ferland, *Historic Crimes and Justice in Portsmouth, New Hampshire* (History Press, 2014), 48–49.

GOING VIRAL

Robert E. Bartholomew, *Hoaxes, Myths, and Manias: Why We Need Critical Thinking* (Prometheus Books, 2003), 49–59.

Martin Van Buren Ingram, *An Authenticated History of the Famous Bell Witch* (Pioneer, 1894).

Pat Fitzhugh, *The Bell Witch: The Full Account* (Armand Press, 2000).

Gladys Hutchison Barr, *The Bell Witch at Adams* (D. Hutchison, 1969).

THE RED COATS

"The Strange and Curious Tale of the Last True Hermit," *GQ*, August 2014, http://www.gq.com/story/the-last-true-hermit.

Tyler Resch, *Glastenbury: The History of a Vermont Ghost Town* (Arcadia, 2008).

Charles A. Stansfield Jr., *Haunted Vermont: Ghosts and Strange Phenomena of the Green Mountain State* (Stackpole Books, 2007), 22.

Joseph A. Citro, *Weird New England: Your Travel Guide to New England's Local Legends and Best Kept Secrets* (Sterling, 2005), 74–75.

Andrea Lankford, *Haunted Hikes: Spine-Tingling Tales and Trails from North America's National Parks* (Santa Monica Press, 2006), 196–200.

Melanie R. Anderson and Lisa Kröger, *Shirley Jackson, Influences and Confluences* (Routledge, 2016), 127–128.

Andrea Lankford, *Haunted Hikes: Spine-Tingling Tales and Trails from North America's National Parks* (Santa Monica Press, 2006), 196–200.

Melanie R. Anderson and Lisa Kröger, *Shirley Jackson, Influences and Confluences* (Routledge, 2016), 127–128.

ABOUT THE AUTHOR

One of the most successful podcast producers in the world, AARON MAHNKE began his career in 2015. His first podcast *Lore* has been downloaded half a billion times, adapted for television by Amazon, and published as a major book series from Penguin Random House. Aaron has also produced a number of other wildly popular podcasts, including his chart-topping *Cabinet of Curiosities* and his award-winning supernatural audio drama, *Bridgewater*.

lorepodcast.com
facebook.com/lorepodcast
Instagram: @amahnke & @lorepodcast
Threads: @amahnke & @lorepodcast

ABOUT THE ILLUSTRATOR

M. S. CORLEY is a professional illustrator and book cover designer fascinated by folklore, the supernatural, and all things strange. Besides *The World of Lore: Monstrous Creatures* and *The World of Lore: Wicked Mortals*, he has also created illustrations for *Darkness There: Selected Tales* by Edgar Allan Poe, *Never Bet the Devil & Other Warnings* by Orrin Grey, and others. He haunts Central Oregon with his wife, daughter, son, and cat named Dinah.

mscorley.com
X: @corleyms

ABOUT THE TYPE

This book was set in Tribute, a typeface designed by Frank Heine for the Emigre type foundry in 2003. It was modeled on a printed specimen of typefaces cut in 1544 and 1557 by the French punchcutter François Guyot. While Guyot's approach to the design of his Renaissance Antiquas tended toward the idiosyncratic, Heine enhanced the readability of Tribute by giving it stronger stroke widths and decreasing the overall contrast between the thick and thin strokes.

DISCOVER MORE FROM
DEL REY &
RANDOM HOUSE
WORLDS!

READ EXCERPTS
from hot new titles.

STAY UP-TO-DATE
on your favorite authors.

FIND OUT about exclusive
giveaways and sweepstakes.

CONNECT WITH US ONLINE!
@DelReyBooks

DelReyBooks.com
RandomHouseWorlds.com